THE CHRIST PARTY
IN THE CORINTHIAN COMMUNITY

EARLY CHRISTIANITY AND ITS LITERATURE

Shelly Matthews, General Editor

Editorial Board:
Ronald Charles
Jennifer A. Glancy
Meira Kensky
Joseph A. Marchal
Anders Runesson

Number 29

THE CHRIST PARTY IN THE CORINTHIAN COMMUNITY

Ferdinand Christian Baur

With an introduction by Ernst Käsemann

Translated by
Wayne Coppins, Christoph Heilig,
Lucas Ogden, and David Lincicum

Edited by
David Lincicum

SBL PRESS

Atlanta

Copyright © 2021 by SBL Press

All rights reserved. No part of this work may be reproduced or transmitted in any form or by any means, electronic or mechanical, including photocopying and recording, or by means of any information storage or retrieval system, except as may be expressly permitted by the 1976 Copyright Act or in writing from the publisher. Requests for permission should be addressed in writing to the Rights and Permissions Office, SBL Press, 825 Houston Mill Road, Atlanta, GA 30329 USA.

Library of Congress Control Number: 2021947810

Contents

Preface vii

Abbreviations xi

Introduction
    Ernst Käsemann 1

Part 1: The Christ Party in the Corinthian Community 17

Part 2: The Apostle Peter in Rome 79

Bibliography 137

Ancient Sources Index 143

Modern Authors Index 148

Subject Index 149

Preface

Ferdinand Christian Baur (1792–1860) was arguably one of the intellectual architects of modern scholarship on the New Testament.[1] Many of his contemporaries and successors disputed his results, but his method of a thoroughgoing historical approach to the material at hand, his thematization of conflict as an engine for development in early Christianity, and his critical sifting of received opinion all distinguish his work, and even many of those who disagreed with his concrete arguments nevertheless adopted many of his broader assumptions.

This little book contains a translation of Baur's long 1831 essay on "The Christ Party in the Corinthian Community, the Opposition between Petrine and Pauline Christianity in the Earliest Church, the Apostle Peter in Rome."[2] Why take the time to read an essay that is almost two centuries old? It was not to be Baur's final word on the subject. The essay belongs to a period in his career when he was just beginning to venture into the critical study of the New Testament. Indeed, all of his major works on New Testament themes would be published over the next several decades, and he would even change his mind on details of his presentation of this material by the time he came to incorporate parts of it into his epochal book on the

---

1. For important studies of Baur in English, with good bibliographies for further study, see Peter C. Hodgson, *The Formation of Historical Theology: A Study of Ferdinand Christian Baur* (New York: Oxford University Press, 1966); Horton Harris, *The Tübingen School: A Historical and Theological Investigation of the School of F. C. Baur* (Oxford: Oxford University Press, 1975; repr., Leicester: Apollos, 1990); Johannes Zachhuber, *Theology as Science in Nineteenth-Century Germany: From F. C. Baur to Ernst Troeltsch* (Oxford: Oxford University Press, 2013); Martin Bauspiess, Christof Landmesser, and David Lincicum, eds., *Ferdinand Christian Baur and the History of Early Christianity*, trans. Robert F. Brown and Peter C. Hodgson (Oxford: Oxford University Press, 2017).

2. Ferdinand Christian Baur, "Die Christuspartei in der korinthischen Gemeinde, der Gegensatz des paulinischen und petrinischen Christenthums in der ältesten Kirche, der Apostel Petrus in Rom," *TZTh* 4 (1831): 61–206.

apostle Paul.³ But if it was not a definitive conclusion, it has come, through the passage of time, to mark a new departure in the study of Christian origins.⁴

In Baur's history of theology in the nineteenth century, he offered a retrospective view of his own efforts in this essay:

> This is where I may mention my own efforts at research into early Christianity. I started my investigations long before Strauss, and thus began from an entirely different point. My engagement with the two Corinthian epistles first provided the occasion to bring more sharply into focus the relationship of the Apostle Paul to the older apostles. I became convinced that in the letters of the Apostle himself, sufficient evidence is available to see that this relationship was something entirely different from what previously had been assumed--that, where people supposed a thorough harmony of all the apostles is to be found, rather an opposition exists, an opposition that, from the Jewish-Christian side, went so far as to call into question the authority of the Apostle Paul. A closer investigation of the Pseudo-Clementine Homilies, a writing whose importance for the history of the earliest period I had especially noted along with Neander, allowed me to see more deeply into the significance of this opposition in the post-apostolic period. It became increasingly clear to me that the opposition of the two parties, which in the apostolic and post-apostolic periods are to be distinguished much more sharply than hitherto has been the case, the Pauline party and the Petrine or Judaizing party, had a decisive influence not simply on the configuration of the sayings of Peter but also on the composition of the Book of Acts.⁵

---

3. Ferdinand Christian Baur, *Paul the Apostle of Jesus Christ: His Life and Works, His Epistles and Teachings*, 2 vols. (London: Williams & Norgate, 1873): the section on the Corinthian correspondence incorporates parts of this article (Baur, *Paul*, 1:268–320), as does "Appendix 1: On the Literature of the Legend of Peter" (Baur, *Paul*, 2:291–96). Note also a series of articles on the Corinthian correspondence: Baur, "Einige weitere Bemerkungen über die Christuspartei in Korinth," *TZTh* 4 (1836): 3–32; Baur, "Beiträge zur Erklärung der Korintherbriefe," pts. 1 and 2, *ThJb* 9 (1850): 139–85; 11 (1852): 1–40, 535–74.

4. Of course, the essay is not an absolute beginning; for a series of essays that explore predecessors to Baur's argument in this essay, especially as it pertains to the disputed phenomenon of "Jewish Christianity," see F. Stanley Jones, ed., *Rediscovery of Jewish Christianity: From Toland to Baur*, HBS 5 (Atlanta: Society of Biblical Literature, 2012).

5. Peter C. Hodgson, ed., *Church and Theology in the Nineteenth Century*, trans. Robert F. Brown and Peter C. Hodgson (Eugene, OR: Cascade, 2018), 364.

This summary in Baur's own words offers a useful window onto the significance of this essay: where much of previous study of the New Testament or early Christianity had emphasized the unity of the ancient church, Baur's essay cleared the way for exploring the importance of diversity and conflict in the formation of early Christianity.

The introduction that follows, by Ernst Käsemann, takes up Baur's novelty and offers a punchy and sympathetic exposition of Baur's achievement by one of his most notable successors.[6] This essay by Käsemann originally appeared as the introduction to volume 1 of a five-volume set of Baur's *Ausgewählte Werke*, the volume devoted to his New Testament research.[7] We gratefully acknowledge the permission granted by Friedrich Frommann Verlag (Günther Holzboog) to translate the essay for this volume.

The slimness of this book belies the long gestation of this translation. The idea to translate the essay first arose in conversations with Martin Bauspiess in Tübingen in 2008 and 2009, and Martin was a significant encouragement to the project, especially in its early stages. Lucas Ogden subsequently contributed significantly to the translation of Baur's essay. Wayne Coppins and Christoph Heilig retranslated and standardized both the introduction and the main essay and rescued the project from the place where it languished in disrepair. An excellent graduate student in Classics at Notre Dame, William Stover, kindly produced translations of the modern Latin quotations. Throughout, this has been a collaborative venture, and it is gratifying to see the project come to fruition. We express our warm thanks to Larry Welborn for initially accepting the volume into the Society of Biblical Literature's History of Biblical Studies series and for his encouragement along the way. When HBS was discontinued, Larry recommended publication in SBL Press's Early Christianity and Its

---

6. In Roy A. Harrisville and Walter Sundberg, *The Bible in Modern Culture: Baruch Spinoza to Brevard Childs*, 2nd ed. (Grand Rapids: Eerdmans, 2002), 122, the authors write, "On the wall in Ernst Käsemann's living room study hung a copy of the University of Tübingen's portrait of Baur, a gift to the New Testament scholar upon his retirement. Once outside Baur's direct influence, the one-time pupil of Bultmann finally came to write of Baur as the true 'progenitor' of a criticism at the root, a criticism conceived not merely as a scientific method but as a presupposition for the life of the spirit. One summer day he pointed to that portrait on his study wall and said, 'greater even than Bultmann.'"

7. Ernst Käsemann, "Einführung," in *Historisch-kritische Untersuchungen zum Neuen Testament*, by Ferdinand Christian Baur, vol. 1 of *Ausgewählte Werke in Einzelausgaben*, ed. Klaus Scholder (Stuttgart: Frommann, 1963), viii–xxv.

Literature series. Thank you to Shelly Matthews, general editor of ECL, for welcoming this work to her series. Many colleagues have generously answered queries along the way, and at the risk of unintentionally neglecting to mention someone, gratitude is due to James Carleton Paget, Luca Grillo, Peter Hodgson, F. Stanley Jones, Robert Morgan, Annette Yoshiko Reed, and Johannes Zachhuber. Bob Buller, Nicole Tilford, and the staff at SBL Press performed miracles of editorial oversight and saved the reader from numerous errors. Jen Guo generously produced the indexes with her characteristic acumen, intelligence, and industry.

A few comments about the way we have approached this translation are in order. Any substantive additions to Baur's text have been marked with square brackets. Baur often quotes bibliographic information in the main body of the text, and we have silently relocated this material to the footnotes. When he quotes from ancient texts, we have presented the Greek and Latin as Baur does (rather than standardizing to modern critical editions), unless there is an obvious error, although we have sometimes adjusted Baur's accentuation. On the whole, we have not translated the Greek quotations from the New Testament but have supplied translations for other ancient texts. We have drawn from the Loeb Classical Library, from the Ante-Nicene Fathers, and from other standard English translations wherever possible and have credited translators by name in parentheses after the citation; unattributed translations have been produced for this volume. We have retained the Greek and Latin original text alongside the translation for ancient material, but when Baur quotes from modern Latin sources we have simply supplied a translation without the original (which in any case is available in Baur's German text). Chapter and verse numbers have sometimes been added where Baur neglected to supply them. Where Baur offers interpretative paraphrase rather than direct quotation of his sources, we have indicated this by the use of italics. We have used CE rather than AD but have not updated Käsemann's or Baur's gendered language. References to the original German pagination of Baur's essay have been inserted in brackets throughout the text, as a means of facilitating access to the original.

Abbreviations

Primary Texts

1 Apol.	Justin, *Apologia i*
1–2 Clem.	1–2 Clement
Ann.	Tacitus, *Annales*
Apol.	Tertullian, *Apologeticus*
Bibl.	Photius, *Bibliotheca*
Dom.	Suetonius, *Domitianus*
Ep. Clem. Jas.	Letter of Clement to James
Ep. Pet. Jas.	Letter of Peter to James
Fug.	Athanasius, *Apologia de fuga sua*
Haer.	Irenaeus, *Adversus haereses*
Herm. Sim.	Shepherd of Hermas, Similitude(s)
Herm. Vis.	Shepherd of Hermas, Vision(s)
Hist. eccl.	Eusebius, *Historia ecclesiastica*
Hist. rom.	Dio Cassius, *Historiae romanae*
Hom.	Pseudo-Clement, *Homiliae*
Ign. *Rom.*	Ignatius, *To the Romans*
Jejun.	Tertullian, *De jejunio adversus psychicos*
Marc.	Tertullian, *Adversus Marcionem*
Mort.	Lactantius, *De mortibus persecutorum*
Pan.	Epiphanius, *Panarion (Adversus haereses)*
Praescr.	Tertullian, *De praescriptione haereticorum*
Rec.	Pseudo-Clement, *Recognitiones*
Strom.	Clement of Alexandria, *Stromateis*

Secondary Resources

ACW	Ancient Christian Writers

AEWK	*Die Allgemeine Encyclopädie der Wissenschaften und Künste.* Edited by Johann Samuel Ersch and Johann Gottfried Gruber. 167 vols. Leipzig: Dieterich, 1818–1889.
ANF	*The Ante-Nicene Fathers: Translations of the Writings of the Fathers Down to A.D. 325.* Edited by Alexander Roberts and James Donaldson. 10 vols. 1885–1887. Repr., New York: Scribner's Sons, 1916.
GCS	*Die griechischen christlichen Schriftsteller der ersten [drei] Jahrhunderte*
HBS	History of Biblical Studies
LCC	Library of Christian Classics
LCL	Loeb Classical Library
NPNF2	*Nicene and Post-Nicene Fathers,* Series 2
OECT	Oxford Early Christian Texts
SBT	Studies in Biblical Theology
ThJb	*Theologische Jahrbucher*
TQ	*Theologische Quartalschrift*
TZTh	*Tübinger Zeitschrift für Theologie*

Technical Abbreviations

AD	*anno Domini* (in the year of our Lord)
ad loc.	*ad locum,* at the place discussed
ca.	circa
CE	Common Era
cf.	*confer,* compare
ch(s).	chapter(s)
ed(s).	editor(s), edited by, edition
e.g.	*exempli gratia,* for example
esp.	especially
etc.	*et cetera,* and so forth, and the rest
i.e.	*id est,* that is
N.B.	*nota bene,* note carefully
n(n).	note(s)
n.p.	no publisher
orig.	original
pt(s).	part(s)
repr.	reprinted

ser.	series
trans.	translator(s), translated by
vol(s).	volume(s)

Introduction

Ernst Käsemann

F. C. Baur's early investigations on the New Testament present an internally closed picture of primitive Christian history as a historical process determined by antitheses and equilibrium. Since this is something that did not exist before him and we can no longer rid ourselves of the question that he posed in such a way, we all stand on the foundation that he laid. To be sure, the program set forth by him has been so strongly overhauled by subsequent scholarship that in its positive statements it remains important to a large extent only from the perspective of the history of theology. The fundamental problems that drove Baur have, however, remained alive, as have the concrete ones for the most part. We, too, stand before them and have to recognize that we have by no means solved them in a satisfying way. On the contrary, the more deeply we penetrate the circumstances of primitive Christianity and the more individual insights we gather, the more difficult it becomes to capture and order the whole. Baur continues to remind us of an unfulfilled and indispensable task. But it is worth it even for the beginner to read him again and again. One learns from him to question in a manner that is precise, consistent, unswerving, and wholly oriented to the subject matter, and this is a skill that one can only obtain by observing a great model and with persistent practice. For Baur himself, however, this was only a presupposition and aspect of that methodology that he called "historical criticism" and that he also actually established for the first time with his question about the reality of primitive Christian history. The present selection of writings[1]

---

1. [This essay, written in Tübingen, Easter 1962, originally served as an introduction to the first volume of Baur's selected shorter writings, in which a reprint of Baur's essay on the Christ party appeared: Käsemann, "Einführung," viii–xxv. In this introductory essay, Käsemann refers to the four individual essays the collection comprises in turn.]

wants, above all, to provide a means of access to this methodology in its original form. For a generation that has undeniably entered a general crisis of historical understanding must return to the beginnings of historical criticism, to its necessity and to its difficulties, in order to find its way into the open air and to be able to do its work in a clearer and better way.

The shorter writings presented in selection here should be read. Therefore, a detailed reproduction of their content is dispensable. Nevertheless, it is in the interest of the reader that a critical approach show to him from the start not only the peculiar character but also the problems of Baur's undertaking. In doing so, one will have to consider that Baur's work at first feels its way forward in an extremely tentative way and does not yet have the same fullness and decidedness as the later writings. The picture that is conveyed here therefore needs completion and at times correction from his major works.

Like every historian, Baur took the detail as his starting point and then returned to it again and again. After all, historians passionately scrutinize the past for the reality that is, as such, always concrete. This reality can be obtained only when one separates it from mere appearance, thus also historically only in the distinguishing of the spirits.[2] For Baur, 1 Cor 1:12 was the Archimedean point from which the history of primitive Christianity disclosed itself. In contrast to the legendary way in which this history was portrayed for eighteen hundred years, the Corinthian parties were proof that in the beginning it was not all united, but that it moved from antagonism to a conciliation that still remained hidden to it and was reached only in early Catholicism via a balancing out of the oppositions. To be sure, the starting point and teleology could be precisely determined only if one could explain the mutual relationship of the four groups named in 1 Cor 1:12, namely, those of the adherents of Paul, of Apollos, and of Cephas and the group of the people of Christ. Here the difficulty lay (and lies) above all in the fact that it is difficult to determine what exactly one should imagine in the case of the Christ party. Baur rightly considers the choice of Christ as a party leader among others to be as unthinkable as a nonconformist assemblage that rejects every apostolic authority.[3] The enigma seems to be unraveled if one understands this party as an extreme wing of the Petrines. It would then have boasted of a direct relationship

---

2. [Cf. 1 Cor 12:10; 1 John 4:1–2.]

3. Baur, "Christuspartei"; also reprinted in Baur, *Historisch-kritische Untersuchungen*, 1–146. [An English translation of this essay follows below.]

to the earthly Messiah Jesus and of his teaching, which was taken up in a nomistic way, and based on this an exclusivist claim to validity that placed especially Paul, but also Christians converted after Easter more generally, into the shadow of its leadership. This interpretation of Baur's, which can point almost only to a dubious exegesis of 2 Cor 10–13 as additional support, is untenable. Not the Petrines, who probably represented only a small minority in Corinth that was itself terrorized, but the adherents of Apollos, who had fallen for radical enthusiasm, constituted the real antagonists of Paul. There never was a Christ party at all. The slogan that supposedly characterizes it, "I am of Christ," is to be understood as an ironic outperformance of the other slogans that were circulating; that is, on the basis of specific Pauline rhetoric.

Nevertheless, one may not simply regard Baur's interpretation as a false inference that could have been avoided. It has reasons for which Baur himself can hardly be blamed, unless one demanded that he should have entirely leaped over the premises that were regarded as valid in his time. In the same way that the meaning and significance of early Christian eschatology were misunderstood for nearly the entire nineteenth century, so also the discovery of the characteristically Hellenistic world, its language and ways of thinking, remained outstanding until the end of the century—on the theological field at any rate. Therefore, Baur has no choice but to read the New Testament as a peculiar record of classical Greek culture and, concretely, to relate the concept of *pneuma*, which was central to his interpretation of Paul, to the divine self-awareness, and derivatively to Christian self-awareness. But in this framework the Corinthian enthusiasts cannot appear as people who, in their pneumatic self-understanding, believe themselves to have received in baptism a heavenly power and nature, who strive to represent the angel-like condition of the reality of resurrection, and thus despise bodily discipline and earthly order. Rather, they are regarded as spiritualists who oppose a sensually oriented Christianity, and who from this perspective regard, for example, bodily resurrection to be meaningless and unbelievable. Thus, in opposition to Jewish Christianity, the Greek element connects itself with the Christian message. Paul himself exemplifies the transition between the two views insofar as the Damascus vision led him, in distinction from the other apostles, to the spiritualized interpretation of the exalted Lord and of Christianity as a whole. Finally, as native Greeks, Apollos and his adherents are said to go a step further. In the same way as the people of Christ are assigned to the Petrinists, they are assigned as extremists to the Paulinists, so that, in Baur's view, two main groups stood over against each other in Corinth. Against the presuppositions of that time, such an argumentation and interpretation are internally consistent and even convincing. The time was not yet ripe for a genuine alternative. Baur would have had to leap over his own shadow to recognize it. When the eminent historian does, however, leap out from the shadow of his own time, he must nevertheless pay his tribute to the fate of never being able to fully get clear of it.

As important as historical detail was and remained for Baur, where arguments had to be made, he was not a man who contented himself with this. For him the concern was ultimately with the intellectual connections into which exegetical insights and historical facts can be placed. His discovery cried out to be expanded in an investigation of church history and thought through in a systematic way. If the early catholic church arose out of an antithesis and, viewed radically, grew out of the two different origins of Jewish Christianity and of Paulinism, then a dogmatic-historical program inevitably followed from this, which had to reach far beyond the bounds of the New Testament. At the same time, a hermeneutical key to the New Testament writings was found, which allowed them to be ordered in highly differentiated ways and with varying proximity to the two poles. The task was to determine the respective "tendencies" of each writing within the primitive Christian or New Testament field of tension so that historical criticism now obtained a dogmatic-historical depth through tendency criticism.[4] Within such a perspective, dogmatic conflict had to be declared to be the real driving force of primitive Christian history, and the relationship of the various "doctrinal concepts" had to be made the central object of historical-theological research.[5] Finally, this history had to be brought out of the isolation in which it had thus far existed vis-à-vis the time that followed. It now appeared as a transition to the early catholic church, as an epoch among others, though of course an immensely

---

4. [*Tendenzkritik.*]

5. [Here Käsemann refers to Baur's invocation of *Lehrbegriffe* or "doctrinal concepts" as a formative driver of early Christian conflict, which the latter also retained as an organizing concept in Baur, *Lectures on New Testament Theology*, ed. Peter C. Hodgson, trans. Robert F. Brown (Oxford: Oxford University Press, 2016; orig. ed., Leipzig: Fues, 1864). The role of such *Lehrbegriffe* has been contested since William Wrede's notable essay "The Task and Methods of 'New Testament Theology,'" in Robert Morgan, *The Nature of New Testament Theology*, SBT, 2/25 (London: SCM, 1973), 68–116.]

important one. Every one of these perspectives contained unforeseeable tasks and promises. Again it was characteristic of Baur that he was not satisfied with the program that had been set up by him and with individual advances into the newly discovered world, but rather reached for the whole. In gritty, detailed work, the historian now had to pursue the play of historical forces in effect, counter-effect, and equilibrium, according to the respective constellations and phases, in order to subordinate it to the topic that had been discovered and to lead the way from all contrast to the harmony of a historical teleology and necessity. We have long since divided and distributed the load that he bore like a giant on his own shoulders, and yet each of us groans under the burden that has been assigned to him or her. The present selection of writings has missed its goal if it does not first of all bring us to this realization.[6] It contains only a narrow slice of Baur's work. It basically highlights only the development of the Paulinism of the beginning period and the hostile forces as they are reflected in that mirror. The reader is left to familiarize him- or herself with this in detail. However, the material and methodological difficulties of the conception require that we briefly discuss a number of decisive aspects here.

It is self-evident that Baur found his thesis confirmed by Galatians. More interesting is his attempt to understand Romans in light of it as well. It is worthy of reflection that Baur starts from the fact that even to the apostles, Christian truth was not given in its entirety from the outset in such a way that it would merely have to be deduced in individual cases. Apostolic function and inspiration manifest themselves—especially in the case of Paul—in such a way that historical involvement compels one to reflect on the "principle" that must be called truly Christian in the concrete situation, and to formulate it anew in the act of a decision. Accordingly, Romans was not originally the first Christian dogmatic treatise, which it then became for later generations, especially in the West, but rather a genuine letter arising out of community conflicts. The Pauline universalism is fundamentally rejected by Jewish-Christian particularism, and the apostle has to defend himself against this rejection. Romans 9–11 now becomes the material center of the epistle and the key point of interpretation, and even today notable considerations from the preceding section of the letter and from the following paraenesis support this assessment. But again the argument is ultimately unconvincing. In the overall context, Rom 9–11 is undoubtedly something

---

6. [See n. 1 above.]

like an excursus; more precisely, it is the application of the proposition of the *iustificatio impii* to the special problem of the chosen people. But the letter is also prompted by the fact that Rome is to be the launching point for the Pauline journey to the West; and, with the presentation of his gospel, Paul has to counter the suspicions regarding his person and his work that were circulating about him or that he feared might exist. There had of course been various groups and theological tensions in Rome, as everywhere else; and precisely there the Christian community had probably originally been strongly influenced by those on the margins of the synagogue and by Jewish-Christians. It remains completely unprovable, however, that a judaizing party in the community was dominant at the time of the writing of the letter. It still seems plausible that Rome offered itself as a transshipment point for different forms of early Christianity and already exercised a balancing-out function at a very early point. But one can attribute hardly more than an exemplary significance to it, as this would also have applied elsewhere. It was not merely in its controversy with nomism on gentile Christian soil that the Pauline gospel was understood only imperfectly and very quickly concealed by other theological streams—this happened even in the Pauline communities from the very beginning. Early Catholicism was not the first factor to exert a leveling influence. Baur underestimates the power of community piety and its normal theology, with which Paul already entered into conflict; and fails to see that even in the New Testament, a sharply defined theology is the exception and largely a defensive phenomenon, not the measure and source of community piety. Because the purity of the antithesis is so important to him, he regards, at first hesitantly but then resolutely, the shorter Pauline epistles to be inauthentic. The Ignatian epistles suffer the same verdict because their theology and the ecclesiastical structure presupposed in them cannot be reconciled with the scheme of primitive Christian development as Baur had reconstructed it. Thus, the variety of primitive Christian reality does not receive proper attention. It is only discovered by the history-of-religion research. The distortions do not emerge so strongly in the two investigations of the pastoral letters.[7] These studies bring together a host of dazzling individual observations and foundational reflections on historical method, which derive the unity and inauthenticity of the letters

---

7. [Käsemann is apparently referring to Baur's *Die sogenannten Pastoralbriefe des Apostels Paulus aufs neue kritisch untersucht* (Stuttgart: Cotta, 1835), and his article, "Über den Ursprung des Episkopats in der christlichen Kirche," *TZTh* 3 (1838): 1–185; the latter reprinted in Baur, *Historisch-kritische Untersuchungen*, 321–505.]

from the antithesis to Gnosticism and view the episcopate, with its supporting institutions taken over from Judaism, as a protective defense of the incipient orthodoxy. The difficulties arising from pseudonymity receive a very good discussion, and the tendency that marks the letters is equally well characterized. The dating far into the second century cannot be accepted in the same way. Baur was compelled to this view because he was not able to see the affinity of the false teaching combatted here with the false teaching in Corinth, above all with respect to the teaching on the resurrection.

Let us draw the conclusion from what has been said quite allusively: Although true historical research into primitive Christianity and the New Testament was first established with the writings presented here, Baur's individual results remain valid only to a very limited extent. We have determined that to a considerable degree this result was virtually inevitable, for at that time the distinctive character and the conditions of the Hellenistic time still lay in darkness. However, this does not mean that one can reduce everything to this common denominator, even though it is certainly true that almost all the errors are connected with this foundational mistake. For just as the luster of Baur's reconstruction is finally owed to its logical consistency, so one will probably also have to designate this consistency itself as a second source of error. For it is, after all, highly questionable whether and to what extent history proceeds logically. With this, however, we stand before the decisive problem of Baur's methodology.

Baur himself was indeed conscious of his having pursued a new path, and therefore he engaged unusually deeply not only with divergent research findings, but no less with methodological questions. The rationalistic manner of interpretation appeared to him to be ahistorical and thus already outstripped by Romanticism. Perhaps he was wrong to give too little attention to it, since his own picture of history could, after all, only have grown out of the resolutely immanent approach of Rationalism. In any case, he takes much more seriously as theological opponents the restorative orthodoxy of his time, whose political influence in terms of both church and faculty he would later experience severely enough. His "extorted justification" against Hengstenberg and his seconds is especially instructive in this regard.[8] The opposing positions can be transposed to our present

---

8. Baur, "Abgenötigte Erklärung gegen einen Artikel der Ev. Kirchenzeitung, herausgegeben von D. E. W. Hengstenberg, Prof. d. Theologie an der Universität zu Berlin, May 1836," *TZTh* 3 (1836): 179–232; reprinted in Baur, *Historisch-kritische Untersuchungen*, 267–320.

time without much displacement. The opponents regard biblical criticism as a sign of advancing unbelief and as a demonically inspired dissolution of the Christian foundations. Baur's defense is twofold. First, he proves to his opponents that even they themselves in no way entirely dispense with criticism. Thus, blanket judgments are not allowed, but must be replaced by concrete interaction with the arguments that have been presented. Of more contemporary relevance is, secondly, the fact that Baur appeals for his approach fundamentally to the Reformation. The opponents miss its intention, so that they find themselves in conflict with their own foundations. In his own self-understanding, Baur regards himself to be indeed a student of the Reformers both with regard to his basic dogmatic position and with regard to his hermeneutics. For the "true protestant criticism," even of the Bible and its parts, arises directly from the central evangelical[9] message and is thus an aspect that constitutes a dividing factor vis-à-vis Catholicism. While the principle of Catholicism is based on authority and stability, the Reformation is decisively, though not exclusively, characterized by the spirit of progress. That such a verdict is purely oriented toward intellectual history and, building on romantic views, anticipates the approach of liberalism, cannot be disputed. In any case, one cannot therefore simply dismiss Baur's appeal to the Reformation without further ado. It touches upon a problem that has not been satisfactorily thought through even up to today. For while such a methodical critique undoubtedly grew out of humanist soil, it is nevertheless not by chance that it was radicalized within Protestantism with a passion that was unthinkable for Catholics. Baur sees the reason for this in the fact that the responsibility of the individual conscience to the truth superseded or even replaced the church's binding judgment and thus led to a criticism of Scripture, not only in detail but fundamentally. His distinction between Judaists and Paulinists undoubtedly reflects, even though on the level of intellectual history, the reformational distinction between law and gospel, just as he, in the same vein, also connects the antitheses of spirit and freedom, flesh and letter, with this distinction. Only a bad Protestantism will fail to hear the voice of its fathers when Baur, with a pathos that is not common for him, coordinates true faith and true scholarship[10] in such a way that he exemplifies Luther's view of the worldly profession of Christians with reference to scholarship:

---

9. [That is, "evangelical" in the sense of being oriented toward the gospel (τὸ εὐαγγέλιον) and so broadly Protestant, rather than referring to a party within Protestantism.]

10. [*Wissenschaft*.]

Both nourish and refresh each other, and just as scholarship profits from faith, so too faith can only gain from scholarship. Only from faith does scholarship learn to purify itself from everything foreign or impure, and to devote itself undividedly and unconditionally to the holy matter of the truth; faith, in turn, owes it to scholarship that it does not devolve into idle rest, but rather is preserved through fresh, vibrant movement in order to become ever more clearly and directly conscious of its divine content. Even though scholarship appears to set itself so antagonistically against faith, when it unsettles it again and again, shakes all of its supports, and seeks again and again to undermine the ground in which it is rooted, it is precisely by this that it renders faith the greatest service. For what matters is not how much one believes, but rather what one believes and how one believes, whether one believes in such a way that in one's faith one also knows how to distinguish the true from the false, the certain from the uncertain, the essential from the less essential.... All doubts, which more recent criticism awakens, are for faith itself supremely beneficial and fruitful; they ought to be seen as a powerful means of upbringing and education for it.[11]

One cannot simply adopt these statements without interpreting them. One must be conscious of the danger of its pointed character and be able to regard corrections to its wording as necessary. In no case may one simply brush it aside or negate it on the basis of alleged or actual experience. It may sound to us today almost blasphemous when Baur opines that it is necessary even in scholarship to put to death the natural human being and that scholarship, too, is folly to the natural human being because it must be grasped spiritually.[12] I do indeed think that these statements are justified, presupposing that one understands them correctly. However, one must ask whether Baur himself has understood and interpreted them rightly. For it cannot, after all, be doubted that he was in a position to formulate them only from the standpoint of the idealism of his own time. The orthodoxy that confronted him could not help him here. In this way, his statements may appeal to the Reformation and at the same time conceal their heritage.

To what extent that really happened can indeed be more precisely determined. For Baur's controversy ultimately applies neither to rationalism nor

---

11. Baur, "Abgenötigte Erklärung," 213 (repr., Baur, *Historisch-kritische Untersuchungen*, 301).

12. Baur, "Abgenötigte Erklärung," 211–212 (repr., Baur, *Historisch-kritische Untersuchungen*, 299–300).

orthodoxy, to which he had only positioned himself in defense as a matter of necessity, but rather to that which he called "negative criticism." This term must be opaque to us, because we are experiencing the triumph of a historical and critical interpretation of the Bible, also taken up by conservative and recently even by Catholic exegesis; mostly, however, precisely in the form of that criticism that Baur called "negative." It was important for him that history should not merely be disenchanted but should also—admittedly with the means of the preceding destruction of the appearance—be reconstructed in its intellectual or spiritual coherence. This corresponds exactly to the program of "demythologizing" that is proclaimed today, since this designates the existential interpretation in its critical function, but seeks to apply the critical function solely as a means, both for correctly apprehending history and in the service of theological truth and the edification of the community. An ethical and, what is more, as we say today, an eschatological interest guides the historical interest here: in the recollection of the past reality in its character as reality, the concern is with no more and no less than the singular and final reality of humanity and the world before God. Baur wants more than the purely philological and historical enlightening of details, no matter how critical. One can explain history without understanding it in its necessity, continuity, and teleology. Interpretation, however, requires that one does not leave the details isolated, but rather, as Baur says, places them in their "objectively" predetermined place. The truth of history, of which he often speaks, lies for him in the objectivity of the given circumstances. For in them are precipitated the workings and effects of the objective spirit, whose movement is history. Again, the manner of expression inevitably seems strange and enigmatic to us, because for the most part we think we have learned that the meaning of the historical is neither to be sought nor found in what is objective. But Baur oriented existence to world history, stressed the objectivity of the conditions, of the truth, of the spirit, of the idea, and did not shy away from using diligently that word that has today become suspect, "fact," in order to be able to point to the activity of God in history, which is a given for humanity and which points beyond the individual. Thus is he able to claim of himself, "to have been guided by no other interest than by the one interest in objective historical truth, which for me is inextricably connected with the true interest in the matter of Christianity."[13] Also in his historical-

---

13. Baur, "Abgenötigte Erklärung," 187–88 (repr., Baur, *Historisch-kritische Untersuchungen*, 275–76).

critical research, he sees his task in "subordinating one's human subjectivity, which in the end is, after all, only the seat of the natural human being, to the objectivity that is determined and ordered by God."[14] For precisely this reason he polemicizes so fiercely and persistently "against the power, so dangerous in historical matters, with which the subjective consciousness wants to control objectivity and to objectify itself in it."[15] That is the actual opponent, which on the Catholic side had chosen stability and authority as its principle, whereas, on the Protestant side, even in critical research, it is not alert to a "total conception" but rather arbitrarily isolates individual facts and makes them the object of its hypotheses. "A historical truth obtains, after all, its secure existence always only in the context of the whole, in which its appropriate place can be assigned to it. Only that which is isolated, broken off, tottering in an unsure stance, can be used for hypotheses, which, however often they are built up, just as often crumble in on themselves."[16] With this, Baur's opinion has probably become clear enough for it to be summarized: history is here understood as a process of the objectively unfolding revelation of the Spirit.[17] In its objectivity it is, as revelation and in its entirety, the object of research, namely, in its historical-critical form. "Historical-critical" implies that no single moment is absolutized or negated, but rather that each moment is understood as a transitional member in the context of immanent historical progress and, precisely in this way, in the context of the revelation—realizing itself in its totality—of the Spirit or the Idea. Thus, for Baur, historical-critical work is obviously much more than a technical method: it is a deeply religious task and the medium of religious assurance. For this kind of work is the material counterpart of historical revelation as an address to the human being called to faith; that is, it is the adequate hearing and understanding of revelation, to the extent that it has gone forth in the past up to now. Historical criticism is the function of living faith on its way from a past

---

14. Baur, "Abgenötigte Erklärung," 207 (repr., Baur, *Historisch-kritische Untersuchungen*, 295).

15. Baur, "Über Zweck und Veranlassung des Römerbriefs und die damit zusammenhängenden Verhältnisse der römischen Gemeinde," *TZTh* 3 (1836): 172 (repr., Baur, *Historisch-kritische Untersuchungen*, 260).

16. Baur, "Über Zweck und Veranlassung des Römerbriefs," 178 (repr., Baur, *Historisch-kritische Untersuchungen*, 266).

17. [*Geschichte wird hier als Prozeß der sich objektiv entfaltenden Offenbarung des Geistes verstanden.*]

that has been made consciously past, to its own present and future. It places precisely this past in the overarching context of the history of the whole.

If, however, this is the case, then in the end, "historical-critical" can only mean "historical-speculative." Baur did not explicitly draw this conclusion in the writings assembled here.[18] He was too careful a historian not to protect himself in the use of his method at the same time, to the best of his abilities, against its dangers. He did not forget that also in the New Testament, the tradition mediates to us only fragments of past history, did not presume to look for more than probability in the historical, conceded to doubt precisely in the name of faith the place that it was due in scholarly investigation, and did not shy away from the sentence: "A criticism that may not also be a skeptical criticism is no criticism at all."[19] His writings prove that he can justly say of himself that he spared no effort in his work and dutifully guarded himself against the overhasty publication of his results. He could write, "To take part in the living process of development of scholarship as a self-acting member, one must also enter into it in such a way that one is prepared to bring to scholarship the sacrifice that it demands. One may not prescribe for it in advance what one wishes to have from it and under which conditions alone one could engage with it. Rather, one must decide, if necessary, even to give up one's subjective ideas and interests in order to receive again what, for example, is true and durable in them through the rebirth of scholarship."[20] Only from this standpoint does he then confess, conversely, "that again and again scholarship generates itself out of itself, that it is in a continual vibrant movement, being propelled by itself, without any human power being able to prevent it from forging a new path, time and again, in order to follow to its ultimate goal what it has once taken hold of and conceptualized."[21] One will hear and see all this and will not doubt in the least that it remained for him unassailably valid. For precisely this reason, however, the basic problem that characterizes his work emerges all the more clearly and urgently: What is the significance of an appeal to the facticity of history when the asserted

---

18. [That is, in the original collection to which this essay served as a preface.]

19. Baur, "Abgenötigte Erklärung," 219, n. (repr., Baur, *Historisch-kritische Untersuchungen*, 307, n.).

20. Baur, "Abgenötigte Erklärung," 211 (repr., Baur, *Historisch-kritische Untersuchungen*, 299).

21. Baur, "Abgenötigte Erklärung," 211 (repr., Baur, *Historisch-kritische Untersuchungen*, 299).

facts have been shown to be untenable to a large extent? It is evident that the view of the whole obtained by Baur did not, as he had hoped, lead him out of "the airy region of hypotheses"[22] and postulates, and into the realm of objectivity. Also with him, against his vigorous will and most honest intention, the subjective consciousness objectifies itself in the projections of his construction of history and forces itself upon history where it wants to serve history. It occurs here in an even more dangerous way than in the case of his opponents, who did not reach for the whole as he did, but rather were content with details and partial complexes. His grandness involves at the same time the depth of his misinterpretation. His method of approach remains ultimately a speculation—a speculation practically and methodically regulated by a man, a historian, a genius—to which he fell victim, precisely by offering to scholarship all the sacrifices that were demanded from him. Thus, it is also the case that while his life's work imparted unusually rich suggestions and insights on every side, it did not enable any unbroken continuation, at least in the area of New Testament. This was not merely—and, if perhaps initially, at least not ultimately—because his school was repressed. One pays Baur too little respect when one does not also make him responsible for the failure, which is evinced in the fact that already the next generation abandoned the actual center of his historical conception as well as his method of approach, and now more or less surrendered to the "negative criticism" against which he had fought. Among New Testament scholars, no one—except for Schlatter and Bultmann—has attempted to grasp and reveal the "whole," and again this may be initially, though not ultimately, connected with the fact that Baur had opened up an infinite perspective, and his students no longer found a way out from the details. His premises, to the contrary, shattered. To be sure, with him theology understood history as the medium of revelation until the end of the First World War, and recent developments allow this thesis to appear probable once more. And yet in the generation following Baur, the field of history was transformed into an infinite chaos of deeply unconnected "facts," in which the teleology of history and the continuity of the Spirit were lost. That "historicality"[23] as the medium of revelation took the place of history signifies this change—and seems at the same time to be a residuum of those grandiose historical speculations of Baur. Also,

---

22. [Cf. Ernst Ludwig Posselt, *Europäische Annalen* (Tübingen: Cotta, 1800), 4:223.]

23. [*Geschichtlichkeit.*]

at the very least it may be asked whether Baur, in the fact that he, in the claim that the Spirit objectifies itself historically, more clearly holds fast to the Reformation testimony of the primacy of the gospel over faith and to the worldwide power of this gospel, does not remain superior to the existential reinterpretation of his speculation. However, just as the generation following him was already no longer in a position to verify historically[24] his picture and speculation of history, so we can no longer follow him in almost every respect also theologically. After all, we have returned against his warning and the view that he dogmatically advocated to the conviction that he, in his "Urspung des Episkopats" ("Origin of the Episcopacy"), characterizes as follows: "A period which, like that of the Reformation, put truth in opposition to error, could be introduced only through an absolute leap, and one would have to see oneself driven in the last respect to the necessity of regarding all of history from the viewpoint of a dualistic opposition."[25] This is probably the only place in his early investigations in which he expressly criticizes the Reformation. It deserves all the more attention. To the absolute leap and the concomitant unavoidable dualism he opposed an immanently historical progress as the self-expression of the Spirit. Whether he was really successful in fully eliminating the dualism may be allowed to rest. That is not the impression one gets when one sees how sharply he allowed subjectivity and objectivity to be methodologically contrasted, and how he himself was constrained, as a historian, to demarcate the "true apostolic divine word" from the human word. For in the end, it is after all easier to describe, in an ultimately speculative program, the subjective (and thus also error) as a transitional aspect of the objective revelation (and thus also of truth) than it is to implement this program historically. Nevertheless, be that as it may, the alternative presented here is possible only on the intellectual-historical plane and is fundamentally questionable theologically. For the fact that we are no longer able to understand history as the objectivization of the Spirit in Baur's sense has as a consequence that history as such loses its revelatory character. Baur thought that docetism and abstraction would then be unavoidable. And indeed, the decisive dogmatic problem is whether this claim can be deemed correct or whether one should not here, with the

---

24. [*Historisch.*]

25. Baur, "Ursprung des Episkopats," 105 (repr., Baur, *Historisch-kritische Untersuchungen*, 425).

Reformation, hold out to history the word as the sole source of revelation and regard history only as a place of encounter with the word.

The problem thus marked out cannot be pursued further here. What is important to note in closing is the recognition that Baur, like scarcely any other, places us before the fundamental question of what meaning the watchword "historical-critical" actually has. But that means inquiring as to how historical work becomes at all possible and meaningful. With this, the worth of historical scholarship and the personal obligation to it need not be cast into doubt in the least. We value and do a lot because we simply cannot leave it. The question to be asked is how we become so aware of historical reality that we are least subject to illusion. From the analysis of Baur's work, it follows that we in no way have this possibility at our disposal according to our own will, since obstructions hinder us that we are as little able to leap over as our own shadow, and that logical consistency can drive us into speculation instead of reality. From this standpoint, he poses for us the methodological problem no less urgently than the dogmatic one. He was the first to really open up to us the world of primitive Christianity, and yet he also made the way, along which he himself had gone, impassable already for the generation following him. Can one draw any other lesson from this than that an access to historical reality that is to be guaranteed by a method does not exist at all? Does not the encounter with it always have the character of a gift, and is this not always the case for all reality? Can a method of approach perform more than an auxiliary service, namely, in preparing for this gift by clearing away the recognizable hindrances as far as possible, while placing recognized reality reflexively into connections that corroborate its own evidence? That would mean that a method of approach is not derivable from principles, but that it is characterized rather as an experiment that, as such, confirms itself through expedience and nothing else. That leads to a second observation. If anyone, it is precisely Baur who proves that there is no scholarship without presuppositions.[26] Even in our methodology, we are bound to our dogmatic premises. What is possible is not presuppositionless scholarship but scholarship that is radically questioning and ready to continually correct itself. That means, however, that we give to ourselves an account of the dogmatic traditions

---

26. [Also perhaps an allusion to Rudolf Bultmann's famous essay, "Is Exegesis without Presuppositions Possible?," in his *Existence and Faith: Shorter Writings of Rudolf Bultmann*, ed. Schubert M. Ogden (London: Hodder & Stoughton, 1961), 289–96, 314–15].

out of which we come and in which we are situated respectively. It is not difficult to show that Baur was not able to go so deeply into this reflection so as to distinguish the Reformation message from the premises of a Protestantism that was divorced from the Reformation through Rationalism. The criticism that he called "genuinely Protestant" shared with the reformational criticism the negation of mere tradition, but not the position that was the criterion of the negation. For this criterion was, for Baur, the self-expression of the Spirit in its totality in the path of immanently historical progress, but for the Reformation it was the gospel of righteousness by faith. It is obvious that this gospel as such cannot determine our historical work with the immediacy that Baur's historical speculation was able to do, even though, in its theological concretions, this gospel allows dogmatic-historical focal points to be recognized in the field of Christian history. This, however, already points to the fact that, as in the Reformation, it can strengthen and clarify the critical function of theology; that is, it urges one to separate the spirits also in the historical sphere, at least fundamentally. It cannot take away from the historian the responsibility that he must himself bear for his work, but rather will radicalize this. It will, however, allow him from the outset to see history as a field of tensions, oppositions, and discontinuities. It will say to him that such tensions, oppositions, and discontinuities cannot ultimately be settled, and will preserve him, at least to a considerable extent, from speculation, which thinks that it must strive for a teleology of world history. In this way it will pull him out of the overconfidence that seeks the truth in the realm of the unlimited and place him instead in the knowledge of his own limitation before a limited reality. It gives freedom for historical work by allowing its limits to be critically recognized in subjective as well as in objective matters.

PART 1
The Christ Party in the Corinthian Community

[61] The two letters of the apostle Paul to the Corinthian community, which are outstanding in so many respects, warrant such great interest largely because they—far more than any other New Testament writing—put us right into the vibrant center of a [62] Christian community that is still taking shape, and provide a clear picture of the circumstances out of which the new life animated by Christianity would develop with its own distinctive characteristics. In a city like Corinth, where Greek learning and Greek sensuality prevailed in equal measure, and a flexibility and factiousness that was native to the Greeks threatened to assert its influence on Christianity as well, it was inevitable that the various elements that everywhere transplanted the germ of an opposition into the midst of the blossoming communities of Christians—an opposition that encroached more and more, and could only gradually be offset again—would give rise to distinctive phenomena.

As one would expect at the outset, and as one can see from both the account of its founding in Acts 18 and the content of the two letters themselves, the Corinthian community was predominantly composed of gentile Christians. However, it also did not lack members who either had been won directly from Judaism or who at least allowed themselves to be very easily influenced by Jewish terms and prejudices. Thus, the apostle felt himself compelled here, as at other times, to present admonitions related to the mutual relationship between Jewish and gentile Christians. However, what testifies to the presence of a Jewish Christian component in the Corinthian community above all else is the well-known passage of 1 Cor 1:11, where the apostle speaks of the contentions that prevail in the Corinthian community and names the individual parties into which the community was divided. Ἐδηλώθη μοι περὶ ὑμῶν—ὅτι ἕκαστος ὑμῶν λέγει· ἐγὼ μέν εἰμι Παύλου, ἐγὼ δὲ Ἀπολλώ, ἐγὼ δὲ Κηφᾶ, ἐγὼ δὲ Χριστοῦ. There is no reason to doubt that it was primarily the gentile-Christian part of the community that joined itself to Paul and Apollos, whereas for those who, also as Christians, remained more loyal to Judaism, the name of Peter was the center of a smaller group. However, the question of where we should place the party named after Christ [63] cannot be easily decided. If its individual characteristics could be determined more precisely, however, then this would certainly shed a welcome light on the circumstances in the Corinthian community in general.

Among the various views that have been set forth concerning the so-called Christ party, there are two views in particular that deserve closer attention: that of Gottlob Christian Storr[1] and that of Johann Gottfried Eichhorn.[2] Here, we must first attend to these two views.

As natural as it appears to regard οἱ τοῦ Χριστοῦ as those who had still experienced the teaching of Jesus themselves or who at least belonged to a sect that was headed by a direct student of Jesus, this view, in the vague form in which Werner Karl Ludwig Ziegler,[3] for example, has presented it, is immediately confronted by the well-founded objection that it fails to explain how the Christ party distinguished itself from the Cephas party, since the latter could, after all, have pointed to the same advantage of the head of its party. Why did the Christ party not also name itself after a teacher who, like Peter, was directly connected with Jesus? The fact that it preferred to name itself after Christ seems to indicate something that even the Petrine party did not have in common with it. It is precisely this—the characteristic feature that distinguishes the Petrine party from the Christ party—that Storr believes he can identify in the kinship relationship in which the teacher at the head of the Christ party stood in relation to Christ. Οἱ τοῦ Χριστοῦ are, as Storr attempted to argue his view with characteristic acumen,[4] those members of the Corinthian community who had made the apostle James, as a relative of Jesus, the

---

1. Gottlob Christian Storr, *Notitiae historicae Epistolarum Paulli ad Corinthios interpretationi servientes* (Tübingen: Fues, 1788). [Storr, 1746–1805, was Professor of Philosophy (1776), then Professor of Theology (from 1777) in Tübingen.]

2. Johann Gottfried Eichhorn, *Einleitung in das Neue Testament*, 3 vols. (Leipzig: Weidmann, 1804–1814). [Eichhorn, 1752–1827, was Professor of Oriental Languages in Jena (1775–1788) and Göttingen (from 1788).]

3. Werner Karl Ludwig Ziegler, "Besondere Einleitung in unsern ersten Brief an die Corinthier," in vol. 2 of *Theologische Abhandlungen* (Göttingen: Dieterich, 1804), 38. [Ziegler, 1763–1809, was professor at Rostock (1792–1809).]

4. Storr, *Notitiae historicae*, 14.

head of their sect. Thus, the advantage that they ascribed to themselves vis-à-vis the Petrine party consisted in the fact that they attached themselves not merely to a direct disciple of Jesus [64], but even to an ἀδελφὸς κυρίου, as Gal 1:19 calls James.⁵ They boasted of a closer external connection with Christ, mediated through James, and this is what the apostle alludes to in 2 Cor 5:16 by means of the expression Χριστὸν κατὰ σάρκα γινώσκειν.⁶ Only on this assumption is it said to become comprehensible why Paul, in 1 Cor 9:5, mentioned the brothers of the Lord, to whom James belonged, and made special mention of James himself alongside Peter in 1 Cor 15:7.

> But if some of the Corinthians have disdained Paul in favor of Peter, and others in favor of the Lord's brother, the reason is evident, because in the first place he has written that he is not altogether universally an apostle—which they contradict—and that he is equal in authority to all the others; but, moreover, he separately added that he is equal in authority likewise to the brothers of the Lord and Peter. For the same reason, because without doubt the authority of Peter would be strongest among one group of Corinthians and that of James among certain others, he is not satisfied to collectively bring up the agreeing testimony of the other apostles alongside his own, but appeals to both Peter and James by name—and only them from the whole number of the apostles—as witnesses of the resurrection of Christ. It is not due to any other reason than that each witness would seem to a certain group of Corinthians to be trustworthy and taking precedence before the others—we hold it to have been a fact settled to a degree as great as the care with which the choice of witnesses whom Paul uses is made in this place.⁷

This view is approved of and adopted by Johann Friedrich Flatt,⁸ as well as by many other scholars, most notably by Leonhard Bertholdt,⁹ Johannes

---

5. Ἰάκωβον τὸν ἀδελφὸν τοῦ κυρίου.
6. Ὥστε ἡμεῖς ἀπὸ τοῦ νῦν οὐδένα οἴδαμεν κατὰ σάρκα· εἰ καὶ ἐγνώκαμεν κατὰ σάρκα Χριστόν, ἀλλὰ νῦν οὐκέτι γινώσκομεν.
7. Storr, *Notitiae historicae*, 14–15.
8. Johann Friedrich Flatt, *Vorlesungen über die beyden Briefe Pauli an die Corinthier...*, 2 vols. (Tübingen: Fues, 1827), 15–16. [Flatt, 1759–1821, was Professor of Philosophy (from 1785) and subsequently of Professor of Theology (from 1792) in Tübingen.]
9. Leonhard Bertholdt, *Historisch-kritische Einleitung in sämmtliche kanonische und apokryphische Schriften des alten und neuen Testaments*, 6 vols. (Erlangen: Palm,

Leonhard Hug,[10] and August Ludwig Christian Heydenreich.[11] However, as plausible as this idea appears, in everything that Storr has put forward there is nothing that actually proves it. The passages to which Storr appeals still make perfectly good sense if neither the ἀδελφοὶ Κυρίου nor James stood in a close connection of this type to the Corinthian [65] community. Like James in 1 Cor 15:7, the ἀδελφοὶ Κυρίου in 1 Cor 9:5 are placed in the series of the others with whom they belong in a class, and the context contains nothing whatsoever that would lead us to assume that they have been mentioned because of a special relation that applies only to them. Likewise, the expression Χριστὸν κατὰ σάρκα γινώσκειν is not crafted in such a way that it must precisely be understood only in the sense of a relationship of kinship, for there is nothing at all in the two letters of the apostle that one would have to understand as standing in opposition to such an exaggerated estimation of external *kinship* relations as something that fed the sectarian spirit of the Corinthian community. Furthermore, if, in accordance with Storr's view, the Christ party was actually the party of James, the question would still arise: "Why did this party not name itself after James, as the rest of the parties named themselves after Paul, Apollos, and Cephas? Why is it the name οἱ τοῦ Χριστοῦ that appears? As common as it is in linguistic usage for the article in such a construction to designate a relationship of kinship, the name itself, Χριστός, does not fit this interpretation. One may note with justification that in this case, instead of οἱ Χριστοῦ, it would read οἱ κυρίου, just as there is, after all, talk of ἀδελφοὶ κυρίου and not of ἀδελφοὶ Χριστοῦ. In the name Χριστός, which is used here, lies an associated concept, which points to a different relationship than that of an external kinship relating to the person of Jesus.[12]

1812–1819), 6:3319. [Bertholdt, 1774–1822, was a rationalist theologian who was Professor of Philosophy (from 1805) and Professor of Theology (from 1809) in Erlangen.]

10. Johannes Leonhard Hug, *Einleitung in die Schriften des Neuen Testaments*, 2 vols., 3rd ed. (Stuttgart: Cotta, 1826), 2:360. [Hug, 1765–1846, was a Catholic theologian and Professor of Theology and Oriental Languages at Freiburg (from 1791).]

11. August Ludwig Christian Heydenreich, *Commentarius in priorem divi Pauli ad Corinthios epistolam*, 2 vols. (Marburg: Krieger, 1825–1828), 1:31. [Heydenreich, 1773–1858, was a Protestant theologian and professor, following a series of pastorates, at the Protestant Seminary in Herborn (from 1818).]

12. Although Jesus as Χριστός is κύριος, in κύριος (cf., e.g., John 20:18, 25) the concept of the historical-personal nevertheless emerges far more than in Χριστός. While Χριστός is also used by itself for Jesus, it always includes at the same time the dogmatic concept of the Messiah or the Redeemer. One could, however, suppose that those who

1. The Christ Party in the Corinthian Community   21

[66] It is undoubtedly precisely this aspect that must form the point of departure for that other view, which Eichhorn was the first to present, as follows:

> While the parties of Paul, Cephas, and Apollos quarreled among themselves, a party of neutrals formed, who claimed that they held neither to Paul nor Apollos nor Peter, but simply to Christ. That this was its origin can hardly be subjected to doubt; it is that much less clear, however, on what it based itself. Presumably not on a particular teacher who would have been a direct student of Christ, [67] for otherwise his name would have been expressly mentioned, like those of Paul, Apollos, and Peter. Likewise, it was presumably not based on a direct instruction by Christ, since the Corinthian Jews, who could, for example, have chanced to hear Jesus while on a pilgrimage to Jerusalem, must have been so extremely small in number that there would hardly have been enough of them to form a party of their own. And if one of them had become the founder of his own Christ party, it would have borne the name of the founder, just like the parties of Paul, Apollos, and Cephas. Thus, it was presumably based on a written instruction, which it drew from the speeches of Jesus that were written down in the *Urevangelium* ("Primitive Gospel").

---

wanted to designate themselves as οἱ Χριστοῦ as relatives of Jesus had wanted, precisely through this expression, to indicate at the same time their close relationship to Jesus as Messiah, Χριστός. [66] However, in this case the concept of kinship would then recede again, and one could at least say that if this were the main thing, it would, as in ἀδελφοὶ τοῦ Κυρίου, more likely be signified by κύριος than by Χριστός. They probably wanted to assert themselves not as relatives of the Messiah but only of Jesus, who appeared as the Messiah. Here, one can compare the passage in Eusebius, *Hist. eccl.* 3.19. In that passage, where it says that the ἀπόγονοι Ἰούδα ["grandsons of Jude"] were accused under Domitian ὡς ἀπὸ γένους τυγχάνοντες Δαβίδ, καὶ ὡς αὐτοῦ συγγένειαν τοῦ χριστοῦ φέροντες ["of being of the family of David, and related to Christ himself" (trans. Lake and Oulton)], it is also not a mere relation of kinship with Jesus that is intended; rather, the actual concept of the Messiah is meant to be expressed here. Thus, one would, at the least, have to modify Storr's view in such a way that it would be assumed that the Χριστοῦ ὄντες had to do not simply with kinship to the person of Jesus but with Jesus as the Messiah. With this modification, however, one can no longer have an interest in restricting the Χριστοῦ ὄντες simply to the actual relatives of Jesus, for others could also boast of having a special relationship to Jesus as Messiah. As far as I know, this objection pertaining to the linguistic usage of κύριος and Χριστός has not yet been advanced against Storr's explanation. But it is undeniable that the particular uses of the designations Ἰησοῦς, κύριος, and Χριστός are by no means arbitrary, and paying closer attention to them in individual passages is highly important for exegesis. See the following remarks on 2 Cor 5:16 [Baur writes "2 Cor 5:26" here].

And why couldn't its adherents—on account of the opposition that was, as a matter of fact, predominant, which the name of the neutrals did not clearly indicate—have preferred to name themselves "students of Christ"?[13]

Apart from Eichhorn's hypothesis of an *Urevangelium*, which is at any rate a very uncertain support for this view, David Julius Pott[14] has sought to ground this same position more securely by a comparison with the passage in 1 Cor 3:22, where Paul, after the preceding reproof of the schisms that had arisen in the Corinthian community, summarizes the main statement of his argument with the words πάντα ὑμῶν εἰσιν εἴτε Παῦλος, εἴτε Ἀπολλώ, εἴτε Κηφᾶς, πάντα ὑμῶν εἰσιν, ὑμεῖς δὲ Χριστοῦ. One could, so he suggests, let the adherents of the Christ party themselves explain their view:

> According to our firm conviction, certainly none of us doubt that the true doctrine of Christ is found in such a degree in the instruction of Paul, as well as in that of Apollos, as in that of Peter, nor whether to make use of it with a view to expanding and strengthening our understanding of Christian matters. Neither preferring the more eloquent Apollos to father Paul, in his particular force and persistent candor, or preferring this one to that one, nor rejecting the teaching even of Peter, the principal apostle, to the extent that the genuine teaching become known to us, so that, since we are singularly engaged with it, not judging in the words of any master except Christ, we worshipers of the true Christ might avoid all these leaders.

Accordingly, one would thus have to regard the view [68] of Χριστοῦ ὄντες as the view that is endorsed by Paul himself. And one would then have to think of the same οἱ Χριστοῦ also with regard to 1 Cor 1:12. Pott says:

> For least of all in that place, since by means of that very same ἐγὼ δέ, employed three times in the immediately preceding context, sects and factions are indicated, in some way we are brought together, so that we should bring back the very words ἐγὼ δὲ Χριστοῦ (in which, moreover,

---

13. Eichhorn, *Einleitung*, 3:107–8.

14. David Julius Pott, *Epistola pauli ad corinthios prima*, vol. 5.1 of *Novum Testamentum Graece: Perpetua annotatione illustratum*, ed. Johann Benjamin Koppe and Christoph Friedrich von Ammon (Göttingen: Dieterich, 1826), 31–32. [Pott, 1760–1838, was Professor of Theology at Helmstädt (from 1787) and Göttingen (from 1810).]

the enumeration of sects passes away) to the sect. Since it was pleasing to Paul, perhaps even on account of the speech that will be received, to designate thus the true disciples of Christ, nor would a great quantity of many words be necessary, even to fully encompass this. Nevertheless, those who, foreign to every pursuit of sects, are zealous to advance in true Christian instruction from any teacher, likewise supersede the aforementioned sects, who by a more powerful authority seem to reach towards Christ alone. And, without doubt, how certainly the apostle, able to refrain so greatly from circumventing, since he knew that they, to whom he was writing, had sufficient knowledge—how would he wish that Χριστοῦ εἶναι be understood? Then, when they were asked, what would they do about the teacher? They would naturally profess themselves τοῦ Χριστοῦ εἶναι, because they would not be able to answer, neither with different words nor with fewer. Then perhaps, for this reason itself, or because the number of factions was increased by others who were wickedly zealous, they were accustomed to being called οἱ Χριστοῦ so that they may keep the appearance of a sect in contrast with themselves.[15]

The source from which those who called themselves τοὺς Χριστοῦ drew their Christian teaching is said to have been the instruction of Paul, Apollos, and Peter. By exhorting the Corinthians themselves in 1 Cor 3:22 τοῦ Χριστοῦ εἶναι, he is said to have wanted precisely by this means to point the partisans of the sects to the teaching of the true teacher, to which οἱ Χριστοῦ already adhered. In order to avoid every appearance of a sect, they did not name themselves after the teacher who first laid the foundation, τοῦ εἶναι εἰ μὴ τοῦ Χριστοῦ, but rather simply τοῦ Χριστοῦ. Insofar as the concern here is first with the claim that the passage in 1 Cor 1:12 is to be explained on the basis of the parallel passage in 1 Cor 3:22, the question arises whether the words of the latter passage, ὑμεῖς δὲ Χριστοῦ, are to be taken in the same sense as the words of the former one, ἐγὼ δὲ Χριστοῦ. For the purpose of answering this question [69], it cannot be superfluous to review briefly the apostle's train of thought in the whole connected section 1 Cor 1:12–3:23. The apostle takes as his starting point the rebuke that he had pronounced over the sectarian spirit of the Corinthians. In 1 Cor 1:14, he says that he is happy that he had not contributed to it through the βαπτίζειν. In particular, this prompts him to comment that the βαπτίζειν is not the chief matter but rather the εὐαγγελίζεσθαι. Through this, he was led to his main theme, to explain what is the chief matter of the εὐαγγελίζεσθαι

---

15. Pott, *Epistola Pauli*, 33.

and its object, Christianity, namely, not human wisdom and artifice, not what otherwise counts as highest according to the usual view of humans, but only the simple teaching about certain historical facts and, above all, the great fact of Jesus's death on the cross. To be sure, in this regard, Christianity, the apostle reminds the Corinthians, comes into the greatest conflict with the prevailing concepts among Jews and gentiles about the religious needs of humans and about what they must regard as their greatest advantage. This, however, reflects the complete difference between the divine and the human standpoints, of which, after all, as the apostle further explains from 1 Cor 1:26 on, the composition of the members who make up the Christian communities provides the most striking proof. All the advantages that usually count among humans are not found among them. But which entirely different advantages does a Christian community possess instead, insofar as it is a society chosen by God and has in Christ the highest principle of its religious and spiritual life? In relation to this, 1 Cor 2:1–2, with reference to the contrast between the σοφία θεοῦ and the σοφία τοῦ αἰῶνος τουτοῦ, develops what is distinctive about the Christian consciousness according to the results of its individual aspects,[16] and the

---

16. The partly objective and partly subjective aspects are: (1) the objectively given, τὰ ὑπὸ τοῦ θεοῦ χαρισθέντα ἡμῖν (1 Cor 2:13 [sic; read 1 Cor 2:12]). If this is the object and content of a teaching, the apostle speaks [70] (2) of the σοφία θεοῦ. But now if this σοφία θεοῦ is really accepted into a person's mind and soul, he receives (3) precisely thereby the πνεῦμα ἐκ τοῦ θεοῦ (1 Cor 2:12). It awakens in him the genuine Christian consciousness. However, the principle of the Christian consciousness itself is ultimately (4) the πνεῦμα τοῦ θεοῦ itself. And just as it alone is what τὰ τοῦ θεοῦ οἶδεν (1 Cor 2:11), so it is also the principle and the efficient cause, ἵνα εἰδῶμεν τὰ ὑπὸ τοῦ θεοῦ χαρισθέντα ἡμῖν. But the πνεῦμα τοῦ θεοῦ, if it is to be active in the human being, must always find something pneumatic already in a person that it can take hold of, for otherwise the distinction made between the πνευματικός and the ψυχικός could not take place at all. With regard to the phrase πνευματικοῖς πνευματικὰ συγκρίνοντες, I agree entirely with the apt observation made in the studies edited by Dr. Klaiber (Eduard Elwert, "Ueber die Lehre von der Inspiration, in Beziehung auf das Neue Testament, ein Versuch," in vol. 3.2 of *Studien der evangelischen Geistlichkeit Wirtembergs*, ed. Christoph Benjamin Klaiber [Stuttgart: Löflund und Sohn, 1831], 51) that συγκρίνειν must be taken here in its actual meaning, i.e., to make a judgment about certain objects, with regard to the extent to which they belong together or do not belong together; however, I maintain that συγκρίνειν πνευματικοῖς πνευματικὰ is to be understood not in terms of the form corresponding to the content, but in terms of the communication of what is pneumatic to pneumatic people, since this appears to me to be the main idea in light of the immediately following ψυχικὸς δὲ ἄνρωπος οὐ

principle of this consciousness is rooted in the [70] πνεῦμα θεοῦ. However, the Christian consciousness cannot awaken unless there is something spiritual in the disposition of the human being himself that corresponds to the pneumatic reality that the πνεῦμα θεοῦ wants to impart, a certain subjective receptivity for what is pneumatic. In accord with the merely sensuous, purely natural orientation of his spirit, the ψυχικός has no concept of that which the πνευματικός is conscious of. He cannot think his way into the spiritual state of the πνευματικός at all because he does not stand on the same level of spiritual life. Accordingly, the πνευματικός is regarded as a μωρός by the ψυχικός. For precisely this reason, a human being can never become aware of the divine on his own; rather, this must be imparted to him by God. This impartation has come about through Christianity, through which an entirely new and higher consciousness has been awakened in all who have a receptiveness for it. [71] In 1 Cor 2:14, the apostle undoubtedly wanted to take account of the adverse judgments that his opponents in Corinth had permitted themselves to make about him. Since they were still lacking a sense and receptivity for the pneumatic, they also could not understand the higher teachings that the apostle could have given to them, and regarded the condescension demanded of him by the nature of the matter simply as a sign of spiritual weakness. In 1 Cor 3:3–4, the apostle then attributes the factiousness of the Corinthians to the same character of still being on such a low level of spiritual life. It also proceeded, in the apostle's view, from an orientation of mind that was incapable of lifting itself to a higher unity, and for precisely this reason was able to view the individual teachers of the gospel only in their own separate existence for themselves and not in their higher communal relationship to the one principle of all spiritual life; that is, to Christ. Thus, this is the background for the main thought, which the apostle explicates in 1 Cor 3:3–4: Christian teachers are only servants of the purposes of God if they act only in the name of God and in the sphere of activity that God has assigned to them. His sphere of activity among the Corinthians was to lay the initial foundation of Christianity. He is aware that he has done his share, and wishes that now other Christian teachers may be able to give the same testimony about themselves. Yet experience, the best test of the effects of a teaching, will demonstrate, in his view, the character of what they teach.

δέχεται and according to 1 Cor 3:1–2. [Elwert, 1805–1865, was Professor of Theology in Zürich (1836–1837) and Tübingen (1839–1841), before returning to pastoral work and serving as director of the theological seminary in Schönthal.]

After this digression concerning his own person, the apostle returns in 1 Cor 1:26 to the main admonition with which he was concerned, namely, that the Corinthians should guard themselves against all the destructive principles that work against the common spirit of Christianity, and should not allow themselves to be deceived by the apparent wisdom of the world, which unduly exalts human status. Where the concern is with the true interest of the community, where everything is related to Christ and God, the one highest principle of the truthful spiritual life, then the Christian teacher can only regard himself as a servant. This thought, which runs through the whole text [72], also underlies the reminder given in 1 Cor 3:16–18. The one who destroys the unity of the Christians by means of a sectarian spirit opposes the Spirit of God, which is meant to fill the association of Christians like a temple of God, and the one who trusts in worldly wisdom gives humans a status that they cannot have vis-à-vis God. The closing reminder in 1 Cor 3:21–22[17] now also connects precisely with this: πάντα ὑμῶν ἐστιν, εἴτε Παῦλος, εἴτε Ἀπολλὼς, εἴτε Κηφᾶς, εἴτε κόσμος, εἴτε ζωὴ, εἴτε θάνατος, εἴτε ἐνεστῶτα, εἴτε μέλλοντα· πάντα ὑμῶν ἐστιν, ὑμεῖς δὲ Χριστοῦ, Χριστὸς δὲ θεοῦ. It is impossible for these words, coming as they do in the context just provided, to have only the meaning that Pott gives to them: the Corinthians should use everything possible to perfect their understanding of Christianity, seeking to learn from all teachers, whoever they should be. Pott says:

> Yours are Paul, Apollos, Cephas, yea, even certainly the whole entirety of teachers, whether among that part of the whole that embraces ζωὴν καὶ θάνατον, living and dead, or in that part that embraces ἐνεστῶτα καὶ μέλλοντα, now present and coming in the future, let them be mentioned, that is, whenever you might withdraw from the manner of the world: I would wish that you all progress in Christian knowledge wholly from all legitimate (γνησίοις) teachers, however great their number might be, whether they are yet alive, or if they have already died, whether they have reached you now, or at a former time.[18]

Let us allow to rest the certainly very forced and unnatural interpretation that is given to the words πάντα ὑμῶν ἐστιν, εἴτε κόσμος, and so on.[19] Let

---

17. [*Sic*; read 1 Cor 3:21–23.]
18. Pott, *Epistola Pauli*, 158.
19. One has no reason to depart from the usual and natural meaning of the words. While, with πάντα, the apostle initially thinks of the teachers, he immediately expands

1. The Christ Party in the Corinthian Community

us also pay no [73] attention to the fact that, if we make a comparison with 2 Corinthians, where only the same teachers mentioned in 1 Cor 1:13 can be meant, the purpose of the apostle cannot be to exhort the Corinthians simply to cling to every possible teacher without providing any characteristic by which the γνησίοι could be distinguished from the false teachers portrayed with such dark colors in 2 Corinthians. Still, the main words πάντα ὑμῶν ἐστιν can only be taken as follows: everything has its relation to you; that is, all Christian teachers have only the purpose of serving your best interests, whereas you yourselves have your relation to Christ; and Christ, in turn, has his relation to God. If you regard your teachers not as mere humans (as humans, they cannot, after all, have such a worth that you would be permitted to downgrade the status of Christ as the one head), if you regard them as servants of the purposes of God, then they are, after all, only there for your sake; and it is foolish to invert this relationship in such a way that it seems as if you are only there for their sake, in order to pay homage to their eminence. In this way, you thereby place yourself on a standpoint on which you stop with what is only individual and subordinate, and do not know how to trace it back to its highest unity. As your teachers have to pay attention to you, must make you the object and purpose of their activity, so must you pay attention to Christ. He is the highest principle upon which you must acknowledge yourself to be dependent in your whole religious and spiritual life, while Christ himself, in turn, points back to God as the last and highest, the absolute principle. Thus, everything has its final relation to God, [74] and the καυχᾶσθαι ἐν ἀνθρώποις (with which the apostle, in 1 Cor 1:21, connects his last reminder to the preceding discussion about the σοφία τοῦ κοσμου) is something that is entirely void. However, for precisely this reason, everything is repugnant through which a teacher is esteemed in a manner that makes him, as it were, an end in himself and that causes the relationship that his entire activity is meant to have toward the best of the

---

and generalizes his thoughts, as he loves to do, in 1 Cor 3:21–22. "Everything should serve what is best for you according to the purpose of God and under his direction." The expressions in 1 Cor 3:22 spell out in general the concept of πάντα. "Everything that is outside of you, the whole surrounding world in which you live, and likewise [73] every change that can happen to you, whether you live or die, is to serve what is best for you." By generalizing his thoughts in this way, the apostle seeks to inspire in his readers a self-assurance of being objects of the divine purpose that cannot allow them to turn themselves into simply a means for promoting the status of their teachers.

community, to Christ, and to God, to be overlooked. If we now compare with the passage discussed up to now that other passage, 1 Cor 1:12, it is unmistakable that the situation is completely different in the case of the latter passage, and that the one cannot serve as a clarification for the other, apart from the fact that both speak of Χριστοῦ εἶναι, yet with a differing meaning in each case. In 1 Cor 1:12, the context demands for the words ἐγὼ δὲ Χριστοῦ to be taken as the designation of a sect, just as the preceding sentences designate many sects: ἐγὼ μέν εἰμι Παύλου, ἐγὼ δὲ Ἀπολλώ, ἐγὼ δὲ Κηφᾶ. For precisely this reason, those words can only be taken in the sense of an adherent of the so-called Christ party, but not as though the apostle wanted to refer, in opposition to those sects, to the divine unity given in Christ that lies beyond all those sectarian divisions and differences. Thus, if Eichhorn's explanation, according to which οἱ Χριστοῦ are the neutrals, is to be accepted, the neutrals themselves would also be nothing other than a sect. Hence, August Neander has also spoken of the Christ party in this vein.[20] Regarding the party's adherents, he says:[21]

> Thus, they must presumably have claimed to be of Christ in a false sense. Most likely, the Corinthians' presumption of wisdom brought it about that in the midst of disputes over whether the teaching of Paul, Peter, or Apollos was alone the correct and perfect teaching, there also appeared among them some who wanted to understand Christianity [75] better than Paul, Peter, and Apollos, who constructed their own Christ and their own Christianity, whether from oral or written traditions, which they interpreted in their own way according to their preconceived opinions and conceits. And now, in their arrogant sense of freedom, they wanted to make themselves independent from the authority of the chosen and enlightened witnesses of the gospel. They probably considered themselves to have a more perfect teaching than these witnesses, and in such conceit they now named themselves the sole disciples of Christ, in contrast to all others.

This view as well can only be seen as a modification of Eichhorn's opinion. However, just as Eichhorn's view, due to the hypothesis of a Primitive

---

20. August Neander, "Der Apostel Paulus und die Gemeinde zu Korinth," in *Kleine Gelegenheitsschriften praktisch-christlichen, vornehmlich exegetischen und historischen Inhalts*, 3rd ed. (Berlin: Eisner, 1829), 68. [Neander, 1789–1850, was a Jewish convert to Christianity who became Professor of Church History and Doctrine in Heidelberg (from 1812) and then in Berlin (from 1813).]

21. Neander, "Apostel Paulus," 98.

1. The Christ Party in the Corinthian Community

Gospel, is not suited to provide a clear conception of the relationship of the so-called neutrals to the adherents of the other sects, so the actual character of the so-called Christ party also remains in the dark according to the explanation provided by Neander. Even if they wanted to construct their own Christ and their own Christianity in opposition to the sectarian leaders, to whose authority the adherents of the other sects devoted themselves, their relationship to Christ would still have had to be mediated in a somewhat similar way as in the other sects. Furthermore, if they thought they had a more perfect teaching than others and claimed to understand Christianity better than Paul, Apollos, and Peter, it is not clear how they wanted to claim this advantage with a better right than every other of the remaining sects presumably also had. Thus, either οἱ Χριστοῦ are not a sect that could be placed alongside the other named sects in a class—a view that the classification of the various sects given by the apostle in 1 Cor 1:12 apparently contradicts—or they did indeed form a sect as well, though in that case we must then acknowledge that, at least according to the views set forth up to now, we are not in a position to form a clear conception of its tendency and distinctive character.

[76] In order to come, from the last pointed mentioned, closer to what is probable, the suggestion provided by Johann Ernst Christian Schmidt in his study of 1 Cor 1:12 appears to me to be not without significance.[22] According to Schmidt, there were actually only two parties. The Pauline and the Apollonian were one party, and the Petrine and the Christinian, as Schmidt expresses it, were likewise one party. In light of the well-known relationship in which Paul and Peter stood to one another, the former as apostle to the gentiles, the latter as apostle to the Jews, partly in actuality, partly, at least, in the perception of the main parties of the oldest Christian church, there can be no doubt that the two sects that named themselves after Paul and Cephas formed the main opposition. Now if it already follows from this that the two other parties, the Apollonian party and the Christ party, could, in comparison to those, display only a smaller difference, then the relationship between the Pauline and the Apollonian parties themselves—if we seek to give a more precise account of it—probably also leads to this same view. We see from numerous passages that

---

22. Johann Ernst Christian Schmidt, *Bibliothek für Kritik und Exegese des neuen Testaments und älteste Christengeschichte*, 2 vols. (Hadamar: Neue Gelehrtenbuchhandlung, 1797–1798), 1:91. [Schmidt, 1772–1831, was lecturer (from 1793) and professor (from 1798) in Gießen.]

Paul places Apollos entirely on his own side and regards him as a true coworker in the proclamation of the gospel. In the contents of the two letters of the apostle themselves, there is nothing that would allow one to infer a far-reaching disagreement. With this I do not wish to deny what is usually assumed, namely, that the apostle may especially have the Apollos party in view in the section in which he speaks of the great difference between the σοφία κόσμου and the σοφία θεοῦ. On the other hand, it is nevertheless also to be conceded that the direction of thought depicted here must have been more or less predominant in the Corinthian community as a whole, at least insofar as it was comprised of gentile Christians, who even in Christianity could not yet repudiate that fondness, so natural to the Greeks, for everything pertaining to worldly education, which was so highly esteemed at that time. [77] The apostle portrays precisely this mindset, in which one is still entangled in the σοφία τοῦ κόσμου and has still not penetrated into the depths of the genuine Christian life, as a characteristic that belonged to the Corinthians in general on that stage of their spiritual life. Thus, even if we assume that the dominant aspect of this direction of thought—especially insofar as it involved valuing the external form of a speech over its content and subject matter—may have distinguished the Apollos party from the Pauline party, and even if we assume that the adherents of these parties placed the leaders whom they viewed as their heads in a relationship to one another that the leaders themselves could by no means have accepted, it still holds true that the difference cannot have been so fundamental and dogmatically fixed that the two parties could not also be regarded again, over against the Petrine party, as a single party. And if we view the matter from this perspective, it can indeed be assumed that the relationship between the Cephas party and the Christ party would have been a similar one. Indeed, if both parties had to be regarded as one and the same with respect to the central issue, this would certainly not militate against the relationship that must be envisaged between the Pauline and Apollos parties. After all, the apostle's purpose in 1 Cor 1:12 may also be to heap up names in order thereby to illustrate the sectarian spirit that predominated in the Corinthian community, which also expressed itself in the pleasure taken in the proliferation of the names of sects, which designated different colors and shades but not really different parties. Therefore, let us first investigate the question: In what did the main opposition between the Pauline and Petrine parties consist? One usually assumes that the Petrine party was a strictly Judaizing one, and that it opposed in Corinth the Pauline teach-

1. The Christ Party in the Corinthian Community

ing about the Mosaic law, the principle that it had no binding authority for Christians. One of the most recent commentators on our letters, Heydenreich, portrays the adherents of this party in this vein with the words:

> They were [78] the most zealous for the Mosaic law, patrons and defenders of all Jewish institutions. They despised the Christian liberation from this law and the active vindication from such institutions by Paul, and therefore they were eager to alienate the souls of everyone from Paul, hated by them worse than a dog or a serpent.

However, against this view it has been observed—with full justification—that Paul, according to the content of the two letters, does not really appear to have such opponents in view. There is really nothing in them from which one could infer that the main difference between Paul and his opponents was related to the latter's excessive attachment to the Mosaic law, as one would expect by way of analogy with other letters, particularly the letter to the Galatians.[23] [79] For this reason, one again felt

---

23. On this, see especially Storr, *Notitiae historicae*, 72: "It can be seen that the anti-Pauline party of Judaism became more zealous, both those from the rabbis, and, it naturally follows, from their opposing parties as well, in reaction to anti-Jewish fervor. What is even more remarkable is what should become of this matter, for which reason the harshest opponent of Judaism scarcely really reaches his goal in these letters. Though indeed (2 Cor 3:14-15; cf. 2 Cor 4:3-4) there are complaints about those caught in the thinking of Judaism, it is not flippantly that he says (2 Cor 3:6) that he is a minister of a new covenant, not of an old one, of one that has just arrived (2 Cor 3:1), and that some teachers who sell themselves as ministers for Christ (2 Cor 11:12-15) are set on the gospel of Christ being perverted (2 Cor 2:17; cf. 2 Cor 11:3-4). Another similar place besides this is found only with difficulty in 1 Cor 15:56. If any regard at all is given to the Judaizers, it is surely less apparent; and it is seen that, when compared, light is finally shed upon this very place (2 Cor 3:6-7)." What Storr then says cannot suffice as an explanation for this phenomenon. According to Storr, (1) both letters of the apostle are primarily directed to the parties in Corinth who were friendly to him and had written to him; thus he did not concern himself with the Judaizing party. And (2) the Corinthian pseudoapostles were Sadducees who did not judge circumcision to be as necessary as the Pharisees did. As shown above, the latter assertion cannot be accepted; and the former is [79] also inadequate, for, after all, even in the assumed case, a statement by the apostle on principles that had such a significant influence on the situation of the Corinthian community could not, in fact, have been regarded as superfluous. Moreover, the apostle, at least in the second letter, defends himself very strongly against the pseudoapostles themselves. To be sure, the passage in 2 Cor 3, in which Paul distinguishes between the παλαιά and καινή διαθήκη and between γράμμα

compelled, in the case of the—according to the presupposition—Judaizing opponents, to assume at the same time yet another tendency. In this connection, Heydenreich states:[24]

> The suspicion does not shrink back from the appearance of truth, that the teachers of that sect falsely and through deceit offered themselves as the disciples of Peter, although truly, at least in part, they were perhaps followers of the sect of the Sadducees, denying the resurrection of the dead, and thus even the return to life of the corpse of Christ himself.

Hugo Grotius already expressed this view when, in his comments on the words ἐγὼ δὲ Χριστοῦ in 1 Cor 1:12, he stated regarding the Christ party: "Some had come from Judea, who had heard Christ himself teach, and what he had said about the new birth; they falsely and destructively wanted those things that he had said about the resurrection to be the same as what he had said about the new birth: these certainly were converts from the Sadducees."[25] To me it does not appear to be in doubt that the opponents whom the apostle combats in 1 Cor 15 did not stand in any connection to the Cephas and Christ party. These opponents belonged to the party of the gentile Christians, who, in line with their materialistic, sensual way of thinking, denied any continued existence after death, while taking the reasons that they employed against Christians who thought better in this connection from the Christian [80] doctrine of the resurrection. Just as nothing was more absurd to the Greek way of thinking than the Christian doctrine of the resurrection (Acts 17:32), so these ambiguous members of the Corinthian community initially adhered to this doctrine in order to present belief in a life after death in general as something absurd with reference to it. The fact that the apostle does not particularly distinguish between resurrection and immortality—which Storr, as the chief defender

---

and πνεῦμα, is also related to the opponents. However, from this we see only that they were Judaizing opponents, upon whom, as those still entangled in Judaism, the bright day of Christian consciousness and life, the δόξα κυρίου, had not yet risen. But with respect to the specific tendency of their Judaism, one can infer nothing from precisely this passage since nothing is said specifically about the attachment to the νόμος here.

24. Heydenreich, *Commentarius*, 28.
25. Hugo Grotius, *Opera omnia theologica...*, 4 vols. (Paris: n.p., 1641–1650), ad loc.: 1 Cor 1:12. [Grotius, 1583–1645, was an influential jurist and theologian from the Netherlands.]

of that view, especially emphasizes[26]—does not prove that the opponents must have been Sadducean in their thinking. After all, the apostle, as his entire development shows, does not engage in this distinction at all for the very reason that in his view, continued bodily existence belongs to the full concept of a continuing life after death. Thus, nothing can be inferred from his argument in this connection. However, Sadducean opponents can also hardly be assumed a priori, for one must conceive of these false teachers, as anti-Christian as they might otherwise have been, as still being in some sort of close connection to Christianity. How could they have otherwise appealed to the authority of the apostle Peter, if they really did belong, as it is, after all, assumed, to the Petrine party? This is why Flatt as well,[27] building on Storr's view, opines that they had probably belonged previously to the Sadducees and now wanted to carry their opinions over into Christianity: they must have belonged to an anti-Pauline, Judaizing party, which is why Paul is said to have invoked Peter and James. But such a connection between Sadduceeism and Christianity is improbable in itself, and it is also not otherwise historically demonstrable. In this connection, Neander as well expresses the view that

> here there is no point of transition and no point of connection, and no mixing of the Sadducean and the Christian can be conceived. Where one has wanted to find such a mixing in the apostolic age [81] among some opponents of the doctrine of the resurrection, this has been assumed without sufficient justification, for this phenomenon can be derived from completely different grounds.[28]

There is certainly nothing more natural than presuming that in a Greek community, the doubts that arose concerning the Christian doctrine of the resurrection lay not in the theological propositions of a Jewish sect that always remained foreign and hostile to Christianity and did not communicate itself to the outside, but rather in the common prejudice that the Greeks and Romans held against the doctrine of the resurrection; for indeed, there was scarcely any other doctrine of Christianity that they found more difficult to accept than this one, as can also be seen by so many

---

26. Storr, *Notitiae historicae*, 78.
27. Flatt, *Vorlesungen*, 1:351.
28. August Neander, *Allgemeine Geschichte der christlichen Religion und Kirche*, 9 vols. (Hamburg: Perthes, 1825–1852), 1.1:82–83.

other examples. The fact that, among those Christians of the Corinthian community, especially the denial of the truth of this doctrine and the lack of a Christian moral view of the life to come was connected with an Epicurean view of life is made very likely not only by the general character of that community—which still reflects the character of the Greek view of life in so many ways and which also repeatedly gave the apostle cause to communicate other serious reminders of a similar kind, such as with respect to πορνεία—but also especially by 1 Cor 15:32, in which the apostle completely sums up everything that is to be regarded as the main point in this matter. However, the more improbable the assumption of a Sadducean influence becomes through this,[29] the more [82] we still lack a definite distinguishing feature with respect to the relationship between the Pauline and Petrine parties. In the investigation mentioned above, Schmidt wanted to find the main reason for the difference between the two parties in the arrogance with which the Jewish Christians regarded only themselves as true Christians, while not wanting the gentile Christians to be regarded as Christians at all.

> There was a segment among the first Christians who were able to claim Christ for themselves in a special way; these were the Jewish Christians. Christ, the Messiah, came first for the sake of the Jews, to whom alone he was also promised; the gentile Christians owed it to the Jews that Christ came into the world. Could not, among such proud Jewish Christians, the presumption arise that Christ, the Messiah, belonged to them alone, just as this presumption is reflected in 2 Cor 10:7? They called themselves τοὺς τοῦ Χριστοῦ, Christ-adherents, Messiah-adherents, or, the name altered only a little, χριστιανούς. Now if these Christians are Jewish

---

29. Of course, one could object that the mixture of such a materialism with Christianity is just as improbable as the mixture of Sadduceanism with Christianity and that it is not possible to know what Christians of such a way of thinking could still have held with regard to Christianity. But surely such an inconsistency is far more conceivable with regard to the peculiarity of the Greek character, so receptive to impressions of all kinds, than with regard to the rigid Sadduceanism, as rigorously dogmatically sealed as it was. That, however, the opponents of the doctrine of the resurrection opposed by the apostle in chapter 15 [82] belonged to the Christian community themselves, comes to light in 1 Cor 15:12 (πῶς λέγουσί τινες ἐν ὑμῖν, ὅτι ἀνάστασις νεκρῶν οὐκ ἔστι;); and thus we see here yet another proof of how fickle the condition of the Corinthian community still was at that time, and with what great difficulty the apostle had to battle in his efforts to found a Christian community in Corinth.

Christians, then there can be no doubt that they were one party with the Petrine Christians.[30]

However, if we also assume this, then there must still have also been something else underlying this presumption of the Jewish Christians. Otherwise there is no way to imagine how they as Jewish Christians could have found entrance in a community comprised predominantly of gentile Christians with a presumption that excluded the gentile Christians from having a share in Christianity. However, I believe Schmidt is completely right in finding the reason for the opposition between the adherents of Peter and Paul precisely in that [83] which also made Peter's adherents into οἱ τοῦ Χριστοῦ. But now the question presents itself more than ever as to how this can be specified more precisely and correctly than has been done before. In answering this question, we are certainly not taking an arbitrary assumption as our point of departure when we assume that the main aspect that the opposing party stressed against Paul will manifest itself in some way in the letters of the apostle. Now, a main topic of the content of both letters has to do with a justification of Paul's apostolic status, which his adversaries did not want to concede to him in the full sense. What if they did not want to acknowledge him as a true and legitimate apostle because he was not τοῦ Χριστοῦ in the same sense as Peter, James, and the other apostles, since he did not stand in the same direct relationship to Jesus during his earthly life as they did? Peter himself was not involved with the party bearing his name in Corinth, as can already be seen in the fact that Peter himself had not come to Corinth. By contrast, however, as all indications suggest, traveling pseudoapostles who appealed to the name of Peter must presumably have come also to Corinth. In the second letter, in which Paul in general speaks out more openly against these adversaries and combats them more directly, he even calls them ψευδαπόστολοι, ψευδαδέλφοι, ἐργάταται δόλιοι, μετασχιματιζόμενοι εἰς ἀποστόλους Χριστοῦ (2 Cor 11:13).[31] Thus, they wanted to be the true ἀπόστολοι Χριστοῦ, the Χριστοῦ ὄντες. Here, too, the Jewish Christians' own zeal for the Mosaic law was probably the main driving force. However, since they could not expect their tenets to be favorably received if they directly came forward with them in a community of gentile Chris-

---

30. Schmidt, *Bibliothek für Kritik und Exegese*, 90–91.
31. [The term ψευδαδέλφοι does not appear in 2 Cor 11:13, but it does occur in 2 Cor 11:26.]

tians, as was the case for the Corinthian community, they sought to work against the apostle Paul by attacking his apostolic standing altogether, and in this way to open the door for their Judaism. Under this presupposition, the relationship of the Petrine party to the Christ party emerges, as it seems, very [84] simply and naturally. Just as the adherents of Paul and of Apollos could not have been substantially different, there were not two different parties here either, but two different names for one and the same party, so that these two names only designated the claims that this party made for itself. They called themselves τοῦ Κηφᾶ because Peter had the primacy among the Jewish apostles, and τοῦ Χριστοῦ because they presented the unmediated connection to Christ as the main distinguishing feature of true apostolic standing. For precisely this reason, they refused to acknowledge Paul, who had emerged as an apostle only later and in a very peculiar way, as a true apostle who was on par with the other apostles, thinking that he would at least have to be placed far below them.[32] Therefore, they also consciously chose the designation οἱ τοῦ Χριστοῦ, not τοῦ Ἰησοῦ or τοῦ κυρίου. The concept of messiah or redeemer was put first in order to designate as the fully valid communicators of the messianic favor and blessing, of the higher life, whose principle is Christ the redeemer, only those who had received everything that belonged to this from the most unmediated tradition, from a connection with the person of Jesus that could be demonstrated outwardly and actually.

It is now necessary to back up the view put forward here as much as possible by considering a few main passages in the two letters. The first apologetic section in 1 Cor 1–4, in which the apostle gives a [85] defense of his authority and activity, may already include some indications in which he may especially have in view the adherents of the Petrine party,

---

32. While some, such as Zachary Pearce (*Epistolae duae ad celeberrimum doctissimumque virum F[ranciscus] V[alckenaer] professorem Amstelodamensem scriptae...* [London: Clay, 1721], 20), sought to conclude from a passage in the first letter of Clement of Rome to the Corinthians (1 Clem. 47.3: ἐπ' ἀληθείας πνευματικῶς ἐπέστειλεν ὑμῖν (ὁ μακάριον Παῦλος ὁ ἀπόστολος) περὶ αὑτοῦ τε καὶ Κηφᾶ καὶ Ἀπολλῶ, διὰ τὸ καὶ τότε προσκλίσεις ὑμᾶς πεποιῆσθαι ["To be sure, he (that is, the blessed apostle Paul) sent you a letter in the Spirit concerning himself and Cephas and Apollos, since you were even then engaged in partisanship" (trans. Ehrman)] that the words ἐγὼ δὲ Χριστοῦ in 1 Cor 1:12 are in all probability not authentic, it seems to be much more reasonable to find in this text of Clement—if indeed it is to be accorded such great importance—a confirmation of our assumption above that the Petrine and Christ parties are one and the same. [Pearce, 1690–1774, was an English bishop of Rochester.]

who promoted themselves as τοὺς τοῦ Χριστοῦ. When, in 1 Cor 2:16,[33] the apostle emphatically claims about himself ἡμεῖς δὲ νοῦν Χριστοῦ ἔχομεν (inasmuch as the divine πνεῦμα is the principle of his Christian consciousness); when, in 1 Cor 4:1, he points out to his readers that they should regard him as a ὑπηρέτης Χριστοῦ; when, in 1 Cor 4:10, he asserts that he, as the least of the apostles, readily views himself as a μωρὸς διὰ Χριστόν, inasmuch as they alone have good reason to consider themselves φρόνιμοι ἐν Χριστῷ; when, in 1 Cor 4:15, he reminds them that what matters is not μυρίους παιδαγωγοὺς ἔχειν ἐν Χριστῷ but rather πολλοὺς πατέρας; then from such suggestive passages it is already quite natural to think back to the party—mentioned not long before—of those who sought to assert themselves in a very distinctive sense as οἱ τοῦ Χριστοῦ ὄντες in a manner that was harmful to the standing of the apostle, even though these specific connections recede behind the general apologetic tendency of this section, as it has been specified above. In a quick turn, the apostle begins to speak here about his own person. At the same time, the section that starts in 1 Cor 9:1 is very closely connected to the content of the immediately preceding chapter, and the opportunity that presents itself precisely here to make an apologetic argument is used by him in a very clever way. For in the preceding chapter 8, in response to the question that had been presented to him about participating in pagan festivals and consuming sacrificial meat, the apostle had said that there could be cases in which one would be obligated out of concern and consideration for others to refrain from doing what one might regard as fully legitimate for one to do in and of itself. Now the apostle uses this thought to give himself an opportunity to present some aspects that his opponents have interpreted to his disadvantage [86] from an angle from which they would have to appear as voluntarily adopted acts of renunciation that have been undertaken out of consideration for his apostolic calling. He claims that he, too, has certain rights as an apostle, which he could make use of just as other apostles did. However, he adds that he has not done this because a higher concern demanded that he not make use of them. Οὐκ εἰμὶ ἐλεύθερος; οὐκ εἰμὶ ἀπόστολος; οὐχὶ Ἰησοῦν Χριστὸν τὸν κύριον ἡμῶν ἑώρακα; "Am I not free? Am I not an apostle (that is, just as much as any of the other apostles)? Have I not seen the Lord Jesus Christ?" What would be the purpose of the appeal to the ἑωρακέναι Ἰησοῦν Χριστὸν τὸν κύριον ἡμῶν as the justification

---

33. [Baur writes "2:26" but obviously intends to refer to 1 Cor 2:16.]

of the ἀπόστολος εἶναι, if his adversaries did not deny his authentic apostolic character on the grounds that he, unlike they, or rather, unlike the apostles that they placed at the heads their parties, had not seen the Lord and lived in direct connection with him? This was thus meant to be the true distinguishing mark of the Χριστοῦ εἶναι. But the fact that these very opponents of the apostle belonged in a class with the adherents of the Petrine party is made clear from the following words in 1 Cor 9:5: μὴ οὐκ ἔχομεν ἐξουσίαν ἀδελφὴν γυναῖκα περιάγειν, ὡς καὶ οἱ λοιποὶ ἀπόστολοι, καὶ οἱ ἀδελφοὶ τοῦ κυρίου, καὶ Κηφᾶς. The Χριστοῦ εἶναι applied to all of these people in the sense explained above: it applied to all of the apostles who had enjoyed contact with Jesus, and it applied in an even narrower sense to the ἀδελφοὶ τοῦ κυρίου, inasmuch as they, as relatives of the Lord, had an even closer relationship to him. In the narrowest sense, it applied to Peter, insofar as Jesus himself had given him a certain priority in comparison with the rest, and insofar as he most fully represented that entire relationship in his person. Nevertheless, Paul, in the full consciousness of his apostolic dignity and of the rights and claims connected with it, did not consider himself to rank behind even someone such as Peter. As proof that he had the same rights as the other apostles, and specifically the right to live at the expense of the community to whom he preached the gospel, [87] the apostle appeals (1) to what is regarded as right and customary in normal life (1 Cor 9:7–8); (2) to a commandment in the Mosaic law, which, he says, initially referred only to the animals that humans use for themselves, but which lets one reason all the more from the lesser to the greater (1 Cor 9:9–12); and (3) to the usage introduced in the Mosaic sacrificial cult (1 Cor 9:13). However, as well founded as this right is, which he claims is due to him just as it is due to the rest of the apostles, he has nevertheless not made use of it because this appeared to him to be more purposeful for the cause of the gospel and more inwardly rewarding for himself. Thus, in constant consciousness of the central objective with which he was occupied, he claims that he submitted his whole personality to the interest of others and to the consideration that had to be shown for them, and that he subdued his sensuality in such a way that it had to subject itself only to the purposes of the Spirit (1 Cor 9:15–27). The most satisfactory way of clarifying this entire section is probably to presume that the opponents of the apostle interpreted the fact that he did not make claims and his self-denial—which he took upon himself as obligatory in the communities in which he proclaimed the gospel—as an acknowledgement made by the apostle himself with regard to how little he dared to put himself on an equal footing with the other apostles in the use of the rights that were due to an apostle in this connection. In contrast to this behavior, which was interpreted exclusively as weakness and as a lack of self-confidence, they could have believed that they had even less reason to need to restrain the self-serving and self-seeking πλεονεξία, of which the apostle accuses them elsewhere. For the apostle, however, the more these accusations were linked with the main attack on his standing as an apostle, the stronger his interest had to be in defending himself also in this regard, and in placing his behavior in the true light. Just as here, the central argument of the apostle's apology goes back to the ἑωρακέναι Ἰησοῦν τὸν κύριον ἡμῶν— through which, by the way, the apostle, without explaining more closely the peculiar character of this ἑωρακέναι, only wanted to register the general thing [88] that made him equal to the other apostles, namely, that he, too, could in any case claim to have seen the Lord himself—so the apostle appeals also in 1 Cor 15:8, with the same consideration in mind, to the fact that the Lord appeared also to him, as he had to the rest of the apostles. However, while the important discussion that follows about the teaching of the resurrection appears to demand a quasi-documentary certification of the main statement upon which it is based, namely, that Jesus rose from the dead and was really seen as the risen one, this does not exclude the premise that here, too, the apostle consciously took advantage of the opportunity to place himself alongside the disciples who were associated with Jesus during his life with respect to the main point with which the opponents wanted to connect the apostolic authority and to claim their direct beholding of the Lord also for himself as criterion of his apostolic calling. Here the apostle himself even appears to be willing to concede to his opponents that he was—as they wanted to consider him at the very best—only an ἔκτρωμα, ὁ ἐλάχιστος τῶν ἀποστόλων (cf. 1 Cor 4:9: ὁ θεὸς ἡμᾶς τοὺς ἀποστόλους ἐσχάτους ἀπέδειξεν), indeed not even ἱκανὸς καλεῖσθαι ἀπόστολος. It is as if he wanted to say with these words that what they want to assert only to his disadvantage, he will, in turn, gladly accept, since such accusations can also be interpreted in a way that does not diminish his apostolic authority at all. The polemical connection that is already present here then appears to emerge even more clearly in 1 Cor 15:11—εἴτε οὖν ἐγώ, εἴτε ἐκεῖνοι, οὕτω κηρύσσομεν. Here, the apostle himself seems to want to point out the difference between himself and the other apostles, which was being so gladly invoked from certain quarters. Whoever is familiar with the multifaceted character of the relations that the apostle takes care to give to the content of his letters, and whoever has become convinced from so many passages as to how accurately and with what adroitness [89] and skill he is able to combine direct and indirect statements will not be able to find anything forced or improbable in what is postulated here.

The polemical references, for which the apostle had such manifold reason in both letters, are more overt and direct in the second letter than in the first one, but even here it only occurs at the end of the letter, where the apostle, without seeking further detours, confronts his opponents with all candor and fixes his eyes upon them in a sharp and unwavering manner. In the preceding sections of the letter, it is especially 2 Cor 5:16 that takes on a new interest through the consideration of the opponents. By means of various expressions, the apostle reassures the Corinthians from the beginning of his trust-evoking love and seeks to convince them of the purity of his intentions and endeavors. Against the accusations of his opponents, he sets the fruits that his teaching is said to bring forth by means of the ability given to him by God, mediated through the διακονία τῆς καινῆς διαθήκης. The greater the advantages of the καινὴ διαθήκη are, the greater the advantages of the διακονία are as well. However, in sharp contrast to this, the apostle continues in 2 Cor 4:7, stand all kinds of suffering, with which, *I as a weak and frail human must struggle, sufferings that threaten to exhaust my strength at every moment. Yet even more gloriously does the same power through which Jesus was raised again from the dead, the power that overcomes death through life, prove itself in me. For this reason, I do not let myself be hindered in my actions by the sufferings of my calling. After all, sufferings only serve to prepare the inner person, the human's true self, for the future glory.* In chapter 5, this thought now causes the apostle to speak of the time in which the earthly body, under whose burden we groan, will be transformed to a heavenly one (2 Cor 5:1–4). *This confident expectation of a condition in which we, after the journey from this* [90] *body, will be at home with the Lord or will be in the most intimate connection to him—which is a fundamental part of our Christian consciousness—must already now give to our entire activity and efforts the most conscientious relationship to Christ, who is, after all, the one who will pronounce the retributive judgment that exactly corresponds to our moral behavior* (2 Cor 5:5–14). *This consciousness also accompanies me in my apostolic ministry, as you yourselves cannot help but confirm. You can feel free to assert that which my inner conscience causes me to say in this connection against my opponents, to my glory, that my concern is not at all with my own person or my own interest. I work in the spirit of love with which Christ offered himself for us in such a way that we can live only for him, and in such a way that all our previous bonds and relationships have stopped exerting a decisive influence on us, for which reason we regard ourselves as having been moved into an entirely new sphere of consciousness and life. The highest efficient cause through which we have been elevated to this entirely new order of things is the reconciliation that God brought about between himself and human beings through the death of Christ. In that this very reconciliation is the actual content of my apostolic preaching and the object of my activity, it is actually only Christ, in whose name I work, only God, whose voice can be heard through me. How then is my concern supposed to be with my person in such a way that my opponents could rightly accuse me of vain self-praise and self-serving intentions?* The expression Χριστόν κατὰ σάρκα γινώσκειν (2 Cor 5:16), used by the apostle in this context, deserves to be considered more carefully and discussed exegetically here. The ambiguity of the word σάρξ already makes the explanation somewhat difficult. The words are usually interpreted in the sense of *res externae* ("outward advantages"), and the text is then paraphrased as follows:[34]

> Because our only concern is that those for whom Christ died also let the holy purposes of his [91] death itself reach them so that they do not live for themselves but only according to his will, I also do not judge anyone by outward advantages but rather only by whether one conforms to the grand purposes of Christ's death, regardless of whether he is a Jew or Greek, free or slave, and so on. All this no longer comes into consideration (the apostle says this by contrast against his opponents, who thought completely differently; see 2 Cor 5:12; 11:18; cf. 2 Cor 11:22).

Against this explanation, one must mainly object that in the context of the passage, σάρξ must be something that, from a certain perspective, mediates the connection with Christ. After all, the apostle expresses the main thought directly beforehand: all for whom Christ died belong only to him. How then is σάρξ in the following statement ὥστε ἡμεῖς ἀπὸ τοῦ νῦν οὐδένα οἴδαμεν κατὰ σάρκα (in which, moreover, οἴδαμεν cannot really be taken to have the same meaning as κρίνομεν) supposed to be understood in the sense of "outward advantages"? This interpretation still needs to be modified according to the context, for which reason several exegetes understand σάρξ more specifically in terms of the advantage of an external connection and kinship with Christ. For example, Johann Jakob Wettstein writes on

---

34. Flatt, *Vorlesungen*, 2:82.

2 Cor 5:16: "Those false apostles pride themselves on having been relatives and hearers of Christ (1 Cor 1:12). Paul responds that kinship alone is of no benefit."[35] Storr places our text in this same relationship to οἱ Χριστοῦ in 1 Cor 1:12. He says:

> They were altogether those who by some special right, which does not extend at all to Paul, considered themselves to be of Christ, and offered themselves by this title to the Corinthians who were looking at outward appearance, τὰ κατὰ πρόσωπον. It does not seem doubtful to us why the apostle should have designated the καυχωμένες ἐν Χριστῷ (2 Cor 5:12) as those who boast about connection with Christ of some external kind (2 Cor 5:16).[36]

The apostle is said to be dealing with those "who, besides outward trappings and Jewish origins, as well as their own former connection with those apostles who knew Christ, have nothing by which they might be able to be eminently glorified."[37] The words would then have [92] to be taken as follows: *That is why I cannot recognize a connection with anyone, the worth of which is meant to consist merely in having been connected with Christ outwardly.* Or, strictly speaking, as the context requires: *That is why I cannot recognize any connection with Christ that is meant to obtain its worth only through an outward relationship.* However, also in this case the term σάρξ is not yet grasped from the angle from which it needs to be grasped in light of the connection between the first and second sentences in 2 Cor 5:16. Therefore, to me, Johann August Nösselt's comments seem to bring us closer to the right interpretation. He remarks:

> When taken together with καινὴ κτίσις in 2 Cor 5:17, κατὰ σάρκα cannot mean anything other than "something very old, or a former custom to be put aside," which, according to the related passage in Gal 6:15, must be defined more precisely: "τὴν σάρκα refers to external things, of which the Jews were accustomed to boast, to which Jews he in fact says in Gal 6:16 that their opposition is τὸν Ἰσραὴλ τοῦ θεοῦ; that is, the true Israelites

---

35. Johann Jakob Wettstein, *Novum Testamentum Graecum*, 2 vols. (Amsterdam: Officina Dommeriana, 1751–1752), 2:191, on 2 Cor 5:16. [Wettstein, 1693–1754, was a pastor and lecturer in Basel (from 1720), and taught in Amsterdam after his removal from the pastorate in 1730.]
36. Storr, *Notitiae historicae*, 11.
37. Storr, *Notitiae historicae*, 20.

according to the judgment of God, who follow this rule of manifestly new human beings, which he had mentioned."[38]

However, when Nösselt draws the following conclusion from this, "ἀπὸ τοῦ νῦν οὐδένα οἴδαμεν κατὰ σάρκα is said in this sense: We do not recognize him as now a Christian, who stands out in regard to external things, in which the Jews think there is the greatest praise, but the one of a spirit resigned to Christ excels in superiority," then this again gives no consideration to the fact that according to the preceding context, which speaks of ζῆν τινι, σάρξ can only be what mediates the connection with Christ in a certain sense. In this regard, in keeping with the entire context of the passage, since ζῆν τῷ ὑπὲρ αὐτῶν ἀποθανόντι (2 Cor 5:15) is a new, completely distinctive life, it seems to me that σάρξ can only express the concept of what is inborn, hereditary, and passed down, and thus what is sensual and outward. Therefore, σάρξ is the life of the individual as defined by natural descent, the connection with the [93] nation to which the individual belongs, and, precisely in this regard, especially by the conceptions and views that become traditional in the common national life and that exert an overwhelming influence on the individual. However, if σάρξ is what is handed down through the national life and propagated, then in opposition against the new life that is meant to be awakened and grounded through Christ who has died for us, it designates a mindset that is trapped in the old traditional circle and dominated by what is sensual and merely natural. This includes everything that still adheres to the παλαιὸς ἄνθρωπος before he becomes a νέος ἄνθρωπος. Thus, in relation to the person of the apostle, one can almost say that here σάρξ stands for Judaism with all of its old traditional national prejudices, with its entire distinctive mindset. Therefore, it seems to me that the full meaning of our text can only be as follows: *Ever since I, because Christ died for me, began to live only for him and came into union with him, I know of nothing else that could, as a consequence of the outer connection in which I stand toward the nation in which I was born, determine and control my mindset, and precisely in this way I have left all the relations of Judaism, to which I previously belonged, everything that by virtue of my birth can be assigned to the σάρξ in me.* Accordingly,

---

38. Johann August Nösselt, "Commentatio de Christi cognitione secundum carnem ad locum 2 Corinth. V, 14–17," in vol. 2 of *Opusculorum ad interpretationem sacrarum scripturarum* (Halle: Hendel, 1787), 196. [Nösselt, 1734–1807, was assistant professor in Halle from 1760, and full professor from 1764.]

οὐδείς means: *no one to whom I belong as a consequence of a connection that determines my mindset*. Instead of οὐδείς, the apostle could just as well have said οὐδέν: *I know of nothing, of no outward condition, that determines and controls me*. However, he says οὐδείς with a view to the personal relation that is entailed in the phrase ζῆν Χριστῷ (2 Cor 5:15).[39]

[94] If we take the meaning of σάρξ specified here as a basis, then the meaning of the second half of the verse also can no longer be in doubt. Exegetes who understand the outward relationship that mediates the connection of the individual with Christ, which σάρξ designates, in terms of having known Jesus outwardly, such as Grotius, Wettstein, and Flatt,

---

39. Concerning this meaning of σάρξ, see Leonhard Usteri, *Entwickelung des Paulinischen Lehrbegriffes in seinem Verhältnisse zur biblischen Dogmatik des Neuen Testamentes: Ein exegetisch-dogmatischer Versuch*, 2nd ed. (Zürich: Orell, Füssli & Co., 1829), 122, and the texts cited there; i.e., Rom 7:5; 11:14; Gal 3:3; 6:12; Phil 3:3. [Usteri, 1799–1833, was a Swiss Reformed theologian who served as Professor and Director of Gymnasia in Bern.] In the first edition of his *Pauli ad Galatas epistola, latine vertit et perpetua annotatione* (Leipzig: Reclam, 1821), Johann Georg Benedict Winer derived the meaning for σάρξ [94] as "Mosaic instruction" in the following way: originally σάρξ meant "every tendency towards sin, the corruptness of human nature," and then "the law of Moses, which uniquely pertains to this encompassing corruptness." However, this explanation of the term is very one-sided and not satisfactory. Accordingly, in the third edition of the commentary (*Pauli ad Galatas epistola, latine vertit et perpetua annotatione*, 3rd ed. [Leipzig: Reclam, 1829], 144), Winer gives the following explanation as to why Paul "generally uses the expression σαρκός with a view to indicating a Jewish matter. Surely nearly all the studies and trappings of the Jews were divided up into things that concern the body, either directly (circumcision, descent from Abraham) or indirectly (sacrifice, abstinence from certain foods), but Christ has come in order to organize people for worshiping God ἐν πνεύματι καὶ ἀληθείᾳ." However, several things must be taken together, and the term has very different shades of meaning, with one or another of them coming to the forefront at a given time. Still it seems to me that when σάρξ simply means Judaism, the basic concept is that which is inborn and grounded in the natural connection of national life. The σάρξ is originally the corporeal, with everything that conditions and determines bodily existence and that stands in some sort of connection with it, since, after all, τὸ γεγεννημένον ἐκ τῆς σαρκὸς σάρξ ἐστιν (John 3:6). Only then are the concepts of the fleshly, worldly, outward, and imperfect attached to this, inasmuch as it is only with Christianity that the natural, bodily, national life is elevated to the truly religious, spiritual, and universal. When Usteri (*Entwickelung des Paulinischen Lehrbegriffes*, 122), commenting on our text, says that "σάρξ designates all external, national, and political considerations with special reference to the smug Jewish prejudices," then I can allow this specific connection only to the extent that it is already contained in the general meaning of σάρξ that has been specified above.

assign the following words a sense that Wettstein has expressed most precisely [95] and completely. Paul answers the false apostles who claimed to be relatives and students of Jesus: "Christ is not lowly, he was a Jew of such a kind—teaching Jews, circumcised, lying in a stable, poor, despised, and ultimately nailed to a cross, but exalted above everyone, and the common savior of all nations of men, and the most just judge."[40] According to this view, Paul would say with these words: *If I had also personally known Jesus during his life on earth, I would nevertheless no longer be able to regard the conception that Jesus's entire outward appearance would have to give me as the true and actual one. I would have had to abandon this conception, upon which my opponents place such great weight due to their outward connection with Jesus, due to their personal acquaintance with him, because the conception no longer fits with the conception that the state of the exaltation of Jesus gives to me concerning his dignity and majesty.*

But could Paul have really wanted to say this? Even if the so-called state of humiliation, which actually would be the κατὰ σάρκα Χριστός, contrasts greatly with the state of exaltation, Paul nevertheless probably could not say that he actually forgot about the former in light of the latter, or that he could no longer put any weight on the former. In that case he would, after all, also not be able to give Jesus's death on the cross the significance that he does in fact always give to it, since Jesus's death can, in fact, only be related to the κατὰ σάρκα Χριστός in this sense. If, in addition, we consider the fact that the apostle, if this had been the meaning of his words, would actually have had to say εἰ δὲ καὶ ἐγνώκαμεν κατὰ σάρκα Ἰησοῦν, or at least Ἰησοῦν Χριστόν, ἀλλὰ νῦν ἐκ ἔτι γινώσκομεν τοιοῦτον ὄντα, then this very thing can lead us to the correct interpretation. Here too the term Χριστός, which is not used by the apostle unintentionally, must not be overlooked. ὁ κατὰ σάρκα Χριστός cannot refer to Jesus's earthly appearance, with regard to which it could not possibly be the apostle's intention to detach himself from the recognition of its value, as he would have done with the words ἀλλὰ νῦν ἐκ ἔτι γινώσκομεν. [96] Rather, the κατὰ σάρκα Χριστός is only the Christ or messiah of Judaism. According to this, the apostle says something that provides a meaning that is both grammatically natural and satisfactory in itself: *If, however, it was also the case* (εἰ δὲ καὶ ἐγνώκαμεν should not be understood hypothetically, as it is usually taken; according to the grammatical construction, the most likely meaning is a categorical

---

40. Wettstein, *Novum Testamentum*, 2:191, on 2 Cor 5:16.

one that says something positive) *that I previously did not know any other messiah than the messiah of Judaism, one who left me with all the prejudices and sensual inclinations peculiar to my own nation and was not capable of lifting me up to the new level of spiritual life in which I now stand, inasmuch as I live for Christ, who died for me and for all, then now I can, nevertheless, no longer acknowledge this conception of the messiah as the true one. I have distanced myself from all prejudices, from all sensual conceptions and expectations that through the natural descent from my nation had also passed to me, had been transmitted to me as a born Jew.*[41]

If we relate the text [97] dealt with here to the goal of our study, precisely this interpretation of it could appear less favorable than the usual

---

41. The main thrust of this interpretation, which is the only one that seems to me to fit appropriately with the linguistic use and the context, has already been expressed by Nösselt ("Commentatio de Christi cognitione," 196): "Even if we previously looked at Christ as an upholder or a restorer of outward happiness, which they either wish for themselves or expect to be brought about by Christ, now we no longer suppose that Christ should be like this, or rather we consider that dignity is maintained in these Christian things, but in this, since people are made new, being equipped with the mind and works of Christ." However, Nösselt displaced the correct aspect of the view of this passage by presupposing that 2 Cor 5:16 is to be understood as "according to the rightly established rule concerning the truth of the Christians." He presumes that the apostle is speaking of ἐγνωκότες κατὰ σάρκα Χριστόν, of Judaizing Christians; and, in order to tell them "that they should disregard Jewish vanity and attend to Christ with a pure mind," he says ἀλλὰ νῦν οὐκέτι γινώσκομεν; i.e., οὕτως. According to Nösselt, these words are to be understood to mean "but now henceforth it is not fitting for such (lovers of Judaism) to be Christians." However, neither γινώσκομεν [97] nor ἀπέθανον (2 Cor 5:14) contain an "ought," and it is not at all necessary to understand it in this way, as soon as we do not assume—which is not justified by the text—that Jewish Christians are spoken of here. Rather, Paul speaks first only about his own person and his connection with Christ. Especially objectionable is the explanation given by Christian August Gottfried Emmerling, the most recent commentator on the second letter (*Epistola Pauli ad Corinthios posterior graece perpetuo commentario* [Leipzig: Barth, 1823], 61). He writes of this passage (2 Cor 5:16): "The sight of the Lord clearly pierces through the boastful, and, to use 1 Cor 9:1, that glory, if it is such, declares itself possible to use, thereby showing the glory of the matter to be vain and foolish, let not the quantity of which be greater." [Emmerling, 1781–1827, was a Lutheran pastor in Probstheyda, near Leipzig.] The verse 1 Cor 9:1 does not belong here, as Nösselt ("Commentatio de Christi cognitione," 200) already noted correctly. The ἑωρακέναι Ἰησοῦν Χριστόν (1 Cor 9:1) had an importance to Paul that makes it impossible to accept the idea that he speaks now of the same matter in such a disparaging way, as one would have to assume according to the words ἐκ ἔτι γινώσκομεν.

one. However, it certainly cannot be denied that the apostle, in using the expression Χριστόν κατὰ σάρκα γινώσκειν, wanted to cast a sidelong glance at his opponents, who promoted themselves as τοὺς τοῦ Χριστοῦ ὄντας in a special sense. This reference can be joined rather well with the interpretation given here, even though, right afterwards, σάρξ is not to be understood directly in terms of the outer connection to Jesus but primarily in terms of the inherited nationality. By refusing to concede the high value to κατὰ σάρκα Χριστόν γινώσκειν that his opponents wanted to give to it, he exposes his opponents—who, after all, also put no small weight on their authentic Jewish pedigree (2 Cor 11:22)—as people who in essence still see things entirely from the viewpoint of Judaism and the Jewish concept of the messiah when they think they need to deny true apostolic status to him because he was not in the same outward contact with Jesus [98] during his life on earth that the disciples who had originally been called by Jesus himself to be apostles could boast in. However, in the apostle's view, the actual aspect from which the εἶναι ἐν Χριστῷ can alone be derived is not the earthly and national manifestation of Jesus, in which the σάρξ in the sense specified here still has a part, but rather the death of Jesus, insofar as it is only in death that the old life dies off and the new one that is to be awakened in us begins. What fundamentally distinguishes the Jewish national messiah from the Christ of the true Christian consciousness is the suffering and death of Christ, the great significance of his death on the cross, which the apostle presents everywhere as the centerpiece of Christian teaching and which he emphatically stresses against his opponents also in these two letters. Therefore, if the earthly life of Jesus as the Messiah and the visible connection with him during his life on earth are regarded, so to speak, as something that stands alone; and if one does not, instead, understand his entire earthly manifestation in light of his death on the cross, then this is still a Χριστόν κατὰ σάρκα γινώσκειν. One stops with what is directly given by natural circumstances, to which one is, in fact, meant to die. If, however, one sees in his death the great turning point in which the καινὴ κτίσις comes to light, in which the old has disappeared and everything has become new, then everything immediately falls away that seemed to give the opponents, or rather the apostles upon whose authority the opponents based themselves, such a distinctively great advantage with respect to the direct connection with Jesus during his earthly life, but which, in fact, had its basis only in circumstances into which the apostles had entered as born Jews. Therefore he, too, the apostle who was called only so late, can place himself in a series with the witnesses of the resurrection of the Lord. He, too, saw him as the one who, only now, as the one who died and lives again, lets [99] the full significance of the Christian consciousness and life arise in us and establishes the true Χριστοῦ εἶναι in us.

Another verse, 2 Cor 10:7, aligns itself closely with the passage explained up to now. In 2 Cor 10 the apostle addresses the accusation made by his opponents against him, that he lacks a powerful personality. In response, he affirms that he will show that, when it comes down to the main issue, he knows how to act very emphatically and seriously, and with the greatest certainty of success. This very thing is also said to refute the accusation made against him, namely, that he lacks the true sign of one Χριστοῦ ὤν. What if one does not simply look arbitrarily at something outward that supposedly attests Χριστοῦ εἶναι better than the ἐξουσία εἰς οἰκοδομήν, the power and energy with which one works to further the cause of Christianity? In saying τὰ κατὰ πρόσωπον βλέπετε, he is not addressing his opponents themselves but rather those members of the Corinthian community who had partly already given them ear and were partly in danger of letting themselves be further led astray by them. *If you, when looking at my person, orient yourself to what I supposedly am κατὰ πρόσωπον, then this proves that you only look at the exterior, that you judge only by the exterior* (πρόσωπον as in 2 Cor 5:12). These words are usually related to the so-called Christ party, and Storr and Flatt understand them, according to their idea of the Christ party, in terms of giving consideration to outward family relations. Since the apostle speaks of Χριστοῦ εἶναι, it is certainly very natural to relate this to those who regarded themselves to be particularly τοὺς τοῦ Χριστοῦ. However, in this passage, too, I cannot find anything from which one could infer that οἱ τοῦ Χριστοῦ formed a party of their own. Rather, the apostle is dealing with his opponents in general, to the extent that vis-à-vis him, they boasted of a closer outward connection with Jesus or with Jesus's original disciples, and particularly with Peter, the first of the apostles, and wanted to find the true criterion of Χριστοῦ εἶναι in this. The fact that [100] Χριστοῦ ὄντες belonged in a class with the Petrine party and the entire Judaizing party is, however, made especially clear by the connection with the material that follows, where the apostle speaks of the ὑπερλίαν ἀπόστολοι (2 Cor 11:5). What he now in 2 Cor 10:7 with regard to the Χριστοῦ εἶναι holds against his opponents seems to me to have to be understood as follows: *If someone so confidently declares himself to be a true disciple of Christ, standing in genuine connection with* him, and according to his subjective opinion—because he believes[42] he has to view the matter in such a way—regards the external connection with Christ as the actual sign of the true connection with Christ, then he must also grant me the right to define the true connection with Christ according to another sign that I consider to be true. In this respect, I can in any case claim for myself—with the same right as my opponents for themselves—Χριστοῦ εἶναι. Which sign of Χριστοῦ εἶναι the apostle means with regard to himself is clear from what follows. *This right to see myself from my own point of view as Χριστοῦ ὄντα cannot be denied me, but it would still have to be granted if I took my claims even further. If I claimed an even greater authority for my office than I actually do, my claims would still be true and well founded. I would not have to fear being put to shame, because I use my authority to act as an apostle only* εἰς οἰκοδομήν *and not* εἰς καθαίρεσιν ὑμῶν, *because I seek to act only for the advancement of the true good of the community. With such good reason I believe can claim that I am* Χριστοῦ. Thus, what the apostle, in opposition to the κατὰ πρόσωπον βλέπειν of his opponents, wants to defend as the true sign of Χριστοῦ εἶναι is the purpose of οἰκοδομήν, the truly Christian nature of his apostolic ministry that benefits the whole community, as he explains further, starting in 2 Cor 10:13. [101] *I am, however, not at all putting myself in the same class as those who commend and exalt themselves with vain ambition and according to entirely arbitrary standards that they themselves established, seeking their own praise at the expense of the achievements of others. My praise resides in what I have actually done for the cause of Christianity in my apostolic course, within the boundaries of the sphere of activity that has been assigned to me by God, insofar as I was the first to bring Christianity to Corinth, hoping to have planted it there in a way that the effects of this will open up to me an even greater sphere of activity. I do not have a need to seek my praise in a foreign region, and in the cause of Christianity nothing else can be of value but what has really been achieved.* The contrasts in which the apostle speaks here allow one to surmise with justification that his opponents not only challenged his reputation, but also claimed for themselves the merit of being the true founders of the Corinthian church. They had come to Corinth only after the apostle, but because they did not recognize Paul as a true apostle,

---

42. This associated concept is both in ἑαυτῷ and πρόσωπον, which includes the idea of what depends on personal, subjective concerns.

as Χριστοῦ ὄντα, they tried to take the praise that he actually deserved for themselves, at least insofar as they claimed that they were the first to plant true Christianity there.

With 2 Cor 10:7, already the section begins in which the apostle turns directly against his opponents, pouring his heart out freely about his relationship to them. Starting in 2 Cor 10:11, the tone that he uses against them becomes increasingly stronger and more spirited. A cutting irony comes into his speech, and the picture he sketches of his opponents is presented to us with ever more detailed and repelling features. In 2 Cor 11:1, he addresses his readers, saying: *You have been listening so patiently to what the fools say (my opponents, who exalt themselves, being full of vain pretension). Surely you will also listen to me for a brief moment if I speak to you as a fool using the same kind of language (saying something to justify myself and for my praise,* [102] *which can only appear to be foolish to my opponents from the high standpoint from which they look down at me). I am zealous for you with godly zeal (I am seized as by a holy zeal at the thought of you transferring the love to which I have the proper claim, as the founder of the Christian community in Corinth, to others who are only working against my aims). I engaged you to one man in order to present you to Christ as a pure virgin. However, as the snake deceived Eve by its craftiness, I am afraid that your thoughts might also be drawn away from simple faithfulness to Christ. If someone came proclaiming another Jesus, which I did not preach, or if you could receive another spirit or another gospel than you received (if it were possible for there to be another Christianity that would have to be held for the authentic and true one but had not yet been made known to you through me, and was now proclaimed for the first time to you by such teachers; that is, if I had either not conveyed the truth to you at all or had done so only in a very incomplete or corrupt way), then you would be completely right to accept this.* (This is what brought the apostle into the most decisive opposition to his opponents. What was at issue between the two parties was nothing less than true and false Christianity. His opponents were really proclaiming another Jesus and another form of Christianity by accusing the apostle of not proclaiming the true one.) *This, however, is a completely unthinkable presupposition. Only the form of Christianity that I preached to you is the true one that deserves to be believed in completely. For I do not believe myself to be inferior to the oversized apostles in any respect.* The ὑπερλίαν ἀπόστολοι could be the very same people as the opponents of the apostle who are later called ψευδαπόστολοι (2 Cor 11:13). Since, however, these ψευδαπόστολοι in Corinth specifically appealed to the authority of the apostle Peter, had come to Corinth from Palestine, and were undoubtedly connected in some way with [103] the Palestinian Jewish apostles, the ὑπερλίαν ἀπόστολοι are presumably the apostles, while the ψευδαπόστολοι professed to be their students and delegates. Thus, the expression ὑπερλίαν ἀπόστολοι is meant to designate only the overestimation with which the authority of these apostles was asserted against Paul. The expression οἱ δοκοῦντες στῦλοι εἶναι, which is used in Gal 2:9 for James, Peter, and John, indicates this as well. It initially says only how they were generally regarded by a certain party that sought to dominate public opinion. Accordingly, the apostle says: *As much as one may want to use the high reputation of these apostles against me, this cannot take anything away from the truth of the Christianity that I teach.* In what follows, the apostle then goes on to explain how he considers it only right for him to be conscious of his apostolic calling, since alongside the correct insight into the nature of Christian teaching, he has demonstrated his pure zeal for the cause of Christianity through his entire behavior toward the Corinthian community and through his whole life. For, the apostle ensures: (1) *In the most selfless way, I have not once asked you to financially support me, while my opponents, who are so well acquainted with all the arts of deception and seduction,*[43] *are only interested in making a profit off you and using you for their own selfish purposes* (2 Cor 11:7–20). (2) *My whole life is a series of afflictions, sacrifices, and dangers, which I have taken on for the cause of Christianity* (2 Cor 11:20–33). Precisely this section removes all doubt that the apostle's opponents in Corinth were born Jews, more specifically of true Israelite descent. Thus, it cannot be disputed that they belonged to the Petrine party [104] and claimed the authority of the apostle Peter for themselves. Continuing in an ironic tone, the apostle voluntarily concedes his opponents' accusation of ἀφροσύνη so that he can, under this guise, place himself on the same level as his opponents, who pride themselves on vain pretentions, and defend himself by being able to say what seemed to be only a vain, foolish act of self-praise, but which was the kind of speech that the Corinthians most liked to hear, being accustomed to the language of his arrogant opponents (cf. 2 Cor 11:19–20 and 2 Cor 11:1). In 2 Cor 11:22, he thus poses the question: Ἑβραῖοί εἰσιν; κἀγώ. Ἰσραηλῖταί εἰσιν;

---

43. οἱ τοιοῦτοι ψευδαπόστολοι, ἐργάται δόλιοι, μετασχηματιζόμενοι εἰς ἀποστόλους Χριστοῦ, as the apostle, in 2 Cor 11:13, calls these persons who are veiled in what is only a masquerade of Christianity, whereas they are, besides this, true descendants of the Pharisees who argued with Jesus in the Gospels.

κἀγώ. σπέρμα Ἀβραάμ εἰσιν; κἀγώ. The apostle wants to say: *If it is a matter of such a καυχᾶσθαι κατὰ τὸν σάρκα* (2 Cor 11:18), *of a καυχᾶσθαι that has only inborn, accidental advantages as its content,*[44] *then I, too, can do the same as my opponents.* However, they do not merely want to be true Israelites, but as such also διάκονοι Χριστοῦ. If it already seems foolish to them that I dare call myself their equal with respect to the advantages named above, then they will regard it as madness[45] that I even claim to have an advantage over them in the fact that I can appeal to something far more real than those advantages—the proofs of my apostolic activity. Thus the same people who, as born Jews, had such a high opinion of themselves, also claimed to be the true διάκονοι Χριστοῦ. The fact that this expression, like ἀπόστολοι Χριστοῦ in 2 Cor 11:13, corresponds exactly to Χριστοῦ εἶναι, which appears repeatedly, is immediately evident. Also in 2 Cor 12, which follows, the apostle continues to defend his apostolic standing. In addition to the two reasons mentioned in 2 Cor 11, he adds a third reason for why he has a right to be confident of his apostolic calling—the extraordinary revelations given to him; [105] namely, a state of ecstasy into which he was placed during the first period of his vocation as an apostle. He clarifies, however, that he does not appeal to this in order to boast. Rather, he says that he carries an affliction in his body, which, alongside that uplifting feeling, also constantly keeps a sense of his human weakness alive in him, causing him to put his entire trust in divine help alone. And, more generally, he says that everything that he said in praise of himself was prompted only by the Corinthians not having said what *they* actually should have said in defense of him against his opponents. They themselves must know best that he could hardly rank behind any other apostle, since he had, after all, proven himself among them by all criteria of a true apostolic conduct and activity, and they did not lack anything that other communities had gained through Christianity. It probably cannot be doubted that the mention of ὀπτασίαι and ἀποκαλύψεις, to which the apostle appeals here, is very closely connected with his apologetic aims and with the character of his opponents, with whom he is engaged. If they, as Judaizing teachers of Christianity in accord with the view that must have been characteristic of the Petrine adherents or the Christ party, presented the outward connection to Jesus and the association with him (as was the case for the disciples who were

---

44. Here σάρξ is used basically in the same sense as in [Gal] 6:12: Judaism as what is inborn.

45. Here παραφρονεῖν apparently indicates more than the preceding ἀφροσύνη.

1. The Christ Party in the Corinthian Community

called and trained for their vocation by Jesus himself) as the true criterion of Χριστοῦ εἶναι and of the apostolic calling, then the apostle Paul, if he was to go back to the last and highest point to which his calling to the office of apostle was linked, could set over against what was experienced externally by the other apostles only an inner experience, those extraordinary appearances, which, as inner vision and revelation of the divine, as facts of his immediate consciousness, had awakened faith within him, that ἑορακέναι Ἰησοῦν τὸν κύριον ἡμῶν, to which he had already appealed in 1 Cor 9:1 and which, in any case, belongs in a class with the ὀπτασίαι [106] and ἀποκαλύψεις κυρίου mentioned here, even though it is unlikely that the ecstatic state described in 2 Cor 12:2–4 is identical with the appearance narrated in Acts 9, which effected the conversion of the apostle. For the opponents of the apostle, such ὀπτασίαι καὶ ἀποκαλύψεις may have appeared to possess in themselves only ideas of imaginary visions, which—in contrast to the externally factual relationship in which the other apostles had lived together with Jesus and according to the principle that Peter had already established at the election of the apostle Matthias (Acts 1:21)[46]— could not make any claim to objective truth. Only for the apostle Paul himself were such appearances, which were granted to him in his own inner life, no less firm, irrefutable facts, and as much as he would have liked to avoid speaking of them, in order to avoid every appearance of vain self-exaltation, here, where he could not remain silent about anything that could serve to justify and secure his apostolic reputation, he simply could not refrain from also appealing to them against his opponents. However, the more—as he himself could not hide—this authentication of his apostolic calling belonged only to the sphere of his own immediate consciousness, the more earnestly he had stressed ever anew in all the contents of his two letters the key factual proof that could least be denied the character of objective reality, namely, the great tests in which he had authenticated his apostolic activity as well as to his great success in furthering the cause of Christianity. One may compare 1 Cor 3:8–15, 9:15–16, 15:10,[47] and what was cited from the second letter above (2 Cor 11:5–33).

[107] Thus the polemic that had begun in purely objective terms in the first letter with the claim that the sectarian nature of the Corinthian com-

---

46. δεῖ οὖν τῶν συνελθόντων ἡμῖν ἀνδρῶν ἐν παντὶ χρόνῳ ᾧ εἰσῆλθεν καὶ ἐξῆλθεν ἐφ' ἡμᾶς ὁ κύριος Ἰησοῦς, ἀρξάμενος ἀπὸ τοῦ βαπτίσματος Ἰωάννου ἕως τῆς ἡμέρας ἧς ἀνελήμφθη ἀφ' ἡμῶν, μάρτυρα τῆς ἀναστάσεως αὐτοῦ σὺν ἡμῖν γενέσθαι ἕνα τούτων.

47. περισσότερον αὐτῶν πάντων ἐκοπίασα.

munity was based in the sensuousness of its orientation and in its inability to raise itself up to a higher perspective, to an all-encompassing unity, after the apostle, in the course of both letters, had confronted his opponents in an increasingly personal manner, and had finally considered it necessary to grasp the point of controversy that was at issue at its leading edge and to oppose the external criteria that were being used against him with equally positive internal criteria, ended in the second letter with the discussion of an aspect that was entirely dependent on his own subjective awareness, or at least had its objectivity only in the powerful impression that an inner fact made on the apostle's immediate consciousness. In the end, everything that the apostle depends on for the defense of his apostolic calling is based on this consciousness of the divine πνεῦμα, to which the apostle repeatedly returns in the two letters to the Corinthians, especially in such variegated contexts, on a principle by virtue of which ὁ πνευματικὸς ἀνακρίνει μὲν πάντα, αὐτὸς δὲ ὑπ' οὐδενὸς ἀνακρίνεται (1 Cor 2:15), on the consciousness of νοῦν Χριστοῦ ἔχειν (1 Cor 2:16).

The same Judaizing opponents, whom the apostle opposed so emphatically in both of his letters to the Corinthian community, are also encountered in other letters from the same apostle in various places where he thought it necessary to take them into consideration, whether directly or indirectly. One of the more specific texts of this sort is Phil 3:1–2, where the apostle combats false teachers who attached great value to circumcision and to everything that belonged to ancestral Judaism, and in this sense placed a trust in the σάρξ conflicting with the faith in Christ's death on the cross. For this reason, while the apostle, as in 2 Cor 12:22, placed himself alongside them in claiming the same advantages with regard to his person, [108] he sought thereby to express even more emphatically how little he cared about these outward things with regard to what really mattered here. It is, however, above all the letter to the Galatians that provides a parallel to the polemical tendency of both letters to the Corinthians, shedding further light on the character of the attacks that the apostle had to defend himself against. The opponents whom the apostle combats in the letter to the Galatians fit perfectly into the same class as those whom he dealt with in his letters to the Corinthians, though they sought to counteract the apostle in different ways corresponding to the different circumstances. In Galatia, where, as in the rest of the Near East, the number of Jews and Jewish Christians was significant, they could more openly come forward with the main aim—with which in Corinth, at least as far as we can infer from the letters of the apostle, they believed they must still hold back—of presenting Judaism with its laws and customs as the only way for everyone, including gentiles, to enter into the messianic kingdom established by Jesus. The combatting of these Judaizing false teachers makes up a main part of the letter to the Galatians, and this cannot be called into question. What has usually been given less attention, however, is the fact that these very false teachers combined with their Judaism attacks on the apostolic status of the apostle Paul, which could have had no other tendency than the one that the apostle had to defend himself against before the Corinthian community. It also resides entirely in the nature of the matter that such a significant difference, as the question that arose between the apostle and his opponents as to whether or not Judaism was an essential and integrating part of Christianity,[48] [109] led back to the higher question as to which side the true apostolic authority was located on, on the side of Paul or on the side of the other apostles. Although this difference will not have affected the Jewish apostles themselves, it was still generally known that the decisive act of breaking through the barriers of Judaism was the work of the apostle Paul alone and that the other apostles had not themselves worked towards this goal, but rather had only agreed to it in a yielding manner (as the behavior of the apostle Peter in Gal 2 undeniably demonstrates). And the more the other apostles restricted themselves to the conversion of Jews, for whom a complete renunciation of the authority of the Mosaic law could not be made obligatory even after they crossed over to Christianity, the easier it was for the idea to arise that Paul alone was the actual advocate and proponent of the principle that made Judaism antiquated, and even that there was a certain opposition between Paul and the other apostles here. How natural it must have then been to raise the question directly connected with this: What authority at all can an apostle have who—in contrast to the other apostles—was not schooled by Jesus himself for the office of apostle, but had only later dared to claim apostolic authority for himself, as if by his own power? In this way, in the same connection in which the apostolic authority of Paul could be invalidated, the authority of the Jewish apostles and the Judaism represented by them must have appeared to be secured. Therefore, I can only regard it as an opposition to the unfavorable view, which was spread by his opponents against the apostolic authority of Paul when, in Gal 2:2, 2:6, and 2:9, the apostle repeatedly refers to the first of the

---

48. The μεταστρέψαι τὸ εὐαγγέλιον τοῦ Χριστοῦ that Paul speaks of in Gal 1:7, or the question of whether another εὐαγγέλιον is possible παρ' ὃ εὐηγγελισάμεθα ὑμῖν, with which one must compare the parallel in 2 Cor 12:4.

Jewish apostles—James, Cephas, and John—with the expression οἱ δοκοῦντες, οἱ δοκοῦντες στῦλοι εἶναι. They are called δοκοῦντες (just as the word δοκεῖν is generally used, after all, for what is valid in the public opinion) inasmuch as their authority was asserted in a way that denigrated the authority of the apostle Paul. That is, they alone were to be [110] regarded as the στῦλοι, the proper bearers and bulwarks of true Christianity, and anything that could make a claim to Christian truth should be linked to their names alone.[49] But what could such great weight be placed upon with respect to these apostles over against the apostle Paul if it were not that sign of true apostolic authority to which the so-called Christ party in Corinth appealed, namely, that they alone, along with the others who belonged with them in a class, could be regarded as true apostles because they alone, as the direct students of Jesus who had accompanied him, had received the objectively valid qualification for the office of apostle? For this reason, the apostle begins his defense of his apostolic standing, to which he was compelled by his opponents, with the main goal, on which everything depended here, with the assurance that he, though it was by a different way, had nevertheless been called to be an apostle by a no less valid way, through an equally direct divine intervention. [111] There are two points that are distinguished in the discussion provided in Gal 1 and 2. In their mutual

---

49. In precisely this vein, the term στύλος also seems to be taken from the conceptual framework of the Jewish Christian party. In the Clementine *Hom.* 18.14, for example, the oldest patriarchs Adam, Enoch, Noah, Abraham, Isaac, and Jacob, and, according to *Hom.* 17.4, also Moses, are referred to as the seven pillars of the world: εἰ δέ, ὡς φῂς, Peter says to the magician, ἔσται διὰ τὸ εἰδέναι διὰ τοῦ Ἰησοῦ νῦν πᾶσιν ἀποκαλύπτεσθαι (τὸν υἱὸν θεοῦ—this has to do with the recognition of Christ as the Son of God) πῶς οὐκ ἀδικώτατον λέγεις; ἐκείνους μὴ ἐγνωκέναι ἑπτὰ στύλους ὑπάρξαντας κόσμῳ καὶ δικαιοτάτῳ θεῷ εὐαρετῆσαι δυναμένους, καὶ τοσούτους δὲ νῦν ἀπὸ τῶν ἐθνῶν ἀσεβῶς ὄντας κατὰ πάντα γνῶναι; οὗτοι παντὸς κρείττονες γνῶναι οὐ κατηξιώθησαν ["But if, as you say," Peter says to the magician, "it will be possible to know Him, because He is now revealed to all through Jesus (the Son of God—this has to do with the recognition of Christ as the Son of God), are you not stating what is most unjust, when you say that these men did not know Him, who were the seven pillars of the world, and who were able to please the most just God, and that so many now from all nations who were impious know Him in every respect? Were not those who were superior to every one not deemed worthy to know Him?" (trans. Smith, Peterson, and Donaldson, modified)]; they are thus called pillars in the sense of those who facilitate the true knowledge of the truth, which the prophet of truth reveals. After all, already according to Prov 9:1, Wisdom—who, according to Wis 7:27, imparts herself to holy souls and makes them friends of God and prophets—also builds her house on seven pillars.

1. The Christ Party in the Corinthian Community

relation, they contain the proof that his apostolic authority is no less divine than that of the earlier apostles. Paul contends that he does not owe his Christian convictions to any one of the earlier apostles, but neither do the contents of his teaching contradict what the earlier apostles themselves would have to recognize as Christian truth.[50] Proving the second point

---

50. The apostle's aim in Gal 1 and 2 is certainly not simply to show that he did not receive his teaching from humans, not even from the apostles themselves. This questionable assumption is generally made by those who defend the opinion that the trip mentioned by the apostle in Gal 2:1 is the same as the one in Acts 11:30 (cf. in particular Friedrich Gottlieb Süskind's discussion of chronology for the book of Acts, etc. [Süskind, "Neuer Versuch über chronologische Standpunkte für die Apostelgeschichte und für das Leben Jesu," in vol. 1 of *Archiv für die Theologie und ihre neuste Literatur*, ed. Ernst Gottlieb Bengel (Tübingen: Osiander, 1816), 157]). [Süskind, 1767–1829, was Professor of Theology in Tübingen (from 1798), and then senior court chaplain and consistorial councilor in Stuttgart from 1805.] Rather, an exact examination of the entire section makes clear that the apostle is concerned in general with demonstrating the autonomy and independence of his apostolic authority and activity through compelling proofs. He does this in two ways, both negatively and positively. Negatively, he shows that at the point in time that was decisive and formative for his apostolic calling, he did not have any close contact at all to the older apostles or to the Christian communities in Judea, which were under their influence at that time. Positively, he appeals to how his apostolic authority within the particular sphere that belonged to him as apostle to the gentiles had been recognized by the Jewish apostles in a way in which he had had the opportunity to assert forcefully his independence from them, and in particular from Peter, their leader. He demonstrated that he was not a student who was dependent on their instruction, so that they instead had to accept the principles he propagated and make them their own. Therefore, it cannot have been the apostle's intention to give a complete enumeration [112] here of his trips to Jerusalem. Rather, he only desires to emphasize the details that would have to count as decisive proof for the independent nature of his apostolic standing. These are what he relates here. Only for the early period of his apostolic ministry was it important to give assurance that he did not have any kind of connection to the older apostles that could be seen as the source of his teachings. Once he had already taught and been active as an apostle independently from the other apostles, then it was not of consequence if he was with them later in Jerusalem or not (after all, he could have still received his teaching from them also indirectly). What was now of decisive importance was the manner in which his principles had to be recognized by the other apostles. This also clarifies that in Gal 2:1, he does not bring up his trip to Jerusalem as a further one that followed the one already mentioned, but rather only because of the specific negotiations that took place at that time. The apostolic authority that he had exercised in practice until then now received its theoretical testing, namely, one that was all the more valid given that he had been active as an apostle for such a long time (διὰ δεκατεσσάρων ἐτῶν) in the

[112] was necessary because there can only be one Christian truth in any case, and a contradiction between the apostles themselves would have undermined Christian truth as a whole. [113] But it was also necessary for the apostle to emphatically insist on the first claim so that his apostolic authority would be just as direct and objectively valid as that of the other apostles. If they had any more specific part in his conversion to Christianity and in his conviction of its truth, then his authority would be only a mediated one that was derived from a higher source. He would lack precisely the one requirement that has to be regarded as the one that actually constitutes apostolic authority: the direct connection to Christ, the source of all Christian life, without any human mediation, not even from any of the other apostles. This was the only way that he could regard himself as entitled to stand alongside the other apostles with the exact same dignity and believe himself to be completely secured of his own sphere of influence. For the more strictly the entire sphere of the apostolic activity was divided into the περιτομή and the ἔθνη, and thus fell, so to speak, into two separated areas (Gal 2:9), the more necessary it must have seemed to return to the highest and most direct point on which, for himself, the consciousness of his apostolic calling was based. This is why he so emphatically insists that he received nothing from human beings, absolutely nothing in the way of instruction and teaching, that he did not adhere to flesh and blood, to weak, fallible humans, to which the apostles, as mere mediating organs of the

---

meantime. In addition, with the appeal to his first trip to Jerusalem, Paul certainly did not merely want to say that he had not received his teachings from one of the other apostles (he says that he spoke very briefly with only two apostles, so that it is also not comprehensible from these circumstances how his teaching could have been the result of his instruction from the apostles at that time; see Süskind, "Neuer Versuch," 157, against which some objections can still be raised). Rather, at the same time he also wants to note that, though he had not received his teachings from them, he had nevertheless been received favorably by Peter (cf. Gal 1:18)—who counted in place of the rest—and had thus been acknowledged as an apostle. His entire relationship to the other apostles is meant to appear, on the one hand, in terms of him being completely independent from them, and, on the other hand, as presupposing no real opposition between them. See Carl Schrader, *Chronologische Bermerkungen über das Leben des Apostels Paulus* (Leipzig: Kollmann, 1830), 50–51. [Schrader, 1795–1872, was a Lutheran pastor in Hörste (1825–1836) and Holzhausen (1836–1850), before being dismissed from his position because of his involvement in the so-called *freireligiöse Bewegung* ("free-religious movement"), a movement critical of the state church and its traditions.]

divine truth, as the example of the apostle Peter in Gal 2:11 shows, did not constitute an exception. This is why he provides such an exact and extensive proof that he only came into contact with the apostles in Jerusalem after he had already become completely resolute in his Christian conviction, to the point that nothing more could be added to the heart of it. In contrast to the παραλαβεῖν παρὰ ἀνθρώπου and the διδαχθῆναι, to absolutely every merely [114] mediated instruction, and insofar as apostles such as James, Peter, and John, as the δοκοῦντες, were set against him, also in contrast to the instruction given to those who accompanied Jesus, Paul derived his qualification for the apostolic office from an ἀποκάλυψις Ἰησοῦ Χριστοῦ, a divine intervention that presented itself to him only as an inner fact of his consciousness (εὐδόκησεν ὁ θεός ... ἀποκαλύψαι τὸν υἱὸν αὐτοῦ ἐν ἐμοί [Gal 1:15–16]). To make it objective, he could appeal here—in the same vein, this is the main aspect of the speeches of the apostle in Acts 22 and 26— only to the obvious and sudden character of the great change that had happened to him, which was transformative of his most inner being.

In this way, already in that first period when Christianity had hardly begun to cross beyond the narrow boundaries of Judaism and to open itself to a more favorable sphere of activity in the gentile world, two opposing parties had formed with a very specific opposition of views. As would be expected, and as the apostle Paul explicitly notes in Gal 2:12, where we see it appear for the first time in Antioch with the same tendency that it doggedly pursued since then, the party that directly opposed the apostle Paul had come forth from Jerusalem, where James the younger, the brother of the Lord, was greatly respected as the one who presided over the Christian community. It is to his and Peter's authority and that the pseudoapostles of this party especially appealed when spreading their teachings, even though it is hardly conceivable that the apostles to the Jews themselves could have approved of this and have recognized alleged emissaries of this sort. In light of this party's earnest efforts to spread its influence outwardly and to aggressively oppose everywhere the apostle Paul's reputation and more lenient teaching (of which we have so much evidence before us in the writings of the New Testament), it is not surprising to find it later in various manifestations [115], which, in turn, shed some light on those first attacks against which the apostle Paul had to defend himself. The very same anti-Pauline spirit finds expression in the vehement accusations that the Ebionites made against the apostle Paul, only with an even greater bitterness, as would be expected from a party adhering so narrow-mindedly and fearfully to its Judaism. In Paul, they saw only an apostate from the law, a false teacher, whose letters they rejected in their entirety (Irenaeus, *Haer.* 1.26; Eusebius, *Hist. eccl.* 3.27). Moreover, if it had pleased Epiphanius (*Pan.* 30.25 [2.25.1]), he would have been able to report a great deal of their defamations against the apostle Paul: περὶ τοῦ ἁγίου Παύλου ὡς βλασφημοῦντες αὐτὸν λέγουσι, πόσα ἔχω λέγειν; ["And how much do I have to say about their blasphemies of St. Paul?" (trans. Williams)]. As hated heretics and reformers in religious issues are gladly looked upon as though they had never been members of the religion against which they sinned so gravely, so the Ebionites also claimed of Paul that he was not a Jew by birth but a Greek, who, being born of pagan parents, had only later become a proselyte to Judaism. Moreover, with regard to the cause of his especially hostile attitude toward the Jewish religion, they had a story that can remind us of other accusations made in the same spirit. They claimed (according to Epiphanius, *Pan.* 30.16 [2.16.9]) that when Paul came to Jerusalem later and stayed there for some time, he courted the daughter of the high priest. This was the reason why he became a proselyte and let himself be circumcised. Since, however, his desire went unfulfilled, he wrote out of anger and resentment against circumcision and the Sabbath and the law in general.[51] This is how forcefully the Ebionites' well-known adherence to Judaism expressed itself in the whole [116] scope of its claims. However, long after the apostolic era, we still find the other main point of the opposition raised against Paul, which was directly aimed at dogmatically denying any objective validity to his apostolic standing. Rather than having been forgotten, it reappears in the form of a quite developed theory. The homilies that have been handed down to us under the name of the Roman Clement are undeniably not merely a Jewish Christian work but a product from the end of the second century or the beginning of the third that stands in some sort of closer connection with the sect of the Ebionites. In this highly peculiar text, the principle is basically established that the only revelation that can be regarded as true and credible is one that is not mediated through appearances and visions but through external impartation and instruction. The two main protagonists in a heated debate with each other, the magician Simon and the apostle Peter, also have the opposite opinion in this regard. Simon defends one opinion and Peter the other in a passage that contains

---

51. In roughly the same way, zealot-like papists derived the abolishment of celibacy in the Evangelical Church, and probably also the entire work of the Reformation, from Luther's desire to marry.

1. The Christ Party in the Corinthian Community

so much that is relevant for the goal of our study that the most important statements merit special attention here. The magician Simon counters the apostle Peter (*Hom.* 17.13), saying:

> You have boasted that you have perfectly understood your teacher (the true prophet, Christ) because you personally saw and heard him before you, and that it is not possible for anyone else to have the same in an appearance or vision [ὁράματι ἢ ὀπτασίᾳ]. I will now show you that this is not true. Whoever hears someone else clearly is not completely convinced by what he hears. For his spirit must ask if this is not a lie—as the one speaking to him appears to be a mere man. The vision, on the other hand, grants to the one who sees, in the moment it is seen, the conviction that it is something divine.[52]

Peter responds:

> You claim that someone could receive more through a vision [117] than through a genuine action [ἢ παρὰ τῆς ἐνεργείας]. For this reason, you believe yourself to be better instructed about Jesus than I am. The prophet alone merits full belief, for one knows in advance that he is truthful, and he gives, as the one who inquires desires, the answer to the questions posed to him. However, the one who believes a vision or an apparition and dream has no security: he does not know whom he believes. For an evil demon or a deceptive spirit can, after all, simulate what is not, and when he asks who is appearing to him, the one who has appeared can say whatever he wishes. He stays as long as he desires and disappears like a suddenly flashing beam of light, without giving the desired answer to the questioner. In a dream, one cannot even ask what one would like to know, for the one who is sleeping does not have his spirit under his own power. This is why, when we are dreaming, we ask many different things in dreams out of curiosity and, without asking, learn what is of no interest to us; and when we wake up, we are discontented that we did not hear and ask what was important to us.

In response to the magician's objection that, even if not all visions should be believed, the apparitions and dreams sent by God cannot be untrue, and that only the righteous and not the godless can see a true apparition,

---

52. [This and the following long citations from the *Homilies* are here translated from Baur's German.]

Peter responds that he cannot concede this, and continues to develop his theory in *Hom.* 17.16 by saying:

> I know that there are many idol worshipers, people who are sexually immoral, and who commit sins of every kind, yet see apparitions and true dreams, and some of them also see demonic appearances. I do not claim that the eye of a mortal can behold the fleshless form of the Father or Son, for it shines in the purest light. It is thus not out of envy that God does not let himself be seen by humans joined with a fleshly nature; whoever sees him cannot remain alive, for the superabundance of light destroys the flesh of the one who sees it, unless God's unspeakable power transforms the flesh into the nature of light so that it can see the light, or the [118] nature of the light passes over into the flesh so that it can be seen by the flesh. For only the Son can see the Father without a transformation needing to take place. However, this does not take place in the same way for the righteous. At the resurrection of the dead, when their bodies are transformed into light, they themselves will become like angels, and they will be able to see him. However, even when an angel is sent to appear to a human, he transforms himself into flesh so that he can be seen by the flesh. For who can behold the fleshless nature not merely of the Son but also of an angel? When, however, someone sees a vision [ὀπτασία], he should consider the possibility that it may come from an evil demon. It is certain that even the godless also see apparitions and true dreams, and I can also prove this from Scripture. In Scripture it is written that the godless Abimelech, when he wanted to seduce the wife of righteous Abraham, heard from God in his sleep that he should not touch her (Gen 20). Likewise, the godless Pharaoh also saw fruitfulness and famine announced to him in a dream, and the explanation was sent by God to Joseph, who explained its meaning to him (Gen 41). Nebuchadnezzar, the idol worshiper who commanded the worshipers of God to be thrown into the fire, saw a dream that encompassed all the periods of world history (Dan 5). Moreover, let no one say that the godless cannot see an apparition when awake. Nebuchadnezzar himself, who had the three men thrown into the fire, saw a fourth figure in the oven and said, "I saw a fourth figure as a son of God" (Dan 3). All of these persons were godless, and yet they saw visions and apparitions and true dreams. From the fact that someone beholds visions, dreams, and apparitions, it cannot be concluded that he is truly a pious man. For the true wells up for the pious out of the indwelling pure mind, not sought in a dream but given to those who are good with consciousness and insight [τῷ γὰρ εὐσεβεῖ ἐμφύτῳ καὶ καθαρῷ ἀναβλύζει τῷ νῷ τὸ ἀληθές, οὐκ ὀνείρῳ σπουδαζόμενον, ἀλλὰ συνέσει ἀγαθοῖς διδόμενον]. This is how [119] the Son was revealed by the Father to me, too. Hence, I

know what meaning the revelation has [τίς δύναμις ἀποκαλύψεως] from my own experience. For as soon as the Lord asked me (Matt 16:14), it rose up in my heart; and I myself do not know how it happened to me, for I said, "You are the Son of the living God." It was only the one who called me blessed for that reason who told me that it was the Father who had revealed this to me. Since then I have understood what revelation is, namely, to become aware of something without outward instruction, without visions and dreams [τὸ ἀδιδάκτως ἄνευ ὀπτασίας καὶ ὀνείρων μαθεῖν, ἀποκάλυψίς ἐστι]. This is also how it is, for in the truth that God has planted in us, the seed of all truth is contained [ἐν γάρ τῇ ἐν ἡμῖν ἐκ θεοῦ τεθείσῃ σπερματικῶς πᾶσα ἔνεστιν ἡ ἀλήθεια]. This is either hidden or revealed only by God's hand, in that God acts in accord with his knowledge of each individual's worthiness. However, receiving messages in visions and dreams from outside is not the character of revelation but a demonstration of divine wrath. Accordingly, it is also written in the law that God, being angry with Aaron and Moses, said (Num 12:6-7): "If a prophet rises up among you, I will reveal myself to him through apparitions and dreams. Not so, however, with my servant Moses, for I speak with him visibly [ἐν εἴδει] and not in dreams, and as one speaks with his friend." You see how apparitions and dreams are expressions of wrath. But what is shared with a friend is communicated from mouth to mouth, directly [ἐν εἴδει] and not through pictures, through dreams and apparitions, as he communicates with the enemy. Thus, if our Jesus appeared also to you, if he revealed himself to you and spoke with you, then he spoke to you in apparitions and dreams and in external revelations for the reason that he dealt with you in anger as against an adversary. Can anyone be instructed through a vision to qualify them for the office of teaching? If you say that this is indeed possible, then I say: Why then did the teacher cultivate [120] continuous association for a whole year with those who were awake, and how can they believe that he has also appeared to you? How then can he have appeared to you, since your thinking does not agree at all with his teaching? If you were really trained to be an apostle by association and instruction, even if only for one hour, then proclaim his speeches, explain what he said and did, love his apostles, and do not argue with me, who was together with him [εἰ δὲ ὑπὸ ἐκείνου μιᾶς ὥρας ὀφθεὶς καὶ μαθητευθεὶς ἀπόστολος ἐγένου τὰς ἐκείνου φωνὰς κήρυσσε, τὰ ἐκείνου ἑρμήνευε, τοὺς ἐκείνου ἀπόστολος φίλει, ἐμοὶ τῷ συγγενομένῳ αὐτῷ μὴ μάχου]. For you have set yourself as an adversary against me, a solid rock, the founding pillar of the church. If you were not my adversary, you would not have maligned me and defamed my preaching so that people do not believe me about what I myself heard from the Lord when I was with him, as if I were condemned, though I should actually be praised. More than this, if you call me condemned, you are bringing an accusation against God, who revealed Christ to me. You are attacking the one who called me blessed because of this revelation. If you really and truly want to be a coworker in the cause of the truth, then first learn from us, just as we learned from him, and when you have become a student of truth, then become our coworker.[53]

According to the theory presented here, the only people who can be credible agents of divine truth are those apostles of Christ who were trained to be his students in personal association with him and equipped for the communication of his teaching. According to the teachings of the Clementines, there must be a continuously persisting cathedra as the seat and container of the divinely revealed truth. Just as Christ, as prophet of the truth—since the scribes and Pharisees sitting on the cathedra of Moses had the key of truth that alone can open the gate of eternal life but did not let anyone enter through it (Matt 23:2; Luke 11:52)—raised himself upon the cathedra of Moses (*Hom.* 3.18–19), so [121] those who have received the teaching of the prophet handed down from the most secure hand must now, on the same cathedra, continually preside. Therefore, James and Peter in particular are the most fully valid witnesses of the truth revealed by Christ, the former as the one who presides over the mother community in Jerusalem; the latter as the one who is responsible for proclaiming this teaching outwardly among the gentiles. When the latter, following his adversary, the magician Simon, from place to place founds Christian communities, he usually names, whenever he is poised to go farther afield, a representative who will administer the church well while sitting on the cathedra of Christ (*Hom.* 3.60). These bishops named by Peter to represent his position are either persons like Zacchaeus (who, according to the Clementines, was named by Peter to be bishop of Caesarea of Straton), who had been together with the Lord himself, seen his miracles, and learned about the administration of the church from him (*Hom.* 3.65), or persons like Clement, the constant companion of Peter and the witness of all his speeches and deeds, persons who had received through this the qualification for such an office in the same way as the disciples in their association with Jesus himself. This excludes every other way of entering the Christian office of teaching and obtaining true apostolic authority—especially the way by which Paul believed he had obtained the conviction that he could place himself with equal status alongside the apostles who were called and

---

53. [This material is taken not simply from *Hom.* 17.16, but from *Hom.* 17.16–19.]

instructed by Jesus himself. After all, if the theory in general contained in the passage quoted above—in the fact that this theory ascribes everything to the personal association and successive instruction through teaching and example, and desires to know nothing of a divine action and awakening that takes place in a single moment—already appears to reflect a certain polemical relationship to the ὀπτασία and ἀποκάλυψις appealed to by Paul, and to the entire way in which he believed himself to be called to the apostolic office and had become conscious of the revelation of the Son of God in his inner being, then [122] the same antithetical tendency against the apostle Paul probably must also be recognized in several specific elements in the Clementines. It is striking how Peter is assigned here entirely to the same sphere of activity that belonged to Paul according to the actual course of events. James is the bishop residing in Jerusalem, who—as he is called in the superscription of the letter of Clement, as κύριος or ἀδελφὸς κυρίου, as ἐπίσκοπος ἐπισκόπων, διέπων τὴν Ἱερουσαλὴμ ἁγίαν Ἑβραίων ἐκκλησίαν, καὶ τὰς πανταχῇ θεοῦ προνοίᾳ ἱδρυθείσας καλῶς ["Lord or brother of the Lord, as bishop of bishops, who rules Jerusalem, the holy church of the Hebrews, and the churches everywhere excellently founded by the providence of God" (trans. Smith, Peterson, and Donaldson, modified)]—is responsible for preserving the treasure of truth, so to speak, in the original ancestral seat, to whom Peter therefore also arranged for his sermons to be sent shortly before his death, so that they would be deposited in Jerusalem in his hands.[54] Peter, on the other hand, has another purpose, as he himself says in *Hom.* 3.59: ὁρμᾶν εἰς ἔθνη τὰ πολλοὺς θεοὺς λέγοντα, κηρύξαι καὶ διδάξαι, ὅτι εἷς ἐστιν ὁ θεός, ὃς οὐρανὸν [123] ἔκτισε

---

54. This same relationship between James and Peter can already be observed in the New Testament. Peter sometimes appears outside of Jerusalem and Palestine, while James never does. According to Gal 1:18, when the apostle Paul came to Jerusalem, the only apostles he met there were Peter and James. The apostle notes this with the words ἕτερον τῶν ἀποστόλων οὐκ εἶδον εἰ μὴ Ἰάκωβον τὸν ἀδελφὸν τοῦ κυρίου. It is as if he wanted to say that it is of course obvious that James was in Jerusalem. Due to the special relationship that he had to the Jewish Christians as the head of the Jerusalem community, he is at times even named before Peter, as in Gal 2:9, where Paul lists the three apostles according to the classification given to them by the Jewish Christians. At the gathering of the apostles in Jerusalem in Acts 15, he appears, as the head of the Jerusalem community, to guide the course of the proceedings by putting forward the motion that is ready to be decided upon. Likewise, in Acts 21:18, he appears as the head of the community. That later authors (cf. Eusebius, *Hist. eccl.* 3.1.23) make him the first bishop of Jerusalem, is common knowledge.

καὶ γῆν, καὶ τὰ ἐν αὐτοῖς πάντα ὅπως ἀγαπήσαντες αὐτὸν σωθῆναι δυνηθῶσιν ["While I am going forth to the nations which say that there are many gods, to teach and to preach that God is one, who made heaven and earth, and all things that are in them, in order that they may love Him and be saved" (trans. Smith, Peterson, and Donaldson)]. He is thus the actual apostle to the gentiles, who is called to spread the teaching of the true prophet. But his sphere of activity is mapped out in advance by the need to follow the magician Simon and refute the errors that his adversary spreads as he hurries ahead of him. For προλαβοῦσα ἡ κακία αὐτῷ τῆς συζυγίας νόμῳ προαπέστειλεν Σίμωνα, ἵνα οἱ ἄνθρωποι ἐὰν τοὺς πολλοὺς θεοὺς λέγειν παύσωνται, καταγνόντες τῶν ἐπὶ γῆς λεγομένων, ἐν οὐρανῷ πολλοὺς θεοὺς εἶναι νομίσουσιν· ἵνα μηδέποτε τὸ τῆς μοναρχίας τιμήσαντες καλόν, εἰς τὸ παντελὲς μετὰ κόλασιν ἀπόλωνται [Hom. 3.59: "evil has anticipated me, and by the very law of conjunction has sent Simon before me, in order that these men, if they shall cease to say that there are many gods, disowning those upon earth that are called gods, may think that there are many gods in heaven; so that, not feeling the excellency of the monarchy, they may perish with eternal punishment" (trans. Smith, Peterson, and Donaldson)]. Moreover, the magician, inasmuch as the teaching he proclaims is only a refined form of polytheism (insofar as Gnosticism, through the teaching of the demiurge as lower god who is distinct from the true God, or even a lower god opposed to him, is shaped in a dualistic or polytheistic manner), leaves behind him a sphere in which Peter as the apostle to the gentiles has to convert the nations from pagan polytheism through the basic teaching of the divine monarchy. Thus, also in this connection, there is no more room left for Paul as the apostle to the gentiles, and while he is simply ignored, purposefully never being named, there is no lack of individual intimations, in which this silent polemic against the apostle is, so to speak, about to remove its mask. When the original text of the following words from the passage quoted above is compared with Gal 2:11-12, who could fail to recognize a relationship to this text, and thus also a rather direct polemic against the apostle Paul? Πρὸς γὰρ στερεὰν πέτραν ὄντα με—Peter says in response to Simon the magician—θεμέλιον ἐκκλεσίας ἐναντίος ἀνθεστηκάς μοι. Εἰ μὴ ἀντικείμενος ἦς, οὐκ ἄν με διαβάλλων, τὸ δι᾽ ἐμοῦ κήρυγμα ἐλοιδόρης. ἵνα ὃ παρὰ τοῦ κυρίου αὐτὸς παρὼν ἀκήκοα λέγων, μὴ πιστεύωμαι· δῆλον ὅτι ὡς ἐμοῦ κατεγνωσθέντος καὶ ἐμοῦ εὐδοκιμοῦντος· ἢ εἰ κατεγνωσμένον με λέγεις, θεοῦ τοῦ ἀποκαλύψαντός μοι τὸν Χριστὸν [124] κατηγορεῖς, καὶ τοῦ ἐπὶ ἀποκαλύψει μακαρίσαντός με καταφέρεις [Hom. 17.19: "For in direct opposition to me, who am a firm rock"—

1. The Christ Party in the Corinthian Community

Peter says in response to Simon the magician—"the foundation of the Church, you now stand. If you were not opposed to me, you would not accuse me, and revile the truth proclaimed by me, in order that I may not be believed when I state what I myself have heard with my own ears from the Lord, as if I were evidently a person that was condemned and in bad repute. But if you say that I am condemned, you bring an accusation against God, who revealed the Christ to me, and you inveigh against Him who pronounced me blessed on account of the revelation" (trans. Smith, Peterson, and Donaldson)]. What Paul says of himself in Gal 2:11, ὅτε δὲ ἦλθε Πέτρος εἰς Ἀντιόχειαν, κατὰ πρόσωπον αὐτῷ ἀντέστην, ὅτι κατεγνωσμένος ἦν, is transferred here to the relationship of the magician Simon to the apostle Peter, and the so-telling expression κατεγνωσμένος, used by Paul in reference to Peter, is placed in the mouth of the magician as the adversary of Peter. What Peter says in chapter 2 of his Letter of Peter to James, preceding the homilies, belongs precisely here: James should use the sermons sent to him by Peter as mysteries for instructing those who wish to take part in the office of teaching. If this does not happen, then the true teaching will be divided into many opinions. He knows this not merely as a prophet but because he has already seen the beginning of the evil.

> Τινὲς γὰρ ἀπὸ τῶν ἐθνῶν τὸ δι' ἐμοῦ νόμιμον ἀπεδοκίμασαν κήρυγμα, τοῦ ἐχθροῦ ἀνθρώπου ἄνομόν τινα καὶ φλυαρώδη προσηκάμενοι διδασκαλίαν. Καὶ ταῦτα ἔτι μου περιόντος ἐπεχείρησάν τινες ποικίλαις τισὶν ἑρμηνείαις τοὺς ἐμοὺς λόγους μετασχηματίζειν εἰς τὴν τοῦ νόμου κατάλυσιν· ὡς καὶ ἐμοῦ αὐτοῦ οὕτω μὲν φρονοῦντος, μὴ ἐκ παρρησίας δὲ κηρύσσοντος, ὅπερ ἀπείη. Τὸ γὰρ τοιοῦτο ἀντιπράσσειν ἐστὶ τῷ τοῦ θεοῦ νόμῳ, τῷ διὰ Μωυσέως ῥηθέντι, καὶ ὑπὸ τοῦ κυρίου ἡμῶν μαρτυρηθέντι, περὶ τῆς αἰδίου αὐτοῦ διαμονῆς, ἐπεὶ οὕτως εἶπεν· ὁ οὐρανὸς καὶ ἡ γῆ παρελεύσονται, ἰῶτα ἕν, ἢ μία κεραία οὐ μὴ παρέλθῃ ἀπὸ τοῦ νόμου. Τοῦτο δὲ εἴρηκεν, ἵνα τὰ πάντα γίνηται. Οἱ δὲ οὐκ οἶδα πῶς τὸν ἐμὸν νοῦν ἐπαγγελλόμενοι, οὓς ἤκουσαν ἐξ ἐμοῦ λόγους, ἐμοῦ τοῦ εἰπόντος αὐτοὺς φρονιμώτερον ἐπιχειροῦσιν ἑρμηνεύειν, λέγουσιν τοῖς ὑπ' αὐτῶν κατηχουμένοις τοῦτο εἶναι τὸ ἐμὸν φρόνημα, ὃ ἐγὼ οὐδὲ ἐνεθυμήθην. Εἰ δὲ ἐμοῦ ἔτι περιόντος τοιαῦτα τολμῶσιν καταψεύδεσθαι· πόσῳ γε μᾶλλον μετ' ἐμὲ ποιεῖν οἱ μετ' ἐμὲ τολμήσουσιν.

["For some from among the gentiles have rejected my legal preaching, attaching themselves to certain lawless and trifling preaching of the man who is my enemy. And these things some have attempted while I am still alive, to transform my words by certain various interpretations, in order to the dissolution of the law; as though I also myself were of such a mind, but did not freely proclaim it, which God forbid! For such a thing were to act in opposition to the law of God which was spoken by Moses, and was borne witness to by our Lord in respect of its eternal continuance; for thus he spoke: The heavens and the earth shall pass away, but one jot or one tittle shall in no wise pass from the law. And this He has said, that all things might come to pass. But these men, professing, I know not how, to know my mind, undertake to explain my words, which they have heard of me, more intelligently than I who spoke them, telling their catechumens that this is my meaning, which indeed I never thought of. But if, while I am still alive, they dare thus to misrepresent me, how much more will those who shall come after me dare to do so!" (trans. Smith, Peterson, and Donaldson)]

This also alludes to Gal 2:12, where it is said of Peter that he drew back (ὑπέστελλε) when the Jewish Christians from Jerusalem arrived, and where, more fundamentally, his entire behavior is presented as lacking sincerity. The only difference is that here the relationships are turned on their head. [125] Instead of Paul presupposing that Peter actually agreed with his view of the Mosaic law and that it was merely a ὑπόκρισις that he denied his true view out of fear of the Jewish Christians who came from Jerusalem, Peter protests here against the presupposition that he conceded more than his true opinion due to a lack of παρρησία about the abolition of the law, and he explains that it would thus be merely an arbitrary interpretation given to his speeches if one were to claim to find this tendency in them. So even if one is not willing to accept that none other than Paul himself is meant by that ἄνθρωπος ἐχθρός ["one who is an enemy"] whose ἄνομος καὶ φλυαρώδης διδασκαλία ["lawless and gossipy teaching"] the gentiles accept, then at least the thought of this apostle[55] to the gentiles should not be excluded entirely here. In the first instance, this ἄνθρωπος ἐχθρός is without doubt the same πλάνος ["deceiver"] as the one spoken of in *Hom.* 2.17. Peter says here that the magician Simon came to the gentiles before him, and that after him he ἐπελθὼν ὡς σκότῳ φῶς, ὡς ἀγνοίᾳ γνῶσις, ὡς νόσῳ ἴασις, οὕτως δή, ὡς ἀληθὴς ἡμῖν προφήτης εἴρηκεν πρῶτον ψευδὲς δεῖ ἐλθεῖν εὐαγγέλιον ὑπὸ πλάνου τινὸς καὶ εἶθ' οὕτως μετὰ καθαίρεσιν τοῦ ἁγίου τόπου εὐαγγέλιον ἀληθὲς κρύψᾳ διαπεμφθῆναι, εἰς ἐπανόρθωσιν τῶν ἐσομένων αἱρέσεων ["has come in upon him as light upon darkness, as

---

55. [Baur's text has *diese Heidenapostel*, but we suggest an error for *diesen Heidenapostel*.]

knowledge upon ignorance, as healing upon disease. And thus, as the true Prophet has told us, a false prophet must first come from some deceiver; and then, in like manner, after the removal of the holy place, the true Gospel must be secretly sent abroad for the rectification of the heresies that shall be" (trans. Smith, Peterson, and Donaldson)]. Neander remarks about this passage:

> At most one could relate this passage again to the teaching of Simon Magus and of Peter and regard it as a subsequent explanation of what was said before, but the chronological specification speaks against this: after the destruction of the temple. Thus, by the false gospel that follows upon the teachings of Simon Magus, the teaching of Paul could indeed be meant. But why did the writer of the Clementines not express himself more unambiguously and precisely in his warnings?[56]

However, I find no support in this passage for the distinction that Neander tries to make here between the teaching of the magician Simon and the false gospel that follows upon it. The false gospel is indisputably precisely the teaching of the magician Simon. [126] I think that the entire relationship to the apostle Paul into which the Clementines place themselves and their Peter has to be envisaged as follows. The magician Simon of the Clementines is apparently not the historical person that we know from Acts and other sources but rather an idealized one. He is the representative of all heretics who, like Simon himself, adopted an anti-Jewish perspective, which is why Peter, in the passage from the Clementines that was just quoted, sees in him the entire series of those who would follow after him with the same false teachings.[57] Specifically, it can be demonstrated that [127] in the teachings

---

56. August Neander, *Genetische Entwicklung der vornehmsten gnostischen Systeme* (Berlin: Dümmler, 1818), 366.

57. That Simon the magician is *the* representative of the gnostic spirit as a whole in the Clementines is not only evident from the fact that the teaching placed in his mouth goes far beyond what we otherwise know of Simon's teaching but also from several passages in which he is portrayed even more explicitly than in the passages above as a mere forerunner. In this regard, the passage *Hom.* 16.21 should be noted in particular. Here the people desire from Peter that he should not spend time refuting the magician but that he should present to them the true teaching straightaway. Peter responds: "If only what Simon says was the end of enticing speeches against God! But according to the word of the Lord, false apostles and sects and power-hungry men will come, who will, as I suspect, going forth from Simon, help him to speak against God." Peter said this with tears, went into the house sighing, and went to bed

that he attributes to the magician Simon, the author of the Clementines has especially the Marcionite system in mind, and that he regarded this system as the outermost point of the path that the magician Simon had set out upon and that had then been traversed by the heretics that followed.[58] In view of the exact relationship that the Clementines have to the teaching of the Ebionites and the well-known hate for the apostle Paul with which this sect was filled, no other conclusion is possible except that the teaching of the Clementines is meant to oppose the principles in particular that Paul had put forth about the relationship of the Mosaic law to Christianity. Just as in the presentation of the Clementines, Marcion collapses with Simon the magician into a single person, so the magician, through the mediation of Marcion, could also be thought together with the apostle Paul. After all, the Gnosis of Marcion did indeed have a Pauline/anti-Jewish foundation, and for Marcion it was

---

without eating. The author apparently has the later gnostics in view here, but due to the time in which he places the action of his writing, he does not yet have them appear themselves but only has them be anticipated by Peter as successors of the Simonian false teaching, while he places their teachings in Simon's mouth. Likewise, in *Hom.* 11.35, Peter says to the presbyters and to the whole congregation: "The Lord and prophet who sent us has told us ahead of time that the devil, since he was not able to gain any ground against him in a discussion of forty days, had decided to send out a whole series of false apostles" (ἐκ τῶν αὐτοῦ ὑπηκόων ἐπηγγέλλετο πρὸς ἀπάτην ἀποστόλους πέμψαι). [127] Therefore, it is said that one must indeed be careful ἵνα μὴ ἡ κακία ἡ τῷ κυρίῳ προδιαλεχθεῖσα ἡμέρας τεσσαράκοντα μηδὲν δυνηθεῖσα, ὕστερον ὡς ἀτραπὴ ἐξ οὐρανοῦ ἐπὶ γῆς πεσοῦσα, καθ' ἡμῶν ἐκπέμψῃ κήρυκα, ὡς οὖν ἡμῖν τὸν Σίμωνα ὑπέβαλεν, προφάσει ἀληθείας ἐπ' ὀνόματι τοῦ κυρίου ἡμῶν κηρύσσοντα, πλάνην δὲ ἐνσπείροντα ὑποβάλλῃ, οὗ χάριν ὁ ἀποστείλας ἡμᾶς ἔφη· πολλοὶ ἐλεύσονται, etc.; ["lest the wickedness which disputed forty days with the Lord, and prevailed nothing, should afterwards, like lightning falling from heaven upon the earth, send a preacher to your injury, as now he has sent Simon upon us, preaching, under pretence of the truth, in the name of the Lord, and sowing error. Wherefore He who has sent us said, 'Many shall come,'" etc. (trans. Smith, Peterson, and Donaldson)]; Matt 7:25. [N.B.: This is not Matt 7:25, but it matches Matt 24:5 (πολλοὶ [γὰρ] ἐλεύσονται...) // Mark 13:6; Luke 21:8.] See further the passage cited above from the Letter of Peter to James.

58. A more precise demonstration of the relationship of the Clementines to Marcion and his teaching will, as I hope, be given by a younger theologian who has carried out an investigation of the purpose of the Clementines and was led to this view of a closer connection of the Clementines to Marcion. [N.B.: Who this "younger theologian" might be remains unclear. It sounds as though Baur has a specific project in mind, perhaps a work that has just been or is about to be completed by an advanced student. But we can trace no one in Baur's circles writing on such a topic this early, and no work appeared that obviously bears a relation to this theme.]

especially Paul who was regarded as ἀπόστολος. Therefore, I do not shy away at all from claiming that the ἄνθρωπος ἐχθρός who appears with the ἄνομος καὶ φλυαρώδης διδασκαλία is nominally the magician Simon in the first instance, but in the end he is just as much Paul as he is Marcion, who follows the Pauline direction to the [128] extreme. It is the same with the πλάνος in *Hom.* 2.17. While this false teacher is the magician for the author of the Clementines according to the most natural sense of his words, here the magician nevertheless also represents in particular the apostle Paul, whose destructive principles concerning the defunct validity of the Mosaic law or whose false gospel it is that is to be counteracted by the true gospel proclaimed by Peter. Therefore, I cannot agree with Neander in taking the words μετὰ καθαίρεσιν τοῦ ἁγίου τόπου ["after the removal of the holy place" (trans. Smith, Peterson, and Donaldson)] as a mere chronological specification. What would be the purpose here of a chronological specification given without any particular occasion? It would be the only such specification that could be found in the Clementines, since it is otherwise characteristic of them to leave us as uncertain as possible about times and places, unless they are absolutely necessary for the narrative. I can see in these words only an allusion to the destruction of Jerusalem, which had already occurred. But to me it mainly seems to refer to Acts 21:28, according to which the Jews fell upon Paul, crying out: οὗτός ἐστιν ὁ ἄνθρωπος ὁ κατὰ τοῦ λαοῦ καὶ τοῦ νόμου καὶ τοῦ τόπου τούτου πάντας πανταχῇ διδάσκων, ἔτι δὲ καὶ Ἕλληνας εἰσήγαγεν εἰς τὸ ἱερὸν καὶ κεκοίνωκε τὸν ἅγιον τόπον τοῦτον. Taking the situation portrayed there into account, the author of the Clementines labels the apostle Paul's procedure, which was so inimically aimed at violently doing away with the Mosaic law and all the institutions of Judaism, as a καθαίρεσις τοῦ ἁγίου τόπου in order to present this wild, truly pagan overthrowing of the law as a prelude to the destruction of Jerusalem and the temple—the τόπος ἅγιος—by the Romans that followed shortly thereafter. However, in my judgment, the fact that, amidst all these connections, the writer of the Clementines never steps forward more openly and unambiguously with his attacks on the apostle Paul, having him clearly in mind [129] but never mentioning him by name, can only be due to the time in which and the purpose for which this writing was composed.[59] The author of the Clementines' purpose was undeniably to secure as much of a Jewish character as possible for Christianity and to bring it back—even in places

---

59. Neander (*Genetische Entwicklung*, 36–37) also finds this striking but without giving a sufficient explanation for it.

where it had already gone decisively beyond Judaism—to the standpoint of Judaism, though not of the usual Judaism but rather of the Judaism that was purified and spiritualized according to Essene-Ebionite principles. From his perspective, this kind of Judaism must have seemed all the more suitable to unite Mosaism with the new form of religion revealed by Jesus in a way that would also be satisfactory in the future. However, at the time in which this attempt was made, Pauline Christianity was already so strong and established and had become so dominant in a large part of the Christian world that this kind of reaction could only be introduced with great caution by a diversely educated person of great intellect, as we must envisage the author of the Clementines due to the impressive nature of his writing, both in terms of form and content. As he himself says (*Hom.* 2.17), it is necessary διαπεμφθῆναι εὐαγγέλιον ἀληθές κρύφα ["the true Gospel must be secretly sent abroad" (trans. Smith, Peterson, and Donaldson)] (whereby this writing designates itself as an intentionally apocryphal work). Accordingly, in order to avoid any unnecessary and alarming offence, the real names should at least be withheld, so that the subject matter itself, which was what mattered, could be kept all the more clearly in focus. How could a more direct attack on the generally so-highly regarded apostle to the gentiles have been appropriately made at that time? However, for those who were receptive, for those who knew how to grasp such a tendency and value it, there were enough allusions in the content of the writing that could inform them of the true purpose of the project.[60]

---

60. An objection to accepting a polemical tendency in the Clementines [130] against the apostle Paul cannot be derived from *Hom.* 3.59, the passage cited on p. 66/123, namely, with the rationale that the teaching of the magician in this passage (which can be compared with *Hom.* 3.3) is referred to as paganism that has been revived in Gnosticism and also further refined. How, one could say, can the magician Simon, as an apostle of paganism, simultaneously represent the apostle to the pagans, Paul? However, as soon as we see the magician as the bearer of a whole series of phenomena, then the one antithesis does not exclude the other one. In addition, it will later be noted that, according to the view of the Clementines, the Pauline Christology could not be very far removed from the gnostic teaching of the demiurge. In the same way, the passage in *Hom.* 11.35 does not justify an objection against the position adopted above. In this passage, the communities are warned: πρὸ πάντων μέμνησθε ἀπόστολον ἢ διδάσκαλον ἢ προφήτην μὴ πρότερον ἀντιβάλλοντα αὐτοῦ τὸ κήρυγμα Ἰακώβῳ, τῷ λεχθέντι ἀδελφῷ τοῦ κυρίου—καὶ μετὰ μαρτύρων προσεληλυθότα πρὸς ὑμᾶς μὴ δέχεσθαι ["above all, remember to shun apostle or teacher or prophet who does not first accurately compare his preaching with that of James, who was called the brother of my Lord—and that even though he come to you with witnesses" (trans. Smith, Peterson, and Donaldson)]. Therefore, as Neander also remarks (*Genetische*

[130] It cannot be a surprise that Judaism—the recommendation and introduction of which in a new form must be seen as the main purpose [131] of the Clementines—also offers other dogmatic points of contact with the teaching of the opponents, which the apostle combats in his two letters to the Corinthians. It was mentioned above that the great emphasis that Paul places on Jesus's death on the cross in both letters must be viewed chiefly also as a counterweight to the Judaizing tendency of his opponents, who could not assign the same value to Jesus's death. In the same vein, the death of Jesus is also placed very much in the background in the Clementines. There is only a single passage in which the death of Jesus is mentioned, and even here it is only a side remark, with no indication of it having a distinctive effect. The passage in question is *Hom.* 3.18, which was already quoted earlier. It speaks of the key of truth, which the scribes and Pharisees held but did not use faithfully. For that reason, *Hom.* 3.19 continues, the teacher raised himself up from the cathedra of Moses, like a father for his children, proclaimed what had from the beginning been secretly entrusted to those who were worthy, extended his compassion to the gentiles, and did not spare even his own blood (ἰδίου αἵματος ἠμέλει). Christ is indeed seen as only a prophet and teacher, and his entire activity is reduced to human behavior that corresponds to his teaching. This purely Pelagian view, which locates the redeeming activity only in the effect of the teaching and example, underlies the whole writing. It is expressed most clearly in the following passage (*Hom.* 8.4–7), which is also noteworthy because a certain polemic against the Pauline teaching of πίστις cannot be missed. Here Peter says:

Entwicklung, 365), one could think that this condition was also met by the apostle Paul through his second trip to Jerusalem (Gal 2). However, once the author of the Clementines viewed the apostle Paul as a πλάνος and pseudoapostle, this testimony (Gal 2:9), which is provided by the apostle himself, could have no credibility in his eyes. See the passage quoted from the Letter of Peter to James on p. 67/124. To the contrary, this very passage in *Hom.* 11.35 reveals a remarkable connection to the Judaizing false teachers attacked by the apostle in the letters to the Corinthians (which Neander also notes; *Genetische Entwicklung*, 365) insofar as they were also unwilling to acknowledge anyone as a teacher of the gospel who did not legitimate himself as a delegate of the Jerusalem Jewish apostles through some testimony or a letter of recommendation. This explains why the apostle asks in 2 Cor 3:1 [Baur actually says 2 Cor 3:2, but he quotes 2 Cor 3:1]: ἀρχόμεθα πάλιν ἑαυτοὺς συνιστάνειν; ἢ μὴ χρῄζομεν ὥς τινες (the καπηλεύοντες τὸν λόγον τοῦ θεοῦ; 2 Cor 2:17) συστατικῶν ἐπιστολῶν πρὸς ὑμᾶς ἢ ἐξ ὑμῶν συστατικῶν; cf. 2 Cor 10:12.

That many are called is not to be credited to those called but only to God, who calls them and causes them to come. That they do not have any claim to a reward is sufficiently evident from the fact that it is not their own work but that of the one who moved them. If, however, after their calling, they do good, which is their own work, [132] then through this they will receive a reward. For the Hebrews, too, when they believe in Moses without observing what is commanded by him are not saved unless they observe what was commanded by him. For in their case, too, their belief in Moses did not happen according to their own decision but according to the will of God, who said to Moses: "Behold, I am with you in the pillar of cloud, so that the people may hear me when I speak with you and may constantly believe you." Since then faith in the teacher of truth is given by God to the Hebrews and to those who were called from the gentiles, so that doing good works remained left to each individual's judgment, it is right for a reward to be given to those who act rightly. For neither Moses's nor Jesus's presence would have been necessary if they of themselves had had the will to be disposed in a way that corresponded to reason. Moreover, salvation cannot be attained by believing the teaching, by calling him Lord. This is why Jesus is veiled from the Hebrews, who have received Moses as their teacher, and Moses is veiled from those who believe in Jesus. Since the teachings of both are one and the same, God accepts anyone who only believes in one of them. However, one believes in a teaching in order to do what is commanded by God. The Lord himself says that this is the case: "I confess before the Father of heaven and earth that you have hidden this from ancient sages, but have revealed it to little children." Thus, God himself has hidden a teaching from the one group because they already know what to do, but revealed it to the other group because they do not know what they should do. For just as the Hebrews are not damned because they do not know Jesus, due to the one who hid him from them, provided that they do what Moses commanded them and do not hate the one whom they do not know, so others, who are from the gentiles, who do not know Moses, due to the one who hid him from them, are not damned, provided that they do what Moses[61] commanded them and do not hate the one whom [133] they do not know. And it does not benefit one to call the teacher "Lord" but not do what servants are to do. Therefore, our Jesus said to someone who repeatedly called him "Lord" but did nothing that he commanded: "Why do you call me 'Lord, Lord' but do not do what I say?" Saying will be of no help, but only doing. Therefore, good works are indeed necessary. If, however, it is

---

61. [*Sic*; read: Jesus. Baur presumably erroneously carries over the reference to Moses from the earlier part of the sentence.]

granted to someone to acknowledge both and to become aware that one and the same teaching is proclaimed by them, then such a person must be regarded as a man who is rich in God, having come to the realization that the old is, with time, new; and the new is old [οὗτος ἀνὴρ ἐν θεῷ πλούσιος κατηρίθμηται, τά τε ἀρχαῖα νέα τῷ χρόνῳ, καὶ τὰ καινὰ παλαιὰ ὄντα νενοηκώς].⁶²

Thus, for the author of the Clementine *Homilies*, a καινὴ κτίσις, a new life principle and a new order of things in which the old has disappeared and everything has become new, has come to light through Christ to such a small extent that he makes Moses and Christ completely equal to each other, seeing in the one only the other. While it was Christ who first made it possible at all to eliminate erroneous additions, which the author of the Clementines assumes are in the written law of Moses, the means were already available before Christ in the secret traditions that had been passed down from Moses until that time among the Jewish teachers, and through which the passages in Scripture that oppose one another can be brought together, and, in particular, the unity of God can be retained.⁶³ Thus, with regard to the pure teaching, the difference in time before and after Christ meant only that what had been passed down secretly among those considered worthy from the beginning had been brought out in the open for everyone through Christ (*Hom.* 3.19).⁶⁴

---

62. Perhaps an allusion to Matt 13:52.

63. See Ep. Pet. Jas. 1 and *Hom.* 16:14.

64. A polemic against the person and teaching of the apostle Paul in the Clementines is also assumed by Daniel Georg Konrad von Coelln ("Clementina," *AEWK* 18:39). [Coelln, 1788-1833, was Professor at Marburg from 1816, and subsequently at Breslau.] [134] In addition to the antithesis against the ἀποκαλύψεις and ὀπτασίαι of Paul, Coelln places here the rejection of the Pauline principle that one must love God more than fear him, according to *Hom.* 18.11, where the fear of God, in the spirit of Judaism, is seen as the fundamental component of religion, and the claim that Adam and Christ do not, as portrayed by Paul in Rom 5:12-13, form an opposition but are identical according to their nature (*Hom.* 3.18), insofar as Christ was first in Adam, and the rule of sin over humans is not to be derived from him but solely from the feminine principle or Eve (*Hom.* 3:17-18). Both of these aspects, however, may be of only secondary importance. On the other hand, the Christology of the Clementines probably does appear as an antithesis to Paul. The author of the Clementines makes a sharp distinction between θεός and υἱὸς θεοῦ. "Our Lord," says Peter in *Hom.* 16.15, "did not call himself God any more than he taught about other gods besides the creator of the world. He was right, however, to declare blessed the one who called him the Son of

[134] Here we have before us, as is self-evident, the directions of two completely opposed systems, which arise from the opposition [135]

God, of the Creator of the universe." When asked by the magician Simon if the one who is from God is not God, Peter declares this to be impossible: "For unbegottenness belongs to the Father, begottenness to the Son. What is begotten cannot be placed on the same level as what is unbegotten or as what is begotten from itself. What is not the same in every respect should not be designated with the same name. What is begotten cannot have the same name as what is unbegotten, not even if the one who is begotten is of the same essence [τῆς αὐτῆς ἐσίας] as the one who begets. For the procession from God and the connection with God so little justifies a claim to be called God that human souls, having come from God and so, to some extent, being of the same essence and also being constantly animated by the breath of God, are nevertheless not called gods. If someone wanted to call them gods, this would be only metaphorical, and only in the same extended sense as all other human souls as well could Christ be called God; [135] but this would then no longer be anything extraordinary, since he would only have what all have. Therefore we call God only what is entirely peculiar to him in the highest nature and communicable to no one [θεὸν λέγομεν, οὗ ἐστιν τὸ ἴδιον ἄλλῳ προσεῖναι μὴ δυνάμενον]." This theory is a visible antithesis to the emerging ecclesiastical teaching about the person of Christ, according to which Christ is understood to be God with respect to his nature. But are not at least the seeds out of which this teaching developed found in the Pauline letters, even if we are right to place no weight upon Rom 9:5? The Christ of the Clementines has something higher and divine within him only to the extent that he, as the true prophet, ἐμφύτῳ καὶ σεννάῳ πνεύματι πάντα πάντοτε ἐπίσταται ["by the inborn and ever-flowing Spirit, always knew all things" (trans. Smith, Peterson, and Donaldson)] (*Hom.* 3.12); or that he, διὰ τὴν ἐν αὐτῷ τοῦ πνεύματος θειότητα ["through the divinity of the Spirit that is in Him" (trans. Smith, Peterson, and Donaldson)], has the πρόγνωσις ["foreknowledge"] (*Hom.* 2.10), or the ἅγιον χριστοῦ πνεῦμα ["Holy Spirit of Christ"] (*Hom.* 3:20). This divine πνεῦμα may be understood as an effect of the divine σοφία (cf. Neander, *Genetische Entwicklung*, 409), but, for precisely this reason, Christ cannot be thought of as the creator of the world according to the Clementines, for the creation of the world is attributed only to σοφία herself, ἣ ὥσπερ ἰδίῳ πνεύματι αὐτὸς (θεὸς) ἀεὶ συνέχαιρεν· ἥνωται μὲν ὡς ψυχὴ τῷ θεῷ, ἐκτείνεται δὲ ἀπ᾽ αὐτοῦ, ὡς χεὶρ δημιουργοῦσα τὸ πᾶν ["But His Wisdom was that with which He Himself (God) always rejoiced as with His own spirit. It is united as soul to God, but it is extended by Him, as hand, fashioning the universe" (trans. Smith, Peterson, and Donaldson)] (*Hom.* 16.12). If the gnostic-Marcionite teaching of the demiurge came into conflict with the basic doctrine of all religion, the teaching of the monarchy of God, by placing alongside the only true God a different creator of the world as a second god, would not also the Pauline Christology have appeared to the author of the Clementines as tending toward polytheism, as a teaching that replaces the fallen κατωπολυθεομανία ["polytheo-mania" (trans. Smith, Peterson, and Donaldson)], as he calls the usual polytheism in *Hom.* 3.3, with a new form of polytheism that threatens the pure monarchy of God?

between Judaism and Pauline Christianity. According to the one system, revelation is only the general disclosure, happening over time, of what was already available, and any communication of what has been divinely revealed occurs only by means of external instruction. According to the other system, revelation is a καινὴ κτίσις, which must be understood in the depths of one's own consciousness as [136] a higher life principle communicated by the divine Spirit. Here Christ is only a teacher; there he is the redeemer in the highest sense. Here all religious value is assigned only to nomistic works; there it is assigned to faith in the death of the redeemer. The more decisively Judaism asserts itself with its nomistic works, the more decisive the opposition to the Pauline understanding of Christianity is. However, even when this contrast recedes the most, and the relationship between πίστις and ἔργα, as in the letter of James, seems to be completely balanced out, the type of thinking from which the anti-Pauline Judaism emerges still shows itself. Moreover, the same James, whom the Jewish Christian party chiefly honored as their head alongside Peter, and to whose name the Clementines ultimately connect their Petrine Judaism, opposes in his letter, at the very least, the abuse to which the Pauline teaching of the δικαίωσις ἐκ πίστεως could so easily be susceptible.

The Pauline letters to the Corinthians and Galatians, on the one hand, and the Clementines, on the other, mark for us the most outermost points on which the polemic made against the apostle Paul in the earliest church, the opposition between Pauline and Petrine Christianity, can be fixed. If we walk through the whole area that lies between these points, in order to pursue as far as possible the traces of this same opposition, then we cannot help but come across the famous saga about the apostle Peter's stay in Rome and the common martyrdom in Rome, which is said to have glorified the two apostles, whom we have here looked at as being in conflict with each other. The very pervasive view among recent interpreters that the apostle Peter's presence in Rome is a fact that can no longer be doubted cannot hold us back from addressing this subject anew against the backdrop of our investigation thus far.

PART 2
The Apostle Peter in Rome

[137] When we consider the sizable number of witnesses that can be adduced in support of this claim, there actually seems to be quite a bit of historical skepticism needed in order not to be convinced by such weighty authorities. Moreover, it was more just the general mistrust against anything that could be used as a historical basis for the claims and pretentions of the Roman hierarchy that moved declared enemies of the pope already in the Middle Ages (such as Marsilius of Padua, Michael of Cesena, and others), as well as Protestant historians in and ever since the Reformation period (such as Matthias Flacius, Salmasius, [138] and others) to either downright reject the entire matter or to at least declare it to be highly suspect.[1] By contrast, it was precisely in relation to this

---

1. See Matthias Flacius, *Historia certaminum inter romanos episcopos et sextam Carthaginensem synodum Africanasque ecclesias de primatu seu potestae papae, bona fide ex authenticis monumentis collecta* [Baur has *collata*] (Basel: Oporinus, 1554), 267: "It is not clearly established that Peter was at Rome. It is clearly false that Peter taught at Rome for twenty-five years, which the papists have written, after he had taught for eighteen years in Jerusalem, and was also in Pontus, as others relate, for five years, and for seven at Antioch; furthermore, he wrote his epistle at Babylon. This is plainly false, since this would mean that he lived long past the death of Nero, who is supposed to have ordered his death. Furthermore, it is evinced that Peter was not at Rome, since Paul, when he was writing to and from Rome, names and greets so many less important Christians, but never writes a word mentioning someone as important as Peter."

Flacius places the greatest weight on Gal 2. See Flacius, *Historia*, 124: "Ultimately, I prefer the letter to the Galatians according to Paul over all the histories of all men about Peter. For there, he first distinctly confirms that the apostleship or episcopacy among the Jews was consigned to Peter, but that among other nations or over the gentiles it was his own. Then he recounts that Peter preached especially to the Jews even until the council of Jerusalem, which was convened about eighteen years after the ascension of Christ, and in the seventh year of the alleged papacy of Peter, and that at a

point that a much larger number of Protestant scholars—especially from the Reformed church, in which excellent work was done in this area of historical research—thought it necessary to demonstrate their impartiality and readiness to acknowledge historical truth whenever it was based on historical witnesses.[2] The first scholar to subject this topic [139] to a

---

later time, he (Peter) had entered into a sacred compact of agreement with him (Paul): that he himself in fact wished to preach to the Jews, but that Paul ought to address the other nations. And there you have the most briefly and truly described account of Peter, which shows that to him the apostleship, episcopacy, or perhaps, the papacy, over and among the Jews in particular, was assigned and entrusted to him by Christ; and that he primarily instructed the Jews, not only before the council of Jerusalem, but also afterwards; and that it was where there were many Jews that he especially set himself down or remained, that being in Syria and other eastern regions. For at Rome there were not many (Jews), since at that time they were not yet as dispersed as they later would be in the overthrow of Jerusalem, and Claudius wholly expelled them from Rome." [Flacius, 1520–1575, was a Lutheran reformer and humanist scholar.]

The Magdeburg centuriators do not express any particular doubt on this matter.

Claude Saumaise (Salmasius), *Librorum de primatu papae, pars prima, cum apparatu* (Leiden: Elzevir, 1645). [Saumaise, 1588–1653, studied in Paris and Heidelberg, and became a prominent Protestant scholar in the Netherlands.]

2. One may compare the series of Protestant scholars evaluating the matter in this way adduced by Friedrich Spanheim the Younger in his 1679 *Dissertatio de ficta profectione Petri Apostoli in urbem Romam, deque non una traditionis origine* (repr. in Spanheim, *Tomus Secundus: Qui complectitur miscellaneorum ad sacram antiquitatem et ecclesiae historiam pertinentium*, vol. 2 of *Opera* [Leiden: Boutestein, 1703]), 336: "In fact, in the camps of the Protestants, the ἐπέχοντες ['those who hold this'] are not few. Indeed, very many, or even most, are hardly reluctant to grant it, being moved by such great authorities. Certainly, it does not seem that such a consensus of the fathers should be so easily belittled by Chamier, but not by David Blondel, who always granted that the Roman church was founded and taught by Peter and Paul. Nor do Theodore Beza (*Annot. ad 1 Peter* 5 [i.e., Théodore de Bèze, *Testamentum Novum, sive Novum Foedus Iesu Christi, D.N. Cuius graeco contextui respondent interpretationes duae...* (Geneva: Stephanus, 1589), 441–42]), Franciscus Junius, Scaliger, Casaubonus, Petrus Molinaeus, Petitus, Usserius, Seldenus, Pearsonus, Fellius, Dodwellus, G. Cave, or Vedelius himself deny the presence of Peter among the Romans; and they defend however many Ignatian epistles, especially that one in which, around the middle, Ignatius says to the assembly of the Romans, οὐχ ὡς Πέτρος καὶ Παῦλος διατάσσομαι ὑμῖν ['I am not enjoining you as Peter and Paul did' (Ign. *Rom.* 4.3; trans. Ehrman)]. And indeed, Patrick Young, in his notes on [*1*] *Clement*, says that the fact that Peter ended his life at Rome by martyrdom is too well known to be doubted. Likewise, Hammond, for instance, considered the matter to be placed beyond doubt by these two witnesses, naturally on the credit of the Corinthians Caius and Dionysius." Immediately after

more precise historical investigation and, as a result of this, to express very decisively the conviction that the common presumption lacked any basis in historical reality, was Friedrich Spanheim.[3] First, Spanheim presents the negative reasons that make the matter seem a priori very hard to believe, such as Luke's silence on the matter in Acts, even though he had so many opportunities to mention it, and Paul's silence in his letter to the Romans and in his letters written during his imprisonment in Rome. The agreement between the apostles Paul and Peter that one of them should see himself as being appointed to the ἔθνη and the other to the περιτομή (cf. Gal 2:9) also makes it improbable that the apostle Peter, who ministered in such faraway countries, took part in the founding of a community that was almost entirely composed of gentile Christians. After mentioning these and similar points, Spanheim then surveys the oldest [140] and most important witnesses, one after the other, evaluating their reliability by applying the general argument—which is separately justified in each case—that witnesses who are so ready to adopt so many traditions that obviously have the character of fables do not deserve to be trusted with regard to this tradition, either. Spanheim feels compelled to derive the origin of the tradition partially from the mystical interpretation that was given to the name Babylon in 1 Pet 5:13, partially from the saga about the trip to Rome made by Simon the magician, whom Peter supposedly followed there, and partially from the ambition of the Roman church, which could only be satisfied with the outcome "that Peter be added to Paul in the foundation of the Roman church but also as a companion in the consummation of martyrdom, the first of all the apostles, πρῶτος in the Gospel, πρωτόκληρος, προήγορος, ἀρχηγὸς ["first-called, defender, founder"], who had set down the first stone in building the church, who would in the

---

Spanheim, Samuel Basnage—in *De rebus sacris et ecclesiasticis exercitationes historico-criticae* (Utrecht: Water, 1692), 548—defended again the opposite view with the explanation: "Because it concerns me, here the authority of such great age moves me, so that it is my duty to cast into doubt the arrival of Peter to the city, mistress of the world, since steadfast rumor, which envelops history in firm defenses, the old age and unspoiled trust of the witnesses, and the weight and number of supporters, march under the banners of this account, so that, if it falters in this matter, faith must be stripped from all of history." [Spanheim, 1632–1701, was a Protestant theologian who taught in Heidelberg and Leiden. Basnage, 1638–1721, was a Reformed theologian who held pastoral appointments in France and the Netherlands.]

3. Spanheim, *Dissertatio de ficta profectione Petri Apostoli*.

first place confirm the faith of all the churches."[4] Spanheim's study—as thoroughly as it seeks to discuss its object and as many accurate points as it undeniably contains—was not able to significantly shake the faith in the old tradition. The church historians who followed continued to hold the view that one could not dare raise objections against such significant historical witnesses. Some of them, such as Johann Matthias Schröckh,[5] even gave assurance that it would be difficult to find another event in ancient history that, by such a unanimous testimony, was rendered uncontroversial to a similar degree as this one. Among more recent historians and critics, only Eichhorn[6] dared to express the opposite claim with his usual confidence. His argument runs as follows: the apostle Peter's stay in Rome in the company of the evangelist Mark is very likely a fable: the presence of the apostle Peter in Rome was based on the composition of his first letter in Babylon (1 Pet 5:13), a name that the most ancient [141] church interpreted as a symbol for Rome, and upon this was built all the fables that the ancient and later Christian world told about his accomplishments toward the Roman church, his primacy there, and his martyrdom in Rome. One may boldly ask where any other proof is to be found. And should historical criticism allow this muddled proof to count?

The controversial nature of this claim prompted in particular the study "On the Apostle Peter's Stay in Rome."[7] According to the results of this study, it is entirely historically certain that the apostle Peter came to Rome, taught and led the Roman church, and, finally, was killed for his faith there; however, he could not have stayed there twenty or twenty-five years, but at most a few months more than one year. The more freely, as is only fair, modern Protestant authors attempt to distance themselves from the partisan polemics of old, the more inclined they usually are to concede that some previously went too far here. One may compare the similar

---

4. Spanheim, *Dissertatio de ficta profectione Petri Apostoli*, 383.

5. Johann Matthias Schröckh, vol. 2 of *Christliche Kirchengeschichte*, 2nd ed. (Leipzig: Schwickert, 1775), 185. [Schröck, 1733–1808, was a student of Mosheim and Michaelis who taught church history in Leipzig (1762–1775) and Wittenberg (1775–1808)].

6. Eichhorn, *Einleitung in das Neue Testament*, 1:554; cf. 3:603–4.

7. Johann Georg Herbst, "Ueber den Aufenthalt des Apostels Petrus zu Rom, zugleich als Beytrag zur ältesten christlichen Chronologie," *TQ* 2 (1820): 567–626. [Herbst, 1787–1836, studied at Freiburg, and from 1817 was a Professor in the Catholic Theological Faculty in Tübingen.]

statement regarding this provided by Johann Karl Ludwig Gieseler[8] and Neander in the most recent period.[9] According to the latter, it is hypercriticism to cast doubt on the tradition authenticated by the unanimous testimony of the ancient church that Peter was in Rome. This tradition, Neander writes, apparently comes from a time in which nobody had yet thought of using the primacy of Peter to exalt the Roman church. In the same way, Gieseler judges that only partisan polemics could have caused some Protestants to want to deny the matter.[10] Although I cannot share this opinion about the reliability [142] of this tradition, I at least know myself to be free of any polemical interest. And I believe in any case that I may present what follows as an attempt to address a topic whose notoriety repeatedly appeals to historical interest and provokes new studies by considering it from a different perspective than the one that has been usual up to now.

The greater the suspicion that the following witnesses supported themselves on the authority of the earlier ones is, the more strictly they can be rightly criticized. Papias—according to Eusebius (*Hist. eccl.* 2.15)—undoubtedly occupies the first place in the series of witnesses that initially come under consideration here. Eusebius recounts there what caused Mark to write his Gospel when he was in Rome. The enormous impression that Peter had made upon the Roman Christians through his glorious victory over the magician Simon produced among them a burning desire

---

8. Johann Karl Ludwig Gieseler, vol. 1 of *Lehrbuch der Kirchengeschichte*, 2nd ed. (Bonn: Marcus, 1828), 89. [Gieseler, 1792–1854, studied in Halle and then held professorial positions in Bonn and Göttingen, where he lectured on church history and the history of dogma.]

9. Neander, *Allgemeine Geschichte*, 1.1:317.

10. The same judgment on this was also pronounced by Berthold (*Historisch-kritische Einleitung*, 5:2690) and by Coelln ("Clementina," 18:42). Also Jacob Peter Mynster, in his treatment on the first stay of the apostle Peter in Rome (Mynster, "Ueber den ersten Aufenthalt des Apostels Petrus in Rom," in *Kleine theologische Schriften* [Copenhagen: Gyldendal, 1825], 144), which will have to be considered later, believes that the cause that led Protestant authors to call into doubt a fact that is attested by the entire Christian primitive period can be found only in the zeal to do so, and these doubts have most recently concentrated themselves in a writing with the bold title *Concerning the Invented Journey of Peter to Rome* (i.e., the treatment of Spanheim, *Dissertatio de ficta profectione Petri Apostoli in urbem Romam*). [Mynster, 1775–1854, was a Danish churchman who held a variety of ecclesial positions, culminating in the bishopric of Seeland in Copenhagen.]

to have a written monument of the Christian teaching presented to them. Due to this urgent request, Mark, the companion of Peter, thus became the author of the Gospel known by his name. Eusebius concludes his account with the words: Κλήμης ἐν ἕκτῳ τῶν ὑποτυπώσεων παρατέθειται τὴν ἱστορίαν, συνεπιμαρτυρεῖ δὲ αὐτῷ καὶ ὁ Ἱεραπολίτης ἐπίσκοπος ὀνόματι Παπίας ["Clement quotes the story in the sixth book of the *Hypotyposes*, and the bishop of Hierapolis, named Papias, confirms him" (trans. Lake and Oulton)]. However, as Storr already noted,[11] it can be doubtful here whether Eusebius appeals to Clement and Papias as witnesses for the entire preceding account concerning the magician [143] Simon and Peter, or only to individual parts of it, namely, to the extent that it relates to the Gospel of Mark. This can appear all the more doubtful since here, too, Eusebius could have meant merely the passage from the work of Papias that is quoted by him (*Hist. eccl.* 3.39), in which it is only stated that the Gospel of Mark was based on what the apostle Peter recounted. However, in the passage in Eusebius, *Hist. eccl.* 3.39, it cannot be missed that Papias himself appeals here to an earlier passage of his work, in which he had spoken of Mark as a companion of the apostle Peter (οὔτε ἤκουσε [Μάρκος] τοῦ κυρίου, οὔτε παρηκολούθησεν αὐτῷ, ὕστερον δὲ, ὡς ἔφην, Πέτρῳ ["Mark had not heard the Lord, nor had he followed him, but later on, as I said, followed Peter" (trans. Lake and Oulton)]). This fits well with the assumption that he spoke in greater detail at another place about the joint stay of Peter and Mark in Rome, and about them being prompted to travel there by the magician Simon. It probably also cannot be presumed that Eusebius, in the previously quoted words, was appealing to the common testimony of Papias and Clement of Alexandria unless they at least shared the fact that they testified about the reason that the Gospel of Mark was written precisely in Rome, since we see from Eusebius, *Hist. eccl.* 6.14, that the passage he has in mind from the *Hypotyposes* of Clement of Alexandria strongly emphasized this aspect (τοῦ Πέτρου δημοσίᾳ ἐν Ῥώμῃ κηρύξαντος τὸν λόγον, καὶ πνεύματι τὸ εὐαγγέλιον ἐξειπόντος, τοὺς παρόντας πολλοὺς ὄντας παρακαλέσαι τὸν Μᾶρκον, etc. ["When Peter had publicly preached the word at Rome, and by the Spirit had proclaimed the Gospel, that those present, who were many, exhorted Mark," etc. (trans. Lake and Oulton)]). I am happy to admit that Eusebius did not encounter the story about the magician Simon in the

---

11. Gottlob Christian Storr, *Ueber den Zwek der evangelischen Geschichte und der Briefe Johannis* (Tübingen: Heerbrandt, 1786), 253.

writings of Papias and Clement of Alexandria in the same detail in which he describes it himself, especially not with regard to what happened in Rome, and that he took at least some parts of it from other authors. However, in light of the close relationship that the one has with the other, the main point we are dealing with—that Peter went to Rome because of the magician Simon—must have already been reported by [144] both of those authors, even though it was recounted in greater detail by the later Clement than by Papias, since Eusebius names Clement first. After all, Mark came to Rome only as a companion of Peter; but what should have caused Peter to come to Rome at such an early time, if he had not been prompted by the magician Simon? But if we are inclined to assume that this connection between the presence of Peter and that of the magician Simon in Rome is meant to have taken place, then for the following reasons it is indeed unclear how this can be justifiably claimed as a historical fact. First, the presence of the magician Simon, which supposedly caused Peter to follow him, as well as the entire scene in Rome, as it is usually told, is obviously a fiction. Second, according to the New Testament authors, Peter cannot possibly have been in Rome during the reign of the emperor Claudius (ἐπὶ Κλαυδίου Καίσαρος ["in the time of Claudius Caesar"]);[12] that is, at the time in which Justin Martyr, the primary witness for the information that the magician was in Rome, has Peter appear in Rome, since Peter could not have made a trip to Rome before the meeting in Jerusalem reported in Acts 15; that is, before the twelfth year of the emperor Claudius's reign,[13] [145]

---

12. *1 Apol.* 26, 56; Eusebius, *Hist. eccl.* 2.13. Justin does not mention the exact year.

13. On this, see the careful chronological study in Herbst, "Ueber den Aufenthalt des Apostels Petrus zu Rom," 591–92. If the trip to Jerusalem mentioned by Paul in Gal 2:1 were not the same as the one mentioned in Acts 15 (as is assumed usually, and certainly with complete justification, against the view of those who regard it as the same trip mentioned in Acts 11:20), but, rather, as the most recent study on this topic (Carl Schrader, *Der Apostel Paulus* [Leipzig: Kollmann, 1830], 72–73, 120–21) has attempted to show, a later trip that has been passed over in Acts, which would not have taken place before 56 CE, then we would obtain through this a new datum for the absence of Peter in Jerusalem at a time in which he is supposed to have already been in Rome. While I do not regard the differences of the facts and circumstances in the two narratives of Acts 15 and Gal 2 to be as significant as Schrader presents them, I nevertheless find the assumption itself to be illuminating in some respects. Specifically, it appears to me more natural to count the fourteen years mentioned in Gal 2:1 not from the conversion of Paul but from the first trip that the apostle made to Jerusalem from Damascus in 42 CE.

whereas the dating of such a trip to the later years of Claudius is ruled out by the Letter to the Romans, which scarcely allows for the possibility that at the time of its composition, an apostle had already proclaimed the gospel in Rome.[14] If, however, following a very popular, though very illogical manner of reasoning, one nevertheless desires to hold on to the basic fact itself and to let go of only the accompanying circumstances pertaining to the time by conceding that Peter could not have been in Rome at the time of Claudius, while still regarding it as justifiable to assume a trip to Rome—which simply has to be placed at a later time—with reference to the same authors, then it is obvious that that the entire assumption no longer has any historical basis, and that if Peter's stay in Rome is to be placed only at a later time, this could be proved only with different sources. Later, we will see whether such sources exist, but with regard to Papias it can rightly be claimed that the report provided by him [146], if it really was connected with the story about the magician Simon, as we must in all probability assume, is a mere saga. Papias was accustomed to getting his reports from oral tradition, and this saga undoubtedly flowed to him from that same source. Since there seems to have been rather lively interaction between the communities of Asia Minor and the Roman community at that time, as the well-known reports of the trips of Polycarp and Hegesippus to Rome demonstrate, we can probably assume that he obtained them in this way. According to Irenaeus,[15] who refers to Papias as Πολυκάρπε ἑταῖρος γεγονώς ["who was a companion to Polycarp" (trans. Lake and Oulton)],[16]

---

14. While the conclusion that no apostle had yet been in Rome up until then cannot exactly be drawn with certainty from Rom 15:20, where the apostle expresses as his principle, εὐαγγελίζεσθαι οὐχ ὅπου ὠνομάσθη Χριστός, ἵνα μὴ ἐπ' ἀλλότριον θεμέλιον οἰκοδομῶ (cf. 2 Cor 10:15, 16), the entire content of Romans nevertheless certainly makes it very likely that the Roman community had not yet enjoyed a more precise apostolic instruction. The apostle repeatedly (cf. Rom 1:9–15; 15:22) speaks of the condition of the Roman community, which unsettles him and had already been prompting him to travel to Rome for quite some time, in a way that does not let one assume that an apostle had been in Rome at that time or even some years earlier. After all, in Rom 15:23 he says that his desire has been already ἀπὸ πολλῶν ἐτῶν ἐλθεῖν πρὸς ὑμᾶς.

15. *Haer.* 5.33; Eusebius, *Hist. eccl.* 3.39.

16. As a contemporary of Polycarp, who died ca. 167 CE, Papias cannot be placed much earlier than the middle of the second century. In the same place in Irenaeus, it also says Ἰωάννου ἀκουστής ["one who heard John"]. Irenaeus means the apostle John, although Eusebius (*Hist. eccl.* 3.39) means the presbyter John.

2. The Apostle Peter in Rome

Papias had a close relationship with Polycarp, at least. Like Hegesippus, Papias most likely belonged to the Jewish-Christian party. His well-known predilection for chiliasm speaks for this, and it may also be noted here that he mainly adhered to those who still stood in a closer relation to the original disciples of Jesus. On this matter, he himself, in Eusebius, *Hist. eccl.* 3.39, says,

> ἔχαιρον, ὥσπερ οἱ πολλοί, ἀλλὰ τοῖς τἀληθῆ διδάσκουσιν· οὐδὲ τοῖς τὰς ἀλλοτρίας ἐντολὰς μνημονεύουσιν, ἀλλὰ τοῖς παρὰ τοῦ κυρίου τῇ πίστει δεδομένας καὶ ἀπ' αὐτῆς παραγινομένας τῆς ἀληθείας. Εἰ δέ που καὶ παρηκολουθηκώς τις τοῖς πρεσβυτέροις ἔλθοι, τοὺς τῶν πρεσβυτέρων ἀνέκρινον λόγους· τί Ἀνδρέας ἢ τί Πέτρος εἶπεν, ἢ τί Φίλιππος, ἢ τί Θωμᾶς, ἢ Ἰάκωβος, ἢ τί Ἰωάννης, ἢ Ματθαῖος, ἤ τις ἕτερος τῶν τοῦ κυρίου μαθητῶν, ἅ τε Ἀριστίων, καὶ ὁ πρεσβύτερος Ἰωάννης οἱ τοῦ κυρίου μαθηταὶ λέγουσιν. Οὐ γὰρ τὰ ἐκ τῶν βιβλίων τοσοῦτόν με ὠφελεῖν ὑπελάμβανον, ὅσον τὰ παρὰ ζώσης [147] φωνῆς καὶ μενούσης.

> [I rejoiced, as many, rather in them who teach the truth, not in them who recount the commandments of others, but in those given to the faith by the Lord and derived from truth itself; but if ever anyone came who had followed the presbyters, I inquired into the words of the presbyters, what Andrew or Peter or Philip or Thomas or James or John or Matthew, or any other of the Lord's disciples, had said, and what Aristion and the presbyter John, the Lord's disciples, were saying. For I did not suppose that information from books would help me so much as the word of a living and surviving voice. (Trans. Lake and Oulton, modified)]

No mention is made here of the apostle Paul; indeed, the great weight that Papias gave to the tradition that went back to the teaching and person of Jesus appears to betray even a certain anti-Pauline tendency, and it would indeed be possible that the words in which Papias speaks of the τὰς ἀλλοτρίας ἐντολὰς μνημονεύοντες ["those who recount the commandments of others"] have such a connection in opposition to the words that have the source of the truth itself in what has been handed down by the Lord. In any case, as we can infer from the quoted passage, Papias adhered to the party that must have had a special interest in keeping in remembrance and spreading what the saga could tell about the actual disciples of the Lord. This could appear to make his information all the more reliable, but we will see on the basis of what follows that it can only serve to awake a prejudice against it.

The Papias passage can be noteworthy for us only insofar as we, with the help of the same passage, can fix the point in time in which the saga—which has prevailed since then—of the stay of the apostle Peter in Rome and his part in the founding of the Roman community comes to light in history. However, it becomes even more noteworthy when we put it together with a passage from the first letter of the Roman Clement [i.e., 1 Clement]. While it may be uncertain whether it speaks for or against this saga at first glance, it becomes indisputably clear that the latter is the case upon closer examination. In chapters 3 and 4 of his first letter to the Corinthians, Clement speaks of the great harm that is created by envy and ill will, with the goal of admonishing to order and unity the community that has again divided into parties. After he has adduced some Old Testament examples as evidence for this truth in chapter 4, he continues in chapter 5:

Ἀλλ' ἵνα τῶν ἀρχαίων ὑποδειγμάτων παυσώμεθα, ἔλθωμεν ἐπὶ τοὺς ἔγγιστα γενομένους ἀθλητάς· λάβωμεν τῆς γενεᾶς ἡμῶν τὰ γενναῖα ὑποδείγματα. Διὰ ζῆλον καὶ φθόνον ἐκκλησίας μέγιστοι καὶ δικαιότατοι στύλοι ἐδιώχθησαν [148] καὶ ἕως θανάτου (δεινοῦ or ἦλθον). Λάβωμεν πρὸ ὀφθαλῶν ἡμῶν τοὺς ἀγαθοὺς ἀποστόλους· Πέτρος διὰ ζῆλον ἄδικον οὐχ ἕνα οὐδὲ δύο, ἀλλὰ πλείονας ὑπήνεγκεν πόνους, καὶ οὕτω μαρτυρήσας ἐπορεύθη εἰς τὸν ὀφειλόμενον τόπον τῆς δόξης. Διὰ ζῆλον ὁ Παῦλος ὑπομονῆς βραβεῖον ὑπέσχεν, ἑπτάκις δεσμὰ φορέσας, ῥαβδευθείς, λιθασθείς, κῆρυξ γενόμενος ἔν τε τῇ ἀνατολῇ καὶ ἐν τῇ δύσει, τὸ γενναῖον τῆς πίστεως αὐτοῦ κλέος ἔλαβεν δικαιοσύνην, διδάξας ὅλον τὸν κόσμον, καὶ ἐπὶ τὸ τέρμα τῆς δύσεως ἐλθών, καὶ μαρτυρήσας ἐπὶ τῶν ἡγουμένων, οὕτως ἀπηλλάγη τοῦ κόσμου, καὶ εἰς τὸν ἅγιον τόπον ἐπορεύθη, ὑπομονῆς γενόμενος μέγιστος ὑπόγραμμος.

[But to stop giving ancient examples, let us come to those who became athletic contenders in quite recent times. We should consider the noble examples of our own generation. Because of jealousy and envy the greatest and most upright pillars were persecuted, and they struggled in the contest even to death. We should set before our eyes the good apostles. There is Peter, who because of unjust jealousy bore up under hardships not just once or twice, but many times; and having thus borne his witness he went to the place of glory that he deserved. Because of jealousy and strife Paul pointed the way to the prize for endurance. Seven times he bore chains; he was sent into exile and stoned; he served as a herald in both the East and the West; and he received the noble reputation for his faith. He taught righteousness to the whole world, and came to the limits of the West, bearing his witness before the rulers. And so he was set free from this world and transported up to the holy place, having become the greatest example of endurance. (1 Clem. 5.1–7; trans. Ehrman)]

The controversy over this passage mainly concerns the words τὸ τέρμα τῆς δύσεως ["the limits of the West"]. The question is whether Italy and Rome or a more distant land of the West—in particular, Spain, where Paul at least intended to travel, according to Rom 15:24—is meant. If the first option is the case, then this passage is an indirect witness for the fact that Peter did not come to Rome, insofar as Clement emphasizes only in the case of Paul as a distinguishing feature that he, in his large sphere of activity, came as far as Rome. If, however, the latter is more likely, as one usually assumes, then one gains even more room for Peter's sphere of activity and can let him—without damage to the priority that Paul is meant to have before him—come all the way to Rome. One of the most recent scholars who has undertaken an investigation of this passage, Carl Schrader, makes the following remark in this connection:

> By saying that Paul became a martyr ἐπὶ τὸ τέρμα τῆς δύσεως ἐλθών ["having come to the limits of the West"], Clement has very much restricted our arbitrariness in the interpretation of these words. We have the choice of assuming that Paul was executed in Spain or England or that, if this happened in Rome, τὸ τέρμα τῆς δύσεως, too, means nothing other than Rome. Clement cannot mean the first of these, for one can see from his letter that what he writes about the apostle's martyrdom was not unknown to the Corinthians, and the information that Paul was not executed in Rome would therefore certainly also [149] have been preserved somewhere else. But there is nothing against the other assumption. After all, τὸ τέρμα τῆς δύσεως need not mean the outermost boundary of the world. It can, indeed, also mean any other boundary of the West. And without forcing the matter at all, one can understand the words of Clement to mean that Paul crossed only the boundary of the West but did not penetrate into its interior because death prevented him from carrying out his earlier resolution. And it must be understood in this way if Paul was executed in Rome and not in Spain or in England.[17]

---

17. Schrader, *Apostel Paulus*, 235.

In opposition to this view, the author of the study "The Last Journey of the Apostle Peter and Paul according to Clement of Rome and Dionysus of Corinth"[18] reminds us

> that τέρμα, which always means the outermost boundary, the end, goal, can be taken to mean border (ὅρισμα) in general and that the above meaning can emerge without force may indeed be doubted. After all, even Greece belongs already to the West, so that this meaning does not fit even for this reason alone. If one does not wish to think of the outermost boundary of the world, then Clement nevertheless cannot mean merely Rome or Italy, since he himself lived there and could not have been unfamiliar with the geographical circumstances of the West that belonged to the Roman Empire, especially since—if the apostle did not come further than to Rome—the praise of Rome among the Corinthians, who were well acquainted with all the conditions, would be diminished rather than increased by such hyperbolism. Even an inhabitant of the Orient, on the border of the Roman Empire, could not at that time call Rome, which was known to all, the border point of the West.

While I agree with these remarks insofar as they concern the word τέρμα in and for itself, I nevertheless believe that if it came down to it, it could indeed be justified philologically to understand the expression τὸ τέρμα τῆς δύσεως to mean not, to be sure, merely Rome but rather Italy as part of the West. Clement compares, so to speak, the apostolic course of Paul with the [150] course of the sun, which rises in the East, illuminates the whole world, and sets in the West, where its goal is. What then, if τὸ τέρμα τῆς δύσεως in this apparently somewhat poetically-rhetorically construed passage is merely equivalent to ἡ δύσις, ἥ (or ἐν ᾗ) τὸ τέρμα ἐστὶν ["the West, which (or in which) is the limit"], either in general or with special regard to Paul?[19] I could much more readily adopt this explanation than

---

18. Maximilian Josef Wocher, "Die letzten Reisen [und Schicksale] der Apostel Petrus und Paulus, nach Clemens von Rom und Dionys von Korinth," *TQ* 12 (1830): 627. [Wocher, 1803–1852, was a Catholic theologian who held junior appointments in the Catholic Theological Faculty in Tübingen before accepting leadership positions at the gymnasium in Ehingen.]

19. One may compare regarding this linguistic usage my learned friend and colleague Prof. Tafel's *Dilucidationum Pindaricarum* [Gottlieb Lukas Friedrich Tafel, *Olympia*, vol. 1.1 of *Dilucidationum Pindaricarum* (Berlin: Reimer, 1824), 83, 94, 459], where it is shown through a series of examples that words such as τέρμα, τέλος, and other similarly poetic and rhetorical terms regularly serve as a mere paraphrase. Ὁδοῦ

the usual claim that precisely this passage demonstrates that for which otherwise no evidence can be produced, namely, the actual carrying out of the intention announced by Paul in Rom 15:24. If, however, one wishes to regard the proposed explanation as artificial and inadequate, and regard the majority view that τὸ τέρμα τῆς δύσεως can only be Spain as the most natural, then fortunately the proof that is to be derived from the passage of Clement, that is, that Peter did not come to Rome, is by no means dependent upon this. And I believe that when the author of the aforementioned study raises the objection to the Schraderian interpretation: "Would not Clement have had to have said the same also about the apostle Peter, since he, just as Paul, came to Greece and Rome? But, precisely in relation to him, does he not stress the special portion of the glory of Paul?," it is permissible to continue in the same vein: Would not Clement have had to have said also the same thing about Peter as he said [151] of Paul, since in the assumed case he would have been active, after all, not merely in the ἀνατολή ["East"] but also in the δύσις ["West"]; why is precisely the distinction of Paul especially stressed that he κῆρυξ γενόμενος ἔν τε τῇ ἀνατολῇ καὶ ἐν τῇ δύσει τὸ γενναῖον τῆς πίστεως αὐτοῦ κλέος ἔλαβεν ["he served as a herald in both the East and the West; and he received the noble reputation for his faith" (trans. Ehrman)]? I do not see any justified objection that one can bring against this argument and thus with full justification conclude from the passage of Clement—who indisputably stood as near as any other of the so-called apostolic fathers to the apostolic period, whose first letter to the Corinthians belongs, according to the consensus view of most scholars, to the most authentic memorials from that time, and who, beyond this, as bishop of the Roman community, deserves all attention—that Clement not only knew nothing about a journey of the apostle Peter to Rome but knew nothing at all about a journey of Peter into the West at the time of the composition of his letter;

τέρμα ["boundary of the way"] is equivalent to ὁδός ["way"], τέλος γήραος ["the end of old age"] to γῆρας ["old age"], or τὸ γῆρας, ὅ τὸ τέλος ἔστι, θανάτου τέρμα ["old age, which is the end, the boundary of death"] to θάνατος ["death"], or the θάνατος ["death"] to τέρμα ["boundary" or "limit"]. If, by the way, one does not wish to assume what cannot (see below) be assumed, namely, that Paul really came to Spain (even if he does not exactly die there, as Schrader unjustifiably seeks to interpret the words of Clement), or to presuppose an error on the side of Clement, for which one has no basis, then only the explanation proposed above can be the right one. [Tafel, 1787–1860, Professor of Ancient Literature at Tübingen, was a philologist who made important contributions to the study of classical and Byzantine texts.]

he knew only in general that Peter died as a martyr but not, as it appears, where and how this happened. For this reason, Peter, as it seems, cannot really have come to Rome, and the saga that has him come there must have arisen only in the time after Clement, in the first half of the second century, between Clement and Papias.[20]

[152] Already through this, the historical foundation is taken away in advance from the second witness in this matter, the Corinthian bishop Dionysius, who has the apostle Peter come to Corinth and Rome. Eusebius introduces him, in *Hist. eccl.* 2.25, where he speaks of the joint Roman martyrdom of the two apostles, with the words:

---

20. If one wanted in addition to appeal to the view that the words of Clement, ἔλθωμεν ἐπὶ τοὺς ἔγγιστα γενομένους ἀθλητάς ["Let us come to those who became athletic contenders in quite recent times" (1 Clem. 5.1; trans. Ehrman)], must be understood locally, as a reference to his martyrdom in Rome, then the context clearly shows that they can refer merely to the time. Clement has previously adduced Old Testament examples, and immediately after these words he adds as an explanation: λάβωμεν τῆς γενεᾶς ἡμῶν τὰ γενναῖα ὑποδείγματα ["We should consider the noble examples of our own generation" (trans. Ehrman)]. It is therefore completely without foundation and empty declamation when Basnage, *De rebus sacris et ecclesiasticis exercitationes historico-criticae*, 553, seeks to rescue the probative force of the passage of Clement through the following commentary: "Examples are freely provided to the Corinthians, not obscure, not hidden in a corner of the world, not remote in place or time, but straightforward and exposed right before their eyes, so that it might be brought together that Peter did not die in lands very remote from Greece by position or knowledge. Assuredly, if it were permitted to take up an argument from circumstances, then everything indeed shows that Rome was the place of execution of both Peter and Paul. The letter of the Roman church places Peter and Paul before the eyes of the Corinthians as an example supplied from its own bosom, which was more able to move souls, since both the Roman and Corinthian churches had been overseen by Peter and Paul as masters. But the letter also relates both the causes of his death and how bitter it was, so that Christians living in Rome might seem to themselves to see the blood of the apostles still steaming and the mangled bodies in the massive theater of the whole world." Salmasius and Spanheim have already rightly asserted the above conclusion from the passage of Clement. Spanheim (*Dissertatio de ficta profectione Petri Apostoli*, 345) says: "Not without cause does ὁ πάνυ ['the renowned'] Salmasius (Saumaise, *Librorum de primatu papae*, 48–49) recount that Clement was ignorant of this journey of Peter to τὸ τέρμα τῆς δύσεως, and of the traversing of the whole world, and of his arrival not only in Italy, but also in Spain [and] Britain, or rather that he was ignorant of the place of Peter's martyrdom and the other circumstances, with that apostle having died, perhaps in Babylon or in the more remote east."

ὡς δὲ κατὰ τὸν αὐτὸν ἄμφω καιρὸν ἐμαρτύρησαν Κορινθίων ἐπίσκοπος Διονύσιος ἐγγράφως Ῥωμαίοις ὁμιλῶν ὧδέ πως παρίστησιν· ταῦτα καὶ ἡμεῖς διὰ τῆς τοσαύτης νεθεσίας τὴν ἀπὸ Πέτρου καὶ Παύλου φυτείαν γενηθεῖσαν Ῥωμαίων τε καὶ Κορινθίων συνεκεράσατε. Καὶ γὰρ ἄμφω καὶ εἰς τὴν ἡμετέραν Κόρινθον φυτεύσαντες ἡμᾶς, ὁμοίως δὲ καὶ εἰς τὴν Ἰταλίαν ὁμόσε διδάξαντες ἐμαρτύρησαν κατὰ τὸν αὐτὸν καιρόν.

[And that they both were martyred at the same time Dionysius, bishop of Corinth, affirms in this passage of his correspondence with the Romans: "By so great an admonition you bound together the foundations of the Romans and Corinthians by Peter and Paul, for both of them taught together in our Corinth and were our founders, and together also taught in Italy in the same place and were martyred at the same time." (Trans. Lake and Oulton)]

In any case, the main thing in this passage is the joint martyrdom attested by Dionysius, which takes place at the same point in time. The phrasing κατὰ τὸν αὐτόν cannot be understood differently, and it is empty sophistry [153] when the author of the aforementioned study[21] seeks to understand this phrasing as referring to the same but not to the identical time. But with regard to the main fact itself, its credibility depends on the probability or improbability of a second imprisonment of the apostle Paul. If we let the bishop Dionysius say in the quoted text what he, according to what has been the almost universal explanation since Valesius, is supposed to have said, namely, that the two apostles met in Corinth and traveled together from there to Italy, then a different trip from the apostle Paul's journey to Rome described in the last chapters of Acts must necessarily be in view, since neither Luke nor Paul, in the letters written during the Roman imprisonment, gives the least hint of the notion that he was on that journey, which, in addition, did not go via Corinth, or that he was in the company of the apostle Peter during his stay in Rome at that time. Only if the apostle became free from the Roman imprisonment mentioned by Luke and came to Rome a second time could he have met with Peter and died with him in Rome as martyr. But what reasons do we have for the alleged second imprisonment of Paul? The testimony of Eusebius, *Hist. eccl.* 2.22? However, Eusebius, or whoever else might be the warrantor of this (τότε μὲν οὖν are the words of Eusebius, ἀπολογησάμενον αὖθις ἐπὶ τὴν τοῦ κηρύγματος διακονίαν λόγος ἔχει στείλασθαι τὸν ἀπόστολον,

---

21. Wocher, "Die letzten Reisen," 646.

δεύτερον ἐπιβάντα τῇ αὐτῇ πόλει, τῷ κατ' αὐτὸν τελειωθῆναι μαρτυρίῳ ["Tradition has it that after defending himself the Apostle was again sent on the ministry of preaching, and coming a second time to the same city suffered martyrdom" (trans. Lake and Oulton)]), has been led, as can be clearly seen from the whole content of the passage, to this assumption only through the difficulty of bringing together all the data contained in Acts and in the letters of Paul regarding his Roman imprisonment, under the presupposition that there was only one imprisonment. But is this difficulty really so great? I regard it as [154] unnecessary to provide a more detailed discussion of this so-frequently discussed controversial question since the concordant view of the recent critics and historians increasingly tends to surrender the presupposition of a second imprisonment, which lacks any historical attestation. While there may still be a certain breadth and differences regarding the way in which the questions that arise need to be answered, in and for itself the main question itself cannot be regarded as unanswerable, and the difficulties that still remain cannot be compared with the great improbability of a presupposition that has no actual historical evidence for it, on the one hand, and is entangled in new, very significant difficulties, on the other hand.[22] If we set—according to the most probable calculation—the arrival of the apostle Paul in Rome in the spring of 62 CE and add to this the two-year duration of his imprisonment spoken of by Luke at the end of Acts, what is more natural than the assumption that the apostle was killed as a victim of the Neronian persecution of Christians that broke out in 64 CE, which Tacitus describes in *Ann.* 15.44? How unlikely is the hypothesis that he was finally liberated from an imprisonment that had already lasted two years, precisely at the point in time that was so fateful for the Christians in Rome? How can one imagine that the same scene repeated itself a short time afterward under nearly the same circumstances (after all, even Hug[23] wants to place 2 Timothy not in the second imprisonment but in the first one)? What series of precarious combinations do all those who want to bring all the data relating to a second imprisonment into a [155] connection that is as satisfactory as possible feel compelled to assume? In one such combination, Mark, who is still with the captive apostle Paul in Rome, according

---

22. I mention here merely the most recent decisive opponent of the assumption of a second imprisonment, Schrader, *Apostel Paulus*, 181–82, who provides a solution to the difficult points that is quite satisfactory for the most part.

23. Hug, *Einleitung in die Schriften des Neuen Testaments*, 2:416.

to Col 4:10, must travel within the period of a year to Babylon,[24] where Peter was at the time (1 Pet 5:13), so that Peter, in the passage mentioned, can pass on a greeting from him. Meanwhile, one has Paul become free from his imprisonment. However, even though now, after his release from the chains and bonds, the point in time would have arrived to carry out his resolution to travel to Spain, and even though an old report—which has great weight due to its age and the place where it was read out in worship services—says that Paul carried out this resolution and traveled to the limit of the world, ἐπὶ τέρμα δύσεως, it is nevertheless regarded as improbable that this happened. Instead, one has Paul go to the East again to visit the communities and his friends, and then, in order to make his way to Spain, return and travel together with Peter—who somehow came along from Babylon—from Corinth to Rome, namely, in the thirteenth year of Nero's reign (since, according to the analysis of the author of this study [i.e., Wocher], Peter could not leave Babylon before the twelfth year of Nero's reign, and both apostles had stayed for some time in Corinth), so that they died, according to the testimony of Jerome, in the fourteenth year of Nero's reign, after Peter had spent at most a few months more than a year in Rome. According to another combination,[25] the apostle Peter wrote his first letter in Babylon in response to the message received in summer 65 CE about the persecution of Christians in Rome, and thereupon undertook—which already is said to be a priori not unlikely (!)—to travel to Rome, where he arrived at the end of that year; or, since he certainly had an interest in visiting the notable Corinthian community, and if he came to Corinth in the fall to spend the winter there, in the spring of the following year. [156] However, rather than being in the company of Paul, he was alone, as the author of this study [i.e., Wocher] believes, whereas Dionysius of Corinth, in the abovementioned passage, only says this: Peter and Paul proclaimed the divine teachings in both communities; and, finally, when they had reached their joint destination (ὁμόσε, not ἅμα or ὁμοῦ)[26] in Rome and likewise proclaimed the divine teaching there, they died as martyrs in that very place at the same time.

---

24. Wocher, "Die letzten Reisen," 623.
25. Wocher, "Die letzten Reisen," 636–37.
26. I do not wish to argue here about the ambiguous ὁμόσε in this passage, which is not very naturally expressed anyway. However, the usual explanation seems more natural to me. κατὰ τὸν αὐτὸν χρόνον also points to a togetherness. Pearson (see Friedrich Adolf Heinichen, *Eusebii Pamphili historiae ecclesiasticae libri X*, 2 vols. [Leipzig:

> Right around this time, in which Peter came to Rome, a new persecution broke out in Rome, not directly at Nero's orders, who was in Greece at the time, but in his absence under the ἡγούμενοι, as Clement puts it [cf. 1 Clem. 5.7], the rulers at that time Nymphidius Sabinus and Polyclitus. At that time, only the apostle Paul could dare to travel to Rome in order to support the hard-pressed community and strengthen them in their faith. He could stay here for a short time and, as a pillar of the church, give it a new attitude. Thus, it was unavoidable that the persecution also struck him, or that it broke out with a new intensity, if it, as one must probably assume, had stagnated somewhat at the start, under the rulers.[27]

It is obvious how many arbitrary and improbable assumptions must be made in these two combinations in order [157] to salvage with some appearance of historical truth the Roman martyrdom of the apostle, which is reported in such a doubtful way by the tradition. However, both combinations, as is always the case with the hypothesis that Paul the apostle was imprisoned a second time, also collide with true history through the fact that to a greater or lesser extent, they are forced to go beyond the actual time of the Neronian persecution of Christians and postulate a second persecution, since all ecclesiastical and profane authors only know of one Neronian persecution that took place in the year 64 CE, the tenth year of Nero's reign, as the result of the great conflagration. If we also assume that according to the findings drawn from the passage in Clement of Rome mentioned above, Peter could not have come to Rome or to Corinth, then it seems all the more a fruitless effort to try to bring the adduced testimony of Dionysius of Corinth in line with the authenticated history, and the suspicion lies very close at hand that one only has Peter, who was traveling to Rome, go via Corinth because, according to 1 Cor 1:13, at the time of the founding of the community there was already a party in Corinth that adhered chiefly to the authority of the apostle Peter and, as a result of those

---

Kayser, 1828], on Eusebius, *Hist. eccl.* 2.25) wants to take ὁμόσε in the sense of *audacter*, "straight ahead," but to me this also does not seem to quite fit the preceding ὁμοίως and following κατὰ τὸν αὐτὸν χρόνον. The context makes one think, in the first place, of traveling together, although I gladly admit that ὁμόσε can also mean the togetherness of direction and of efforts. In any case, one should not forget that the whole weight of the report as a witness for this position would, in the end, depend on a meaning that is merely possible. [Heinichen, 1805–1877, studied theology and classics in Leipzig, and then worked in secondary education while continuing his philological endeavors.]

27. Wocher, "Die letzten Reisen," 640–46.

2. The Apostle Peter in Rome

old factions that had not entirely disappeared, may also have had a particular interest in placing the apostle Peter alongside the apostle Paul later. Here, too, just as in Rome, there was a desire to let the glory of both apostles reflect back upon the community. Therefore Peter, too, had to come to Corinth, so that the Corinthian community could have the glory of having sent both apostles from their midst to the place of their joint martyrdom.

No small value is usually attached to the testimony of the Roman presbyter Caius, which Eusebius, though it is significantly later than the testimony of Dionysius of Corinth,[28] nevertheless places, as a local testimony, before Dionysius's testimony [158] with the words:

οὐδὲν δ' ἧττον καὶ ἐκκλησιαστικὸς ἀνήρ, Γάϊος ὄνομα, κατὰ Ζεφυρῖνον Ῥωμαίων γεγονὼς ἐπίσκοπον (πιστοῦται τὴν ἱστορίαν)· ὅς δὴ Πρόκλῳ τῆς κατὰ Φρύγας προϊσταμένῳ γνώμης ἐγγράφως διαλεχθείς, αὐτὰ δὴ ταῦτα περὶ τῶν τόπων, ἔνθα τῶν εἰρημένων ἀποστόλων τὰ ἱερὰ σκηνώματα κατατέθειται, φησίν· ἐγὼ δὲ τὰ τρόπαια τῶν ἀποστόλων ἔχω δεῖξαι. Ἐὰν γὰρ θελήσῃς ἀπελθεῖν ἐπὶ τὸν βατικανόν, ἢ ἐπὶ τὴν ὁδὸν τὴν Ὠστίαν, εὑρήσεις τὰ τρόπαια τῶν ταύτην ἱδρυσαμένων τὴν ἐκκλησίαν.

[No less than a writer of the Church named Caius, who lived when Zephyrinus was Bishop of Rome (confirms the account). Caius in a written discussion with Proclas, the leader of the Montanists, speaks as follows of the places where the sacred relics of the Apostles in question are deposited: "But I can point out the trophies of the Apostles, for if you will go to the Vatican or to the Ostian Way, you will find the trophies of those who founded this Church." (Trans. Lake and Oulton, modified)]

Right before this, Eusebius appeals, as proof of the credibility of the tradition involving Peter and Paul, to the fact that the places where the two apostles are said to be buried are generally known up until his own time and are designated by this name (πιστοῦται τὴν ἱστορίαν ἡ Πέτρου καὶ Παύλου εἰς δεῦρο κρατήσασα ἐπὶ τῶν αὐτόθι κοιμητηρίων πρόσρησις ["the title of 'Peter and Paul,' which is still given to the cemeteries there, con-

---

28. Dionysius lived in the second half of the second century and is usually assumed to have died around 176 CE. Caius lived in the first half of the third century CE, namely, during the reign of Caracallas (211–217 CE). See Martin Joseph Routh, *Reliquiae Sacrae: Sive, auctorum fere jam perditorum secundi tertiique saeculi fragmenta, quae supersunt*, 4 vols. (Oxford: Oxford University Press, 1814–1818), 1:165; 2:3. [Routh, 1755–1854, was an English classicist and President of Magdalen College, Oxford, from 1791 to 1854.]

firms the story" (trans. Lake and Oulton)]). If we could give credence to the older testimonies with better justification, then the objections against the credibility of Caius's testimony would have no weight. However, given the results of our study thus far, it only arouses new suspicion. For while it is ill-suited for making the matter itself more credible, it is nevertheless noteworthy as a proof of the great interest that the matter had in Rome itself. In any case, what the passage of Caius contains cannot be regarded as factual, for who could believe that the two apostles were buried in a way that brought them such honor at the very places where the execution is said to have taken place? Was one not accustomed to proceed against the corpses of the martyrs in a completely different manner, otherwise in the rage of persecution? One could in any case regard the places mentioned only as the places of the execution, but also in this regard, the saga [159] looks totally as if it only sought out famous localities in order to cling to them and create authority for itself (as, indeed, sagas of this kind generally seek to become as local as possible). To be sure, according to Tacitus *Ann.* 15.44, the Vatican, in the vicinity of which Nero's circus and gardens were located,[29] was the scene of the Neronian persecution of Christians; but with what grounds is it assumed that Peter fell as a victim of this persecution, and with what justification does the saga have him die at the designated place, at the Vatican, whereas it has Paul die, as if outside the city, on the road leading to Ostia? While Caius does not explicitly name the apostles when he mentions the place of their martyrdom, there is no doubt that already at that time, the saga had the apostle Peter die at the

---

29. The circus of Nero was at the foot of the Vatican (Tacitus, *Ann.* 14.14), and his gardens were in the same area. Peter is also said to be buried in that very place, where a church was also later built for him. See Famiano Nardini, *Roma antica di Famiano Nardini*, 4th ed., ed. Antonio Nibby, 4 vols. (Rome: Lomanis, 1818–1820), 3:358, where even the Italian scholar of antiquity remarks: "But if they had buried the bodies of St. Peter and of the martyrs put to death by Nero, and of many successive holy pontiffs, and the cemetery was where St. Peter's Basilica is, it appears strange that the circus might have still been standing there. Perhaps Nero, who vigorously slaughtered the Christians, exercised compassion in destroying his circus to allow them burial? Yet that circus remained standing in Pliny's time. Perhaps he was satisfied that it should serve one purpose for some, and another for others, namely, as a circus for the pagans, and as a catacomb for the faithful?" Therefore, the view—of which Caius speaks—that Peter is buried at this place, could in any case have emerged only a fairly long time after the execution of the apostle. [Nardini, 1600–1661, was a pioneer in the study of Italian archaeology.]

former place and Paul at the latter place. In precisely this way, however, the saga—as it was already present then and as it has developed with increasing fullness in the same tendency since then—shows a deliberateness that casts a rather bright light upon its origin. [160]

If the saga, however, had already then established itself with such weight in Rome, how can it surprise us that from the end of the second century CE onward, there is only one position regarding this in all the writers who had a reason to mention the matter, namely, in Irenaeus, Tertullian, and Lactantius. Yet with these writers, too, the saga still bears in itself a certain sign of its suspicious, unhistorical origin. When the *maxima et antiquissima et omnibus cognita a gloriosissmis duobus Apostolis Petro et Paulo Romae fundata et constituta ecclesia* ["the greatest and most ancient church, known to all, founded and built up at Rome by the two most glorious apostles, Peter and Paul" (trans. Unger and Dillon)] is emphasized so strongly by Irenaeus in the well-known passage *Haer.* 3.3, then the interest that the Roman church had to have in a saga that glorifies it to such a great extent shines forth clearly from these words of this man who stands in direct connection with the Roman church and attributes such great value to the tradition. When, in the same spirit, Tertullian[30] praises the same church as the *felix ecclesia, cui totam doctrinam Apostoli cum sanguine suo profuderunt, ubi Petrus passioni dominicae adaequatur, ubi Paulus Johannis exita coronatur, ubi Apostolus Johannes, posteaquam in oleum igneum demersus nihil passus est, in insulam relegater* ["fortunate church, upon which the apostles poured their whole teaching together with their blood, where Peter suffered like his Lord, where Paul was crowned with John's death, where the apostle John, after he had been immersed in boiling oil without harm, was banished to an island" (trans. Greenslade, modified)], then here the truth lies quite clearly only in the middle, flanked on both sides by completely unhistorical fiction. When Lactantius has Peter come to Rome—admittedly not until the rule of Nero—and has him perform miracles that cause a great sensation, then here the magician Simon is in play again, and it is by no means to the advantage of the saga that that one is referred back to this origin time and again:

> *Quumque jam Nero imperaret ... Petrus Romam advenit, et editis quibusdam miraculis, quae virtute ipsius Dei, data sibi ab eo potestate, faciebat, convertit multos ad justitiam, Deoque templum fidele ac stabile collocavit.*

---

30. *Praescr.* 36.

Qua re ad Neronem delata, quum animadverteret, non modo Romae, sed ubique [161] *quotidie magnam multitudinem deficere a cultu idolorum et ad religionem novam, damnata vetustate, transire, ut erat exsecrabilis ac nocens tyrannus—Petrum cruci affixit, et Paulum interfecit.*

[It was when Nero was already emperor that Peter arrived in Rome; after performing various miracles—which he did through the excellence of God himself—he converted many to righteousness and established a faithful and steadfast temple to God. This was reported to Nero; and when he noticed that not only at Rome but everywhere great numbers of people were daily abandoning the worship of idols and condemning the practice of the past by coming over into the new religion, Nero, abominable and criminal tyrant that he was ... he nailed Peter to the cross and slew Paul. (Trans. Creed)][31]

Here we find talk of a period in which the Roman church was actually founded in truth for the first time, and yet, completely ignoring the achievements of Paul, the saga attributes everything to Peter alone. Can such an obviously partisan and convoluted saga really merit belief? Yet it is precisely this passage from Lactantius upon which the author of the aforementioned essay chiefly bases the result of his investigation, namely, that Peter must, after all, have come to Rome, at least in the final years of Nero's reign, even if only for a short time.[32]

---

31. Lactantius, *Mort.* 2.

32. Wocher, "Die letzten Reisen," 625, 609–10: "This testimony is very weighty. Lactantius lived already in the beginning of the third (?) century. He was in the Occident for a long time with Arnobius in Africa, whose church had unbroken interaction with the Roman church. He was with Crispus for a long time in Gaul, whose bishops had friendly relations with the Roman church since the introduction of Christianity. Lactantius was accordingly (?) entirely in position to receive and to give reliable information about the arrival of Peter." It cannot, however, even be conceded to the author of this study that Lactantius says at all that Peter came to Rome under Nero, and it is therefore incumbent upon us only to determine more exactly the time when the apostle was not yet in Rome. If we look more closely at the context of the passage, then it cannot be missed that Lactantius has Peter come to Rome in the first period of Nero: *discipuli, qui tunc errant undecim, assumtis in locum Judae proditoris Matthia et Paulo, disperse sunt per omnem terram ad evangelium praedicandum, sicut ilis magister Dominus imperaverat, et per annos XXV, usque ad principium Neroniani imperii per omnes provincias et civitates ecclesiae fundamenta miserunt. Cumque jam Nero imperaret, Petrus,* etc. ["Then his disciples, who were at that time eleven, after adding to their number in place of Judas the traitor Matthias and Paul, scattered throughout the world

[162] A tradition that with a deceptive appearance has asserted itself as an historical truth over many centuries is only then entirely refuted and presented in its baselessness when one does not merely deny the historical credibility of the testimonies on which it tends to be based but also accounts for the causes out of which it originally arose. The more probable—according to the nature of the matter—the reasons are that we can give to explain the emergence of a saga, the less we are to assume that the saga is still based on something factual. It is with respect to this area, so it seems to me, that the least progress has been made in contributions to our topic—which is, however, something that needs to be addressed for the inquiry to be satisfyingly complete. The vague appeal—which is not grounded in detail—to the ambition and hierarchical spirit of the Roman church in order to explain the origin of the saga can only awaken a prejudice toward the thoroughness and impartiality of the study, since it can easily be shown that the saga dates back to a time in which that spirit—at least to the degree in which it would have to be presupposed here—had not yet appeared. It is equally inadequate to assume that the mystic reading of the name Babylon in the well-known Petrine passage first gave the impetus for the emergence of the saga, since in such an isolated element, the cause [163] does not appear to have an appropriate relation to the effect that allegedly followed from it; and, while that interpretation could be used—as it really was used (Eusebius, *Hist. eccl.* 2.15)—to seemingly confirm the already-existing saga, in itself it is not enough to make the origin of the saga understandable. Rather, time and again one feels compelled to go back to a specific cause, by virtue of which precisely this interpretation was given to that name in a passage that otherwise contains nothing that recommends that interpretation. As far as this part of the present study is

---

to preach the Gospel as their Lord and Master had commanded them, and during the twenty-five years up to the beginning of Nero's reign they laid the foundations of the church in every province and city. It was when Nero was already emperor," etc. (trans. Creed)]. If Peter, according to the result of the aforementioned study, cannot have come to Rome before the last years of Nero, then this very passage of Lactantius, which speaks only of the first years of Nero, shows that Peter did not come to Rome at all. In any case, the fact that the passage can only be related to the beginning of the reign of Nero makes its convolutedness and worthlessness only all the more clear. Peter's arrival in Rome is set in the time of Nero in order not to separate him from Paul. At the same time, in order to let him also be in the vicinity of the magician, who supposedly already came under Claudius, as a compromise, the beginning of the reign of Nero is assumed.

concerned, I believe it may not be difficult, within in the historical context in which I have attempted to place the saga of Peter here, to find the correct standpoint from which one must proceed here.

After what has been said, it may justifiably be assumed that a saga that took the apostle Peter as an object to be glorified and that does so little to hide the intention of giving a certain preference to the apostle to the Jews over the apostle to the gentiles—and does so, precisely in relation to a community to which the latter had made such decisive contributions and with which he had such a close connection—could only have originated in a community that was mainly composed of Jewish Christians and that granted a very predominant influence to their Judaism. Just as the so-called Cephas party pursued a Judaizing direction in Corinth, so also elsewhere the name of Peter may have been a banner under which the Judaizing party placed itself with the goal of asserting its Judaism. Therefore, the more definitively we can demonstrate a Judaizing element in the Christian community in Rome, the easier it is to explain from this the emergence of a saga that is supposed to bring Peter into such a close relationship to this community. This can be proven, however, rather easily. In itself, there is already nothing more probable than that Jewish Christians formed the first foundation of the emerging Christian community in a city in which, as in Rome, Jews resided in [164] significant numbers and undoubtedly maintained lively communication with their native land; in a city into which Christianity—as far as we know, without the presence of an apostle or of a proclaimer of the gospel from the circle of the first disciples of Jesus, on its own, so to speak—had already penetrated at such an early time, perhaps earlier than elsewhere in the West. As much as there was an aversion against Christianity among the majority of the Jews, it was nevertheless almost always Hellenists, or at least such gentiles that had already attached themselves more closely to the Jewish synagogues as proselytes, among whom Christianity found its first point of connection. It certainly was not any different in Rome, and the first members of the Roman community known to us (who give us the first information about its existence), Aquila and Priscilla, were Jewish Christians. The cause that forced them to leave Rome and brought them into the vicinity of the apostle Paul had been given by quarrels that for a while already had arisen amongst the Jews in Rome, as Suetonius says in chapter 25 of the *Life of Claudius, impulsore Chresto* (undoubtedly because now, after Christianity had found entrance, two parties that were inimically opposed to each other had formed also in Rome, as they had elsewhere, a Christian-Jewish party and an old-Jewish party). However, the apostle Paul's letter to this community provides us with the clearest proof of the dominant Judaism in the Roman community. Not only does the apostle feel compelled, also in this letter, to make admonitions, as these were required by the circumstances of a community in which Jewish Christians and gentile Christians stood over against each other as two joined elements that did not yet belong to a whole (cf. esp. Rom 15:5–13; 14:1–2; 11:1–36, esp. 11:13); but it is also clear to see from the overall tendency and conception of the letter, from the prejudices and errors [165] that he combats, and from the character of the teachings that he presents as essential components of Christianity that in this letter, the apostle sees it as his main task to counter as much as possible the predominant influence that Judaism partly had already really achieved in the community, and partly was threatening to achieve further, in order to gain ground for a purer Christianity that would be freer from the restricting bonds of Judaism and would bring about a λογικὴ λατρεία (Rom 12:1). This is the reason for such an emphatic reminder that the περιτομή, the εἶναι ἐκ σπέρματος Ἀβραάμ, with everything that those born Jewish could assert as an advantage that distinguishes Judaism, has no real religious worth. This is the reason for the development of the two main principles about the δικαιοσύνη ἐκ πίστεως and the δικαιοσύνη ἐξ ἔργων νόμου, and their relation to the main teaching about the great significance of the death of Jesus—a development that penetrates such a large part of the letter, through all aspects of Christian consciousness and life, and that unlocks the whole depth and wealth of Christianity. Everyone who knows the Pauline manner of presentation will readily concede that a polemic-dogmatic discussion, which the apostle so purposefully made the object of his task, all objectivity of its purpose and worth notwithstanding, would nevertheless have had a specific relationship that resided in the circumstances and needs of the community for which the letter was intended. But what else could this be if not what has just been stated? The same conclusion emerges from a comparison of the letter to the Romans with the letter to the Galatians, where the apostle combats the same Judaism that is intruding into Christianity and therefore emphatically stresses the same basic teachings that he develops in the letter to the Romans. Indeed, as one can clearly see from the letter to the Romans itself, already at that time false teachers, who Judaized in a Pharisaic manner, of the same sort as those who had sought to divert the communities in Galatia, Corinth, [166] and other places from the direction given to them by the apostle Paul, had made the same attempt in Rome and had not been without success.

One may compare Rom 16:17–20, which cannot be missed for the correct specification of the tendency of the letter, and which is unjustifiably contested with regard to its authenticity.[33] Just as the apostle saw himself compelled to justify his apostolic authority in opposition to such opponents in other letters, so in the letter to the Romans there is also no lack of specific passages that appear to contain the constellation (such as Rom 15:18–19). All of these aspects that come into consideration here certainly justify us in assuming a strict Judaizing tendency in the Roman community. This is also indicated by another note, which can be adduced as a by no means insignificant confirmation of what has just been said here. In the works ascribed to Ambrose, perhaps from the *Commentaria in XIII. Epistolas Paulinas*, composed by the Roman deacon Hilarius, who lived in the fourth century CE, there is a passage[34] in which the author expressly derives the origin of the Roman community from the Jewish Christians and, with the purpose of "seeking the beginnings of the matters, so that wider notice of these things might be had," states as an introduction:

> It is manifest that the Jews, in the time of the apostles, since they lived under Roman rule, lived in Rome. Of these, those who believed passed on to the Romans that while professing Christ, they should preserve the law. But the Romans, having heard the fame of the virtues of Christ, were quick to believe, although they were careful, and not careful without reason, since having once been led astray, they were at once corrected, and remained in him. For those of the Jews who were believing and considering Christ wrongly were saying that the law had to be kept [167], as if there was not full salvation in Christ. On that account, he (Paul) denies that those followers have spiritual grace. Therefore, as it is given to be understood, those of the Jews who were believing in Christ did not accept that he is God from God, thinking that this was contrary to one God.[35] For this reason, Paul denies that those followers have the spiritual grace of God, and through this lacked confirmation. These were the

---

33. The study of my esteemed friend and colleague Dr. Schmid is especially relevant in this connection. See Christian Friedrich Schmid, *De Paulinae ad Romanos epistolae consilio atque argumento quaestiones* (Tübingen: Fues, 1830). [Schmid, 1794–1852, was Professor of Practical Theology in Tübingen from 1826 until his death.]

34. In the Benedictine [Maurist] edition of the works of Ambrose, *Sancti Ambrosii Mediolanensis Episcopi opera...*, 4 vols., ed. Jacques Du Friche and Denis-Nicolas Le Nourry (Paris: Coignard, 1686–1690), 4:35–36, appendix.

35. It should probably not be regarded as coincidental that the author of this commentary characterizes as anti-Jewish the same teaching of the person of Christ that

2. The Apostle Peter in Rome

ones who had undermined the Galatians so that they turned away from the teaching of the apostles, with whom therefore the apostle was angry, since, having been well taught, there were easily led astray. But there was no need to be angry at the Romans but rather to praise their faith since, having seen no miracles nor any of the apostles,[36] they accepted the faith of Christ, although from a Jewish rite, more in words than in feeling, for the mystery of the cross of Christ had not been explained to them. And so, when some people came who believed correctly, there were questions about eating and not eating meat, and about whether the hope that is in Christ was sufficient, or if the law must also be kept.[37]

In the same connection, the author of this commentary remarks:[38]

He signifies that they pursued a carnal sense, because under the name of Christ they had not followed the things that Christ had taught but rather those that were passed down from the Jews. Indeed, he desires that he himself come more swiftly, so that he might pull them away from that tradition and give to them a gift of the spirit. From this [168] it is to

---

the author of the Clementines regards as standing in obvious contradiction to Jewish monotheism.

36. The author of the commentary thus at the same time contradicts all those statements that have the apostle Peter already come to Rome under Claudius and confirms the remarks made above (85–86/144–45).

37. *Ut rerum notitia habeatur plenior, principia earum requirere.... Constat temporibus Apostolorum Judaeos, propterea, quod sub regno Romano agerent, Romae habitasse, ex quibus hi, qui crediderant, tradiderunt Romanis, ut Christum profitentes legem servarent. Romani autem audita fama virtutum Christi faciles ad credendum fuerunt, utpote prudentes, nec immerito prudentes, qui male inducti statim correcti sunt, et permanserunt in eo. Igitur ex Judaeis credentes et improbe sentientes de Christo legem* [167] *servandam dicebant, quasi non esset in Christo salus plena. Ideo negat illos spiritualem gratiam consecutos. Hi ergo ex Judaeis, ut datur intelligi, credentes Christo, non accipiebant, Deum esse de Deo, putantes uni Deo adversum, quamobrem negat illos spiritualem Dei gratiam consequutos, ac per hoc confirmationem eis deesse. Hi sunt, qui et Galatas subverterant, ut a traditione Apostolorum recederent, quibus ideo irascitur Apostolus, quia docti bene, facile transducti fuerant: Romanis autem irasci non debuit, sed et laudare fidem illorum; quia nulla insignia virtutum videntes, nec aliquem Apostolorum, susceperant fidem Christi ritu licet judaico, in verbis potius, quam in sensu; non enim expositum illis fuerat mysterium crucis Christi. Propterea quibusdam advenientibus, qui recte crediderant, de edenda carne et non edenda quaestiones fiebant, et utrumnam spes, quae in Christo est, sufficeret, aut et lex servanda esset.*

38. *Commentaria in XIII. Epistolas Paulinas*, on Rom 1:10, 13; in Ambrose, *Sancti Ambrosii Mediolanensis Episcopi opera...*, 4:38–39, appendix.

be understood that previously he was not praising their faith, but their ease and devotion toward Christ. Confessing themselves as Christians, with simplicity they carried on under the law, as it was handed down to them. He shows forth his plan and his dedication, which he does not doubt that they know from those brothers who were coming to the city (Rome) from Jerusalem or the surrounding cities because of their religion, introducing his vow to the Romans, just like Aquila and Priscilla. Since he often wanted to come and was prevented, it happened that he wrote a letter, lest they would not be easily corrected, having been held in bad practice for a long time. And he calls them brothers, not only since they were reborn, but also since there were some among them who understood correctly, although only a few.[39]

The author of the commentary appears to have drawn his historical specifications—which fit well with the content of the letter—from a credible source, since he not only places them intentionally at the front as an introduction but also repeatedly returns to them in the commentary itself. He distinguishes accordingly, as one can see from his words, in the Roman community founded by Jewish Christians, as it seems, already in the earlier period, even before the apostle Paul came into contact with it, a double direction of its Judaism, namely, a direction that attached itself strictly to the actual Judaism, which was the original direction, and a freer direction, which was closer to the Pauline spirit, as Aquila and Priscilla had understood it. It seems to be almost certain that the activity of the apostle Paul—who had long carried within himself the pressing wish to come to Rome (Acts 19:21; 23:11), certainly with regard to the conditions of the community that were already known to him—dedicated very specifically to the Roman community; the very extensive letter that expresses the entire character of the Pauline spirit; the two-year imprisonment,

---

39. *Carnalem illos sensum assequutos significat, quia sub nomine Christi non illa, quae Christus docuerat, fuerant assequuti, sed ea, quae fuerant a Judaeis tradita. Se autem cupere citius venire, ut ab hac illos traditione abstraheret, et spiritual illis traderet donum.* — *Hinc datur intellegi, superius non fidem illorum laudasse, sed facilitate et votum circa Christum; Christianos enim se profitentes, sub lege agebant simpliciter, sicut illis fuerat traditum.* — *Propositum et* [168] *votum suum ostendit, quod quidem scire illos non ambigit per eos fratres, qui ab Hierusalem vel confinibus civitatibus causa suae religionis ad Urbem veniebant, sicut Aquilla et Priscilla, votum ejus insinuantes Romanis. Cum enim saepe vellet venire et prohiberetur, sic factum est, ut scriberet epistolam, ne diu in mala exercitatione detenti non facile corrigerentur. Et fratres eos vocat, non solum quia renati errant, sed et quia errant inter eos licet pauci, qui recte sentirent.*

which so little restricted the apostle in his effectiveness for the cause of Christianity (Acts 28:31); all of these had a very benevolent influence upon the community and increasingly began to secure the predominance of the Christianity that was purified through Pauline principles. The apostle, who already met with such a large reception at his arrival in Italy (Acts 28:14–15), surely had, all the more so, [169] a significant party since then, which continued to have an effect along his trajectory and no longer allowed the spirit awakened and nourished by him to be suppressed. Nevertheless, the community appears, especially after the violent disturbance that it undoubtedly suffered through the Neronian persecution of Christians also for the development of its inner relations, to have continued to remain, also subsequently, in a vacillating state between the two opposing directions. Judaism still had a great many friends, and repeatedly asserted its rights and claims. From the first half of the second century, the decisively Judaizing product that pressed for penitence, good works, and observance of the divine law (though it did not exactly emphasize the works in an overly exclusive way), which has come to us under the name of the Shepherd of Hermas, attests for us the spirit that predominated among at least a large part of the community. On the other hand, certain phenomena testify more to the opposite direction, just as Neander[40] also claimed that the opposition against Judaism predominated in the West, especially in the Roman church. The accusation that Tertullian[41] brings against his Roman opponents belongs here—namely, that they deprive the Sabbath of the observance due to it, sometimes continue the fast from Friday into Saturday, and have the even-more-noteworthy custom of strictly separating the Christian Easter celebration, in a direction antithetical to Judaism, from the Jewish Passover celebration. However, it must be taken into account here that one attempted to justify the former (anyway, Tertullian[42] says, after all, only *si quando* ["whenever"]) through the saga that the apostle Peter fasted on a Sabbath in preparation for his disputation with the magician Simon;[43] and the latter appears not to have been a consistent custom of the Roman community from the beginning, since Irenaeus, in his writing to the Roman bishop Victor (in Eusebius, *Hist. eccl.* 5.24), [170] goes back only to the bishop Anicetus in the listing

---

40. Neander, *Allgemeine Geschichte*, 1.2:515.
41. *Jejun.* 14.
42. *Jejun.* 14.
43. See Neander, *Allgemeine Geschichte*, 1.2:516.

of the Roman bishops who did not agree with the custom of Asia Minor, from which John Pearson and Henry Dodwell already concluded with justification[44] that this difference had not existed in earlier times. Just as Victor fervently opposed the Asian Minor Passover ceremony, so there is an occurrence in this same period that could be regarded as proof of how eager people were at that time to completely repress the Judaizing element that continued to exist in the Roman community up until then. For their Judaizing conception of the person of Christ—according to which Christ was not a divine being in terms of his nature but rather only a human being who was gifted with the spirit or wisdom of God above all other human beings—the Unitarians, headed by Artemon, also appealed to its antiquity. Their claim was that all those from earlier times and the apostles themselves had passed on and taught the same thing as what they claim, and that the true teaching had preserved itself until the time of Victor, who was the thirteenth bishop since Peter, but had been distorted under his successor Zephyrinus. For this reason, they designated the now-dominant teaching that Christ was a divine being according to his nature as a teaching that had arisen only recently. But in which other tendency could this reshaping of the theological view and way of teaching have occurred than in an anti-Jewish one? While these circumstances cannot be more clearly grasped, it is nevertheless striking—as Coelln[45] rightly notes—that while the unnamed opponent of the Artemonites in Eusebius, *Hist. eccl.* 5.28, appeals to the fact that the divinity of Christ is taught in a series of older church authors, whom he invokes by name, not one of them can be assigned with certainty to the Roman community, despite the fact that the opposite of the Artemonic accusation could be proven only from the teachers of this community. The Shepherd of Hermas, at least, which presents entirely the [171] Jewish-Christian view of Christ,[46] more likely speaks for the claim of the Artemonites. As further proof of that character

---

44. See Heinichen, *Eusebii Pamphili*, 2:124.
45. Coelln, "Clementina," 18:43.
46. This view is also not excluded by the passage Herm. Sim. 9.12 [89]: *Filius quidem Dei Omni creatura antiquior est, ita ut in consilio patri suo adfuerit ad condendam creaturam* ["The Son of God is older than all creatures, and so he became the Father's counselor for establishing his creation"]. For the author the *filius Dei* is equivalent to the *spiritus sanctus* and thus basically the same as what σοφία is in the Clementines. See Christoph David Anton Martini, *Versuch einer pragmatischen Geschichte des Dogma von der Gottheit Christi in den vier ersten Jahrhunderten nach Christi Geburt* (Rostock: Stiller, 1800), 28; Coelln, "Clementina."

of the Roman community that continued into that time and, in general, of the Judaism that probably predominated in most of the communities of that time, we can adduce what Hegesippus, who stayed for an extended period of time in Rome under the Roman bishops Anicetus, Soter, and Eleutheros, says in Eusebius, *Hist. eccl.* 4.22, with particular reference to the Roman community: ἐν ἑκάστῃ διαδοχῇ καὶ ἐν ἑκάστῃ πόλει οὕτως ἔχει, ὡς ὁ νόμος κηρύττει καὶ οἱ προφῆται καὶ ὁ κύριος ["In each list and in each city things are as the law, the prophets, and the Lord preach" (trans. Lake and Oulton)]. Hegesippus was a Jewish Christian, and the purpose of his trip was to find out on location whether the communities conformed to the nature of Christianity, as he understood it as a Jewish Christian. He wrote down the results of his trip in his five books of ὑπομνήματα ["memoirs"], in which he, according to Eusebius (*Hist. eccl.* 4.22), reported ὡς πλείστοις ἐπισκόποις συμμίξειεν, ἀποδημίαν στειλάμενος μέχρι Ῥώμης, καὶ ὡς ὅτι τὴν αὐτὴν παρὰ πάντων παρείληφε διδασκαλίαν ["how, when travelling as far as Rome, he mingled with many bishops, and that he found the same doctrine among them all" (trans. Lake and Oulton)]. The same Hegesippus may have even gone so far in his Judaism that he did not shy away from declaring himself to be an opponent of the apostle Paul. In his extracts from the works of the Monophysite Stephanus Gobarus (*Bibliotheca*, §232),[47] Photius has also preserved for us the following passage from the ὑπομνήματα of Hegesippus:

> ὅτι τὰ ἡτοιμασμένα τοῖς δικαίοις ἀγαθὰ οὔτε ὀφθαλμὸς εἶδεν, οὔτε οὖς ἤκουσεν, οὔτε ἐπὶ καρδίαν ἀνθρώπου ἀνέβη. Ἡγήσιππος μέντοι, ἀρχαῖός τε ἀνὴρ καὶ ἀποστολικὸς ἐν τῷ πέμπτῳ τῶν ὑπομνημάτων, [172] οὐκ οἶδ᾽ ὅ τι καὶ παθών, μάτην μὲν εἰρῆσθαι ταῦτα λέγει, καὶ καταψεύδεσθαι τοὺς ταῦτα φαμένες τῶν τε θείων γραφῶν καὶ τοῦ κυρίου λέγοντος μακάριοι οἱ ὀφθαλμοὶ ὑμῶν οἱ βλέποντες καὶ τὰ ὦτα ὑμῶν τὰ ἀκούοντα.

["For the good things that have been prepared for the righteous, neither eye has seen, nor ear has heard, nor has it entered into the heart of a person" (cf. 1 Cor 2:9). Yet Hegesippus, an ancient and apostolic man, in the fifth book of his memoirs (I do not know concerning what matter), says it is foolish to say such things, and those who say such things speak falsely, since both the divine Scriptures and the Lord said, "Blessed are your eyes that see and your ears that hear."]

---

47. Photius, *Photii Bibliotheca*, 2 vols., ed. Immanuel Bekker (Berlin: Reimer, 1824–1825).

The words quoted first are from 1 Cor 2:9, and the accusation of false teachings thus appears to refer to the apostle Paul. Neander, however, believes that this assumption is opposed by Hegesippus's satisfaction with the general tradition of the church and his connection with the Roman church.[48] In his view, since Hegesippus would necessarily have had to have been an opponent of both, it must instead be assumed that he might have said this not in opposition against Paul but instead in his fervent zeal against the adversary of the fleshly chiliasm (who could probably use the invoked Pauline passage and other similar ones in order to counter the sensual conceptions of the future bliss). If, however, Hegesippus, as Neander himself notes, filled out the picture of James—who bore the name of a brother of the Lord and enjoyed the greatest veneration among all Jewish Christians as head of the community of Jerusalem—according to Ebionitic taste, in such a way that we have reason to infer Ebionitic principles in Hegesippus, then should it be unlikely that those words contain an opposition against those who, like the apostle Paul, without having seen the Lord and heard his teaching, claim to present the divine truth on the basis of a revelation that been directly imparted to them? As the cited passage reads, it is only found in Paul; and right after this, Paul continues: ἡμῖν δὲ ἀπεκάλυψεν ὁ θεὸς διὰ τοῦ πνεύματος αὐτοῦ (1 Cor 2:10). In the passage from Matt 13:16 that Hegesippus quotes to refute the words of Paul, Jesus speaks to his disciples about the blessedness of those who see and hear him. In this regard, it is completely in accord with the Ebionite principle that only direct association with Jesus can be regarded as the source and criterion [173] of the divinely revealed truth.[49] And if the author of the Clementines did not

---

48. Neander, *Allgemeine Geschichte*, 1.3:1139.
49. Rightly noted by Routh, *Reliquiae Sacrae*, 1:253, on the words of Hegesippus: "Concerning spiritual matters, which were revealed to the faithful through the gospel, Hegesippus leads this way. By no means would I think those proven dogmas concerning the redemption of mankind were defined in this division by the apostle himself, or the mysteries of the gospel, which were hidden from the eyes of the Jews, and only τοῖς τελείοις when the Holy Spirit laid bare the things which were hidden.... I regard it as settled, from many passages of Clement of Alexandria, that the gnostic heretics were accustomed to these words, whether they took them up for themselves from an apostle, or from an apocryphal book, just as they immediately applied δικαίους to divine things, with all others having been excluded, which they uttered on account of its own greatness. Whereby Hegesippus seems to disprove himself on account of those heretics, with the words of Christ having been introduced, in which wisdom, already lying open to the eyes and ears of the disciples, is revealed." Routh appeals to Clement

name the apostle Paul but polemicized clearly enough against him, why should the same indirect polemic, which may have been required by the conditions of the time, not also be assumed in Hegesippus? After all, as already noted earlier, Papias's high estimation of the tradition going back to Jesus himself also appears to have flowed from a view that could not be very inclined toward recognizing the apostle Paul's claim to apostolic credibility. But if men such as Hegesippus and Papias found themselves moved to testify that they were completely satisfied with the views and principles that prevailed in the Roman church, and to adhere especially to the traditions of this [174] church, then by this we may judge what kind of spirit may have been predominant in the Roman church at that time.

However, if, after all that has been said, it cannot in fact be doubted that in the Roman community there was from the very beginning a very significant Judaizing element,[50] which even through the Pauline influence could not be entirely repressed, but rather may well have emerged with greater force at the end of the first century CE, a period that is so dark to us due to a lack of information, and at the beginning of the second century CE, then through this the assumption becomes very likely that the saga of Peter's journey to Rome and his stay and martyrdom there—which appear so uncertain and all the more unfounded the further we go back—owes itself solely to the Judaism of the Roman community. There

---

of Alexandria, *Miscellanies*, book 4 [Clement of Alexandria, *Klēmentos Alexandreōs ta heuriskomena / Clementis Alexandrini opera, quae extant*, ed. John Potter (Venice: Zatta, 1757), 615, 628 (i.e., *Strom*. 4.18.116; 4.22.143)]; and *Miscellanies*, book 5 [Potter, *Klēmentos Alexandreōs ta heuriskomena*, 628, 659 (i.e., *Strom*. 5.4.25; 5.6.40)], where Clement, however, speaks only of the gnostic in his sense. While it is analogous to this, the opposition against the apostle Paul evidently has to be much more likely for a Jewish Christian of Hegesippus's spirit.

50. The fact that the names in the series of the first Roman bishops are almost all Greek is also conspicuous; i.e., Linus, Anacletus, Clement, Evaristus, Alexander, Xystus, Telesphorus, Hyginus, Pius, Anicetus, Soter, Eleutherus. In this whole series, besides Pius, only Clement (who appears to have become the direct successor of the apostle Peter for the first time in the sequence of our Clementines; Coelln, "Clementina," 18:43) has an authentically Roman name. But Clement is explicitly called a gentile Christian. This phenomenon probably can only be explained from the fact that the community was predominantly composed of Jewish Christians or Hellenists. Only with Victor, the first Roman bishop who displayed an anti-Jewish spirit, do the Roman names become more frequent, as in the case of the bishops Urbanus, Pontianus, Fabianus, Cornelius, and Lucius, who followed Victor, with a few interruptions, by bishops with Greek names.

was a party in Rome in whose interest it was to set the authority of Peter, the apostle to the Jews, against the authority of Paul, the apostle to the gentiles. What one knew about Paul as an undoubted fact was also to be applied to Peter. What the life of the one contained in reality was to be transferred to the life of the other through [175] the saga that mediated truth and fiction. However, one was not simply content to place in this way the one alongside the other; the historical prototype should be outshone by the traditional afterimage. If Peter was to have the same standing for a part of the Roman community that Paul had for another, then, like Paul, he had to have come to Rome and worked there for some time. But how could Peter have been in Rome, without sharing with his rival above all the fame of martyrdom, which glorified the memory of Paul? Therefore, while each of the opposing parties contributed their part to honoring the one church, the great preeminence that the Roman church attached to itself was in being founded by the two most glorious apostles; as Tertullian puts it, "Peter and Paul left as legacy the gospel, sealed moreover with their own blood" (trans. Evans).[51] But in order to place the one over the other (as, after all, the preeminence seemed to belong to Peter in every respect), not only should Peter die and be buried at another, more famous place than Paul (as we have already seen), but the way that the two of them died should also be different. Eusebius, *Hist. eccl.* 3.1, shares the news from Origen that Peter, after he had preached the gospel in Pontus, Galatia and Bithynia, Cappadocia, and Asia, finally also came to Rome, and ἐν Ῥώμῃ γενόμενος ἀνεσκολοπίσθη κατὰ κεφαλῆς, οὕτως αὐτὸς ἀξιώσας παθεῖν ["in Rome was crucified head downwards, for so he had demanded to suffer" (trans. Lake and Oulton)], to which Rufinus comments in his translation of Eusebius's *Ecclesiastical History*: "He was crucified upside down, with his head hanging down, since he begged that it be done in that way, lest he seem to be equal to the Lord."[52] By contrast, Tertullian had still simply said, in the aforementioned place: "Peter was made equal to the Lord's passion."[53] That the joint martyrdom still met with a certain objection for a long time can be seen from the proceedings of one of the Roman synods under Bishop Gelasius I, in

---

51. *Evangelium et Petrus et Paulus sanguine quoque suo signatum reliquerunt* (*Marc.* 4.5).

52. *Crucifixus est deorsum, capite demerso, quod ipse ita fieri deprecatus est, ne exaequari Domino videretur.*

53. *Petrus passioni dominicae adaequatur.*

2. The Apostle Peter in Rome 113

which the following is said in relation to Peter: [176] "To whom indeed was given the companionship of the blessed Paul, who, not otherwise, as the heretics chatter, but at one time, on the same day, with Peter in the city of Rome, suffering under Nero, was crowned."[54] It is true that the difference concerned, as it appears, initially only the time and day of the joint martyrdom, concerning which the Catholic Church itself was not quite united even in the fourth and fifth century CE, since it was sometimes the same day but not the same year; sometimes it was the same day and year.[55] But should not, for precisely this reason, the *garrire* ["chattering"] for which the heretics were blamed allow one to infer a more far-reaching opposition? But whatever the case may be regarding this, the saga followed the course that was once taken. Alongside the glory of martyrdom, the fame of the apostle consisted mainly in the fact that he had been active for the cause of the gospel in such a vast sphere of activity. In this respect, too, Peter could not have taken a back seat to him. Rather, to make his presence and activity in Rome credible, he had to be given above all an apparent reason that might have led him there. In this respect, as I believe, the previously touched-upon fiction regarding the magician Simon—which arose from an apparent misunderstanding[56]—accommodated the developing saga in a very welcome way. If the magician Simon finally came to Rome, which one could not doubt since one could see the documented proof with one's own eyes, then how should his apostolic opponent, who contested and refuted him, not have followed him to the outermost destination of the track, where he was ruining the church with his deceptive black magic? [177] How the tradition took form in this regard can be seen from the Clementine *Homilies* and the apocryphal writings that belong to the same group of sagas. The encounter between the apostle and the magician in Samaria recounted in Acts provided the starting point. Just as Peter, according to

---

54. *Cui data est etiam societas h. Pauli, qui non diverso, sicut haeretici garriunt, sed uno tempore, uno eodemque die gloriosa morte cum Petro in urbe Roma sub Nerone agonicans coronatus est.* See Henri de Valois (Henricus Valesius), *Eusebii Pamphili Ecclesiasticae historiae libri decem...* (Paris: Vitré, 1659; with several successive reprints), on Eusebius, *Hist. eccl.* 2.25. [Valois, 1603–1676, was a French philologist and scholar of ecclesiastical historians.]

55. See Valois, *Eusebii Pamphili*, on *Hist. eccl.* 2.25.

56. That a mere misunderstanding moved Simon Magus, who was confused with the Sabine-Roman God *Semo Sancus*, to Rome requires no further demonstration. See Neander, *Allgemeine Geschichte*, 1:779–80.

Acts, was—in contrast to James, who, as the head of the mother community, did not leave Jerusalem—the outwardly active, traveling apostle, namely, in the newly founded communities and in the regions where new communities were to be founded, so one now had every reason to extend his sphere ever further. According to Acts, the main location of Peter's apostolic activity was the area of the Phoenician seaside towns. In exactly this area, in the town of Caesarea Stratonis, the Clementines have Clement meet with Peter, when he was just preparing for a dispute with Simon the magician. After being defeated by Peter, the magician left Caesarea, where Peter founded a Christian community, and went to Tyre (*Hom.* 3.58). Peter sent Clement ahead there with the two youths Nicetas and Aquila, but since the magician had sailed onward to Sidon, they only met Apion Pleistonices, an Alexandrian grammarian, and some other followers of the magician. The arrival of Peter in Tyre drove them away, and Peter then made Tyre, Sidon, Berytus, and Tripolis the setting of his speeches and deeds, converted the citizens of those places, and gave the newly founded communities an orderly constitution. From Tripolis, Peter continued his journey with his companions via Orthosia, Antaradus, Laodicea, and through the cities of the gentiles (*Hom.* 12.1) to Antioch, where new disputes with the magician Simon began, which lasted for several days (*Hom.* 16–17); but in our defective manuscript, *Hom.* 19 breaks off without completing it. From the *Epitome de gestis Petri*, we learn of the further success of the activity of the apostle Peter; that he, after the magician was also completely defeated in Antioch, [178] converted the whole city, founded a very significant community there, thereupon traveled with Clement and his other companions to Rome, named Clement bishop of the Roman community before his death, and gave him (as Clement himself also reports in the letter to James that precedes the homilies) the task of sending a description of his life and the speeches recorded on his travels with Peter to James, the head of the Jerusalem community.[57] That the magician caused Peter to travel to Rome is not explicitly stated in the *Epitome de gestis Petri*, but in general this part of the life story of Peter is only narrated summarily here.[58] That Peter

---

57. [Joachim Périon, ed., *Clementis Romani episcopi, de rebus gestis, peregrinationibus, atque concionibus sancti Petri epitome...* (Paris: n.p., 1555).]

58. The narrative of the *Epitome de gestis Petri* (chs. 144–45) is as follows: "I, Clement, with the brethren remained yet at Antioch in the presence of the teacher, Peter, who was applying himself to the preaching of the gospel and was healing many

2. The Apostle Peter in Rome 115

came to Rome for this reason was almost universally accepted. Eusebius (*Hist. eccl.* 2.14) also does [179] not have a different knowledge of the matter in a passage whose rhetorical overtones clearly reveal the influence of the saga: παρὰ πόδας γοῦν (["close after him"], as soon as the magician had fled before the apostle from the Orient to the Occident, and in Rome had managed with his black magic to be venerated like a god through a statue that was built for him),

ἐπὶ τῆς αὐτῆς Κλαυδίου Βασιλείας ἡ πανάγαθος καὶ φιλανθρωποτάτη τῶν ὅλων πρόνοια τὸν καρτερὸν καὶ μέγαν τῶν ἀποστόλων, τὸν ἀρετῆς ἕνεκα τῶν λοιπῶν ἁπάντων προήγορον, Πέτρον, ἐπὶ τὴν Ῥώμην ὡς ἐπὶ τηλικοῦτον λυμεῶνα βίου χειραγωγεῖ, ὅς οἷά τις γενναῖος τοῦ θεοῦ στρατηγὸς τοῖς θείοις ὅπλοις φραξάμενος τὴν πολυτίμητον ἐμπορείαν τοῦ νοητοῦ φωτὸς ἐξ

---

people from various diseases and afflictions. Then, having traveled through cities, he came even to Rome. And to those who flocked to him, he announced the message of piety, and he brought many into the religion of Christ through baptism, as many men as women, to the point that he persuaded nearly all the most illustrious of noble women, whom they were accustomed to call matrons, to take refuge in holy baptism and to believe in God. Moreover, when life had to be given up by him, and he had to proceed to Christ, the Master, when the course of the gospel was finished (of course, it was notable to him that he was condemned even to the cross so that he might have common passion and glory with his master) with all the brethren joined together, seizing my hand as he stood in the middle of the assembly and the church, he said: 'Hear me, sons and brothers, certainly the end of my course is near, for this is already known to me, but today I ordain this man Clement as your bishop, to whom I entrust my seat of preaching, since from the beginning, even till now, he has been my companion, and so he has heard all my sermons.'" (*Ego Clemens cum fratribus adhuc apud Petrum doctorem mansi (Antiochiae), qui evangelicae praedicationi insistebat, et complures variis morbis ac perpessionibus curabat. Deinde ille urbibus peragratis Romam quoque pervenit, atque iis, qui concurrebant, verbum pictatis annunciavit, multosque per baptismum adduxit ad Christi religionem, tam viros, quam mulieres, adeo ut et brevi tempore nobelium mulierum clarissimis, quasque solent matronas nuncupare, propemodum universis persuaserit, ad sanctum baptisma confugere ac Deo credere. Porro cum ipsi jam vita relinquenda fuit, et proficiscendum ad magistrum Christum, evangelii cursu consummato (id quippe notum illi erat, quodque ipse etiam ad crucem, ut cum magistro passionem et gloriam commune haberet, damnandus esset) una congregates cunctis fratribus, apprehensa manu mea, stans in media concione et ecclesia: Audite me, inquit, filii et fratres: cursus quidem mei finis proper est, id enim et jam mihi est cognitum, Clementem autem hunc episcopum vobis hodie ordino, cui et meam sermonum cathedram credo, quoniam ab initio hucusque comos mihi fuit, sicque omnes audivit conciones meas.*)

ἀνατολῶν τοῖς κατὰ δύσιν ἐκόμιζεν, φῶς αὐτὸ καὶ λόγον ψυχῶν σωτήριον, τὸ κήρυγμα τῆς τῶν οὐρανῶν βασιλείας εὐαγγελιζόμενος.

[In the same reign of Claudius, the Providence of the universe, in its great goodness and love towards men, guided to Rome, as against a gigantic pest on life, the great and mighty Peter, who for his virtues was the leader of all the other apostles. Like a noble captain of God, clad in divine armour, he brought from the east to the dwellers in the west, preaching the Gospel of the light itself and the word which saves souls, the proclamation of the kingdom of heaven. (Trans. Lake and Oulton)]

Having come to the belief that the magician Simon came to Rome, one could not have the apostle Peter end his apostolic course in any more worthy destination than in Rome. In doing so, the opportunity to let Peter appear in an even more radiant light than Paul again presented itself very naturally. Not only did one have him pace through a sphere among the Jews and pagans that could indeed equal that of Paul in expansiveness and fame, but it was also Peter who came, even before Paul, to Rome under Claudius and became, through the great success of his deeds and teachings, the real founder of the Christian community in the capital.[59] The

---

59. In a similar way, also already in Corinth, the Cephas or Christ party wanted to be associated with the fame of founding the Corinthian community; see page 49–50/101 above. In order to make Peter himself the founder of the Corinthian community, it required only the further step of having Peter himself come to Corinth instead of the Petrine pseudoapostles. As we can see from the aforementioned passage of the Corinthian bishop Dionysius, this step really took place, with the same injustice to the true merit of the apostle Paul in Corinth as in Rome. In Eusebius, *Hist. eccl.* 2.25, Dionysius speaks of the ἀπὸ Πέτρου καὶ Παύλου γενηθεῖσα φυτεία ["the foundations by Peter and Paul"], both are said to have come εἰς τὴν ἡμετέραν Κόρινθον φυτεύσαντες (this is what is to be read, and not φοιτήσαντες; see Heinichen, *Eusebii Pamphili*, on *Hist. eccl.* 2.25) ἡμᾶς ["to our Corinth as those who founded us"]. Here I believe I can add a remark that relates to 2 Cor 11:2. It seems to me that the same thing that was noted above about Gal 2:9 applies to this text. The comparison of the Christian community with a bride and the portrayal of its relationship to Christ using the image of marriage (which image is found in the apostle Paul only additionally in Eph 5:23, perhaps likewise due to a special occasion) appears to have been an especially beloved allegory among Jewish Christians. This can be inferred not only from the well-known places in the Gospels (Matt 9:15; 25:1; John 3:29; etc.) and Revelation (Rev 19:7; 21:9; etc.) but also from the Clementines, where *Hom.* 3.26 [*Hom.* 3.27] says of the false prophecy that it βραχείαις ἡδοναῖς τοῦ λογισμοῦ τὴν ἰσχὺν ὑποσυλῶσα τοὺς πλείονας εἰς μοιχείαν ἄγει, καὶ οὕτως τοῦ μέλλοντος καλοῦ στερίσκει νυμφίου·

2. The Apostle Peter in Rome

only problem was that this resulted in a certain inconvenience with regard to the saga, which [180] has Peter suffer martyrdom at the same time with Paul. Since the point in time at which Paul died in Rome was historically determined, one had from the reign of the emperor Claudius until the tenth year of emperor Nero's reign a period that was too long and devoid of content. From this, there arose various modifications of the saga. Either one paid no further attention to Paul and had Peter—after [181] he had devoted himself to proclamation of the gospel and the founding of the community for some time there—die in Rome as a martyr for his faith and vocation (as we find in the *Epitome* and undoubtedly have to assume for the lost presentation of the *Homilies*). Or one ignored the occasion for his journey given to Peter by the magician in order to have him come to Rome from Corinth in the company of Paul, working with Paul in Rome, and then share the same fate (according to Dionysius of Corinth and according to Irenaeus, *Haer.* 3.1, which says that Matthew produced the gospel for the Hebrews in their own language, τοῦ Πέτρου καὶ τοῦ Παύλου ἐν Ῥώμῃ εὐαγγελιζομένων καὶ θεμελιούντων τὴν ἐκκλησίαν ["while Peter and Paul were preaching in Rome and founding the church" (trans. Lake and Oulton)]).[60] Or one also moved the scene that took place with the magician in Rome from the time of Claudius to the time of Nero, a combination that Lactantius apparently followed in the abovementioned passage. While more recent thinkers, such as even Bertholdt[61] and especially Jacob Peter Mynster,[62] in order [182] to unite the different variations of the saga, have

---

νύμφη γὰρ ἔστιν ὁ πᾶς ἄνθρωπος, ὁπότ' ἂν τοῦ ἀληθοῦς προφήτου λευκῷ λόγῳ ἀληθείας σπειρόμεονος φωτίζεται τὸν νοῦν ["spoiling the strength of the judgment by short pleasures leads the greater part into fornication, and thus deprives them of the coming excellent Bridegroom. For every person is a bride, whenever, being sown with the true Prophet's whole word of truth, he is enlightened in his understanding" (trans. Smith, Peterson, and Donaldson)]. See also *Acts of Thomas* (Johann Karl Thilo, ed., *Acta S. Thomae apostoli ex codd. pariss.* [Leipzig: Vogel, 1823], 123–24). When the apostle, in opposition against his pseudoapostolic opponents, who wanted to take the credit of establishing Christianity in Corinth from him, uses here precisely the image: ἡρμοσάμην ὑμᾶς ἑνὶ ἀνδρὶ παρθένον ἁγνὴν παραστῆσαι, τῷ χριστῷ [1 Cor 11:2], is it not probable that he showed similar consideration for the language and circle of ideas of his opponents as in Gal 2:9?

60. Eusebius, *Hist. eccl.* 5.8.
61. Bertholdt, *Historisch-kritische Einleitung*, 5:2690.
62. In the aforementioned study, on the first stay of the apostle Peter in Rome from 1813 in the *Kleinen theologische Schriften*, published in 1825 [i.e., Mynster, "Ueber den

ersten Aufenthalt," 143–66]. Here is the most fitting place to briefly consider this most recent defense of a not merely one-time stay of the apostle Peter in Rome. Mynster ("Ueber den ersten Aufenthalt," 164) summarizes the result of his study as follows: "When Paul first began to spread Christianity in Europe, Peter was undoubtedly still in Asia. However, around the end of the reign of Claudius or at the beginning of the reign of Nero, Peter came to Rome, where he, even though he was not the first to mention the name of Christ there, nevertheless earned the fame given to him by the whole Christian primitive period, namely, that he was the actual founder of the Roman community, which was so important both then and afterward. From there, he appears to have made his way through Corinth, where he had been, as we know from the testimony of Dionysius, and thus we understand how there could be a party named after him in this city. [182] However, we see from the letters to the Corinthians that Peter was no longer there when these letters were written. He was certainly also not in Rome when Paul wrote to this city nor when he wrote his letters from Rome in about 63 CE. And we know nothing about the subsequent fate of Peter until we finally find him in the capital of the world, uniting his witness with that of Paul, and, like Paul, suffering death." If we ask how this result is supposed to be grounded, then Mynster ("Ueber den ersten Aufenthalt," 153) assumes that the honor that Christianity first brought into the European lands undoubtedly belongs to Paul, and that up until the time of the first arrival of the apostle Paul in these regions, we find no trace of the activity of Peter. A few years later, the situation is said to be different. When Paul, toward the end of his stay in Ephesus, undoubtedly in the spring of 58 CE, wrote his first letter to the Corinthians, this community had split into parties. As the name of Apollos was misused in this way, because Apollos had really taught in Corinth in the meantime, so this same cause appears to have been the case with Peter. When Paul, Mynster notes further, wrote his letter to the Romans at the beginning of the following year, a community that was rich in numbers and well instructed was already in Rome, whose faith was praised in the whole world (Rom 1:8); "So, was it Peter who, in the course of this time, had founded or at least formed this community?" Mynster then appeals to Dionysius's testimony that Peter had been in Corinth and Eusebius's testimony that he came to Rome under Claudius at the instigation of the magician Simon, but he is inclined to give at least equal value to Lactantius's testimony that Peter only founded the Roman community at the beginning of the reign of Nero. At the time, Mynster ("Ueber den ersten Aufenthalt," 157) notes, some Jew, who was familiar with Christianity or had accepted it himself, had perhaps spoken with some Jews in Rome; but we can say with considerable certainty that Christ had not yet been proclaimed there. By contrast, soon after this we find [183] in Rome a sizable community, which was renowned in all Christian communities. Thus, who else should we name as the founder of this community than the person whom the whole church tradition thus names, Peter? With this presupposition, Mynster connects the saga that Peter wrote his first letter in Rome ἐν Βαβυλῶνι (1 Pet 5:13) through the supposition that the Silvanus mentioned in 1 Pet 5:12—who, with Paul, had founded Christianity in Corinth according to Acts 18:5; 2 Cor 1:19, but did not, according to Acts 18:18, follow Paul when he left Corinth in the spring of 54 CE—

may have traveled to Rome around the same time (at the end of the reign of Claudius or in the first years of Nero's reign), and through his narration of the spread of Christianity in Corinth perhaps caused the apostle to visit the Corinthian community. It seems to me that it is presumably not necessary to demonstrate in detail how little this attempt is able to give greater probability to the alleged fact. Here I will briefly highlight just a few main points. (1) The assumption that the apostle Peter founded the Roman community or took part in its founding is opposed by—besides Rom 15:20, 2 Cor 10:26, and the whole letter to the Romans—the above-cited assertion of Hilarius that the Roman community at the time of its origin had no apostle in its midst. (2) The assumption that the first beginnings of the Roman community are to be set between 54 and 58 CE, or between the first arrival of the apostle Paul in Corinth and the composition of his first letter to the Corinthians, is at odds with the fact that Paul already met with Aquila and Priscila at his first arrival in Corinth (Acts 18:2), who—according to the whole relationship in which they appear in relation to the apostle in Luke, when we connect the cause of their departure from Rome recounted by Suetonius with this— attest for the existence of a Roman community already around that time or at least the first configuration of this community. To be sure, Mynster ("Ueber den ersten Aufenthalt," 152) comments on that passage by arguing that it does not follow from the words of Suetonius [184] that these unrests took place in Rome itself; that Suetonius undoubtedly wanted to say that the alleged instigators of these unrests had stayed in Rome; and that it is probable that the violent movements among the Jews, which were reported in several provinces and approached the capital at that time, prompted the emperor or those who acted in his name to expel the Jews from Rome so that they would not also begin similar unrests there. However, in opposition to this view, it is undeniable that the *tumultuantes Judaei* ["Jews making disturbances"], who were driven from Rome, must also have been in Rome itself. By contrast, it presents no difficulty to understand the *impulsor Chrestus* ["the instigator, Chrestus"] in relation to the impetus that Christianity or Christ, as the founder of Christianity, as the person whose recognition was at issue, gave to these unrests. (3) If the testimony of Eusebius is meant to prove something, then Peter, if one places no weight upon the fact that other statements already have him come to Rome in the first years of Claudius, must nevertheless still come to Rome in any case under the reign of Claudius. Since, however, according to Acts 15, this cannot have taken place before the twelfth year of Claudius, and Claudius did not reign for a full fourteen years, the time in which Peter could have come to Rome becomes very restricted. Moreover, it becomes even more restricted by the fact that we find Peter in Antioch after the gathering in Jerusalem, if, as it appears, the incident recounted by Paul in Gal 2:11 must be placed in the period that directly followed that conference and not at an earlier point in time. In any case, however, the arrival of Peter in Rome would have fallen still at the end of the reign of Claudius, precisely in the time in which the order that Claudius gave against the Jews must have still been in force; i.e., in the period that is least favorable for the founding of a Christian community in Rome. If, however, as Mynster also regards as preferable, one moves forward from the time of Claudius into the time of Nero, then one can actually only still adhere to the highly

the apostle Peter come to Rome twice, [183] in the ancient period, the long duration of the episcopacy, which Peter administered in his own person [184] in the midst of the Roman community, became increasingly plausible already at an early stage; and from this arose the well-known standard number of twenty-five years, [185] which is first assigned to the stay of Peter in Eusebius's *Chronicon*, in the translation of Jerome.[63] How little all of these so greatly divergent variations allow something factual to be assumed in the saga of the stay of the apostle Peter in Rome requires no further comment. The abovementioned tradition about the origin of Mark's Gospel also undoubtedly arose from this same endeavor of the saga to place the apostle Peter partly alongside Paul and partly to give him even a certain priority. Since it was already customary at an earlier time, as the Marcionite canon proves, to regard the Gospel of Luke [186] as the Pauline Gospel, there also had to be a Petrine Gospel—with regard to this, there was even less room for doubt, since one already knew the evangelist Mark as a friend and companion of the apostle Peter. However, that the saga of the composition of the Gospel of Mark in Rome owes its origin solely to the interest in having Peter not appear inferior to Paul in any merit of

---

uncertain and confused testimony of Lactantius, who explicitly places the journey [185] of Peter to Rome and the founding of the Roman community by him in the first period of Nero; and must then, so that Peter can still be martyred with Paul at the end, let him remain in Rome into the tenth year of Nero's reign, or at least have him come and go. Probably so that he can let the testimony of Eusebius and others still retain some validity, Mynster ("Ueber den ersten Aufenthalt," 158) says that according to an old report (?), Peter met Simon the magician for a second time in Rome. This arbitrary method of removing historical testimonies from their context and granting them validity only insofar as one can use them for one's hypothesis merits the just rebuke of all who are concerned with the truth of history.

63. "In the second year of Claudius, Peter the Apostle, when he had founded the church at Antioch, went to Rome. There, preaching the gospel, he remained the bishop of that city for twenty-five years." *Anno secondo Claudii, Petrus Apostolus, cum primum Antiochenam fundasset ecclesiam, Romam proficiscitur, ubi evangelium praedicans, viginti quinque annis ejusdem urbis episcopus perseverat.* Concerning the premises of this specification, see Herbst, "Ueber den Aufenthalt des Apostels Petrus zu Rom," 608. The suspicion that the *Chronicon*, which does not agree at this point with Eusebius's *Historia ecclesiastica*, owes this specification to the hand of the translator Jerome does not seem to me to be entirely removed by the fact that the Armenian translation of Eusebius's *Chronicon* as well has the number *viginti* and, as a later addition, also the number *quinque* (see the Herbst, "Ueber den Aufenthalt des Apostels Petrus zu Rom," 601).

2. The Apostle Peter in Rome

apostolic activity is proven by all of those circumstances under which the Gospel of Mark is said to have been composed in Rome: the time of composition during the presence of Peter in Rome, the great impression that the complete refutation of the magician had made, the so-fervent wish of Roman Christians to possess a written gospel. This part of the saga, too, displays the same colors as the saga as a whole, and denies just as little as any other feature of the saga the ground from which it has sprung.[64]

---

64. The existing genetic explanation of the saga seems to me to be an adequate counterweight to the common argument, to which one so readily retreats time and again, though one cannot deny that the persuasive power of the individual arguments, taken on their own, leaves something to be desired, namely, that if the saga had no historical basis, it would always remain incomprehensible how its truth could be attested by so many sides without any significant contradiction being raised against it. It is precisely this argument on which Basnage (*De rebus sacris et ecclesiasticis exercitationes historico-criticae*, 558) relies, when he summarizes—with his characteristic rhetorical flare—the *summa* of his *disputatio* in the following passage: "For what reason has the idea that Peter was present at Rome completely filled the entire earth, if it is an invention of idle men? Why does it reach the church in the east and the south, that he met death at Rome rather than at Babylon? That news wanders through the whole earth, Greece furnishes its witnesses in Dionysius, Gaul summons its own in Irenaeus, clearly in the same generation." (*Qua ratione fama de Petro praesente Romae totum pene terrarium orbem replevit, si figmentum est otiosorum hominum? Quid ecclesiae et orientali et australi redibat, quod Romae potius quam Babylone mortem oppeteret? Vagatur ille rumor ubique terrarum; Graecia suos testes in Dionysio suppeditat; Gallia excitat suos in Irenaeo, eodem plane seculo.*) "Carthage and Alexandria, [187] differing in tongues, are in agreement together" (for Alexandria, see the passage of Athanasius [*Fug.* 18; *Sancti Patris nostri Athanasii Archiepiscopi Alexandriae, Opera quae reperiuntur omnia*, 2 vols., ed. Lucas Hostenius (Cologne: Weidmann, 1686), 1:713]: "And Peter, who had hid himself for fear of the Jews, and the apostle Paul, who was let down in a basket, and fled, when they were told, 'You must bear witness at Rome,' deferred not the journey" [trans. Atkinson, Newman, and Robertson]. Πετρὸς δὲ ὁ διὰ τὸν φόβον τῶν Ἰουδαίων κρυπτόμενος, καὶ Παῦλος ὁ Ἀπόστολος ἐν σαργάνῃ χαλασθεὶς καὶ φυγών, ἀκούσαντες εἰς Ῥώμην δεῖ ὑμᾶς μαρτυρῆσαι, ἐκ ἀνεβάλοντο τὴν ἀποδημίαν). "The same thing is confessed and proclaimed by the allies of the Roman church and its enemies, nor does anyone dare to mutter against the tradition in the matter. What fact of history will be certain, if this is not? If Peter suffered martyrdom in a city other than Rome, on what account would the church that witnessed the martyrdom so swiftly cast away the memory of the martyr? Why did no group of the faithful frequent the apostolic tomb? Why did they not contend with Rome over the body or martyrdom of Peter? Without anyone's disagreement, Rome was assuredly established as the one place of the apostle's death." (*Consentiunt una et Carthago et Alexandria linguis discrepantes. Idem fatentur atque profitentur et amici romanae ecclesiae et adversarii, nec*

[187] It has previously been shown how the same saga, which initially only had the intention of placing the apostle Peter alongside the apostle Paul but then [188] gave the former an increasingly decisive preference over the latter, so that it believed it could also completely ignore Paul, finally took another turn in the Clementines and opposed, in the person of the magician Simon, the apostle as a dangerous opponent of the Mosaic law and as the herald of a new paganism. This, too, is nothing but another form of the same saga, since the saga in all its forms asserts the character of Judaism, whose creation it is. Since the polemic against the apostle Paul documented above seems to me to be one of the most important points from which one can more precisely specify the general point of view from which the tendency of the peculiar writing is to be understood, I believe that I can add a few more comments in this connection that are not too far removed from the purposes of this study. When Neander[65] regards the opposition of the simple faith in revelation against Greek philosophy and

---

hiscere quisquam ausus est in ejusmodi traditionem. Quid facti certum erit in historia, si hoc non est? si in urbe, a Romana diversa, Petrus martyrium passus est, qua de causa testis ecclesia martyrii tam cito martyris abjecit memoriam? Cur nullus fidelium coetus Apostolicum sepulchrum celebravit? Cur cum Roma de corpore martyriove Petri nullus certavit. — Unus locus apostolicae morti constitus est Roma scilicet, memine quidem contradicente.) But how little, upon closer consideration, is said with all this! How is it that the saga ambiguously begins only around the middle of the second century with the witness of Papias and Dionysius? Is it something so extraordinary and unbelievable that in the course of a complete century a saga of this kind was formed, even though not as "an invention of idle men" (*fimentum otiosorum hominum*), then indeed in the interest of a certain party for very natural, local reasons? If, however, one wishes to be amazed that no objection was raised by anyone, then let me remind us of the negative opposition of Clement of Rome and of the lack of reason to object, as soon as we make the certainly very natural assumption that one did not know anything further about the end of Peter than what the famous passage in John 21:18, 19 suggests; i.e., nothing definite that could be opposed to the emerging tradition. After all, how little do we know for certain about the fates and deaths of most of the apostles, and how easily can one apply to them what Basnage says in relation to these? How uncertain even our knowledge of the death of the apostle Paul would be, if the accounts of the ancients did not have a firm anchor point in the fact of the Neronian persecution of Christians? Moreover, one can very easily imagine how much, once the saga [188] of the Roman martyrdom of Peter had begun to be formed, precisely the celebrity of the place where it is to have taken place, must have procured a more general entrance for it. Amidst the lack of certain information, who should have disputed the honor to the Roman church without a special occasion?

65. Neander, *Genetische Entwickelung der vornehmsten gnostischen Systeme*, 369.

speculative Gnosis as the predominant idea of the Clementines, this point of view may apply to a certain side of the writing. However, one soon finds oneself compelled to abandon a general carrying out of this perspective when one penetrates further into the writing and perceives how, in the person of Peter, the author of the Clementines opposes the gnostic system of the magician Simon combatted by Peter with a no less gnostic-speculative system, so that one could instead regard the opposition of Judaizing Gnosticism against anti-Jewish Gnosticism, which was related more to paganism, as the basic idea of the writing. While [189] the Neanderian idea is characterized by being too broad, Coelln[66] has drawn the circle too narrowly. Coelln connects the Judaizing Christianity of the Clementines with the disputes that the Unitarians, headed by Artemon, triggered through their Jewish-Christian conception of the Son of God in the Roman community during the reign of Bishop Zephyrinus since 200 CE. In particular, from Praxeas, whose teachings essentially understood the Son of God like the Clementines, we know that he enjoyed great favor with the Roman bishop Victor. If the views of the Jewish Christians regarding the Son of God spread in this way through the Roman community in the second century, if one systematically worked to win the Roman bishops to this view, then it also follows that it was completely in the interest of the party to have the Roman Clement appear as a defender of these ideas, or even as a recorder of the allegedly Petrine doctrinal proclamations in which they were defended. The specified historical circumstances, compared with the spirit and manner of presentation of the Clementines, lets one suspect that this occurred between Eleutherus and Zephyrinus; that is, between 180 and 200 CE, namely, at Rome, from one of the Artemonites or Unitarians there who had come over from Asia Minor (as, for example, was the case with Praxeas) and were thus skilled in the purer Greek expression. I gladly admit that the movements in the Roman community connected with the controversy of the Artemonites, as has already been pointed out above, were not very far removed from the tendency of the Clementines, but I cannot believe that an author who describes such a wide sphere was mainly concerned only to assert the Artemonian understanding of the Son of God. If this were the main purpose, why then the polemic against Gnosticism, which occupies such a prominent place? The quick-witted, diversely [190] educated author, who was so precisely

---

66. Coelln, "Clementina," 18:37–38.

informed of all the religious manifestations of his time, undeniably wanted to bring up all the differences that pertained to the relationship of Christianity to paganism and Judaism, and that had emerged within the sphere of Christianity, especially through the influence of Gnosticism, and to attempt as far as possible to conciliate and balance out all of these oppositions on the foundation of the Judaizing that gave his writing its peculiar stamp. Therefore, the author starts from pagan religion and views it from the double viewpoint of the popular and allegorical interpretations. According to this double aspect, it seems equally reprehensible to him. In its customary popular sense, pagan religion is reprehensible, especially in the fact that it is polytheistic in both theoretical and practical respects: theoretically, because it in no way corresponds to the concept of the absolute (*Hom.* 2.43; 5.22); and practically, because in the polytheistic regions there cannot be a monarchal soul; that is, no soul that in its most strenuous striving comes to rest and inner satisfaction (*Hom.* 2.42), because in polytheism there is, moreover, a necessary attraction to conflict and war (*Hom.* 9.2), through which it proves to be something that is evil in itself (*Hom.* 5.22), and because the divine beings that polytheism sets up have a moral nature that elevates sensual lust and desire to the highest principle (*Hom.* 4.12–13). Moreover, the morally corrupt views of the world, such as fatalism and the system of fate, are also closely connected with polytheism (*Hom.* 4.12–13; 14.2–5; 15.4). However, the allegorically interpreted pagan religion—which presupposes a deep philosophical meaning in the myths, to which allegory is supposed to be the key—also cannot satisfy the religious disposition any better, since it is not only contradictory in itself, but it also, by transforming the gods into mere powers of nature, nullifies the essence of religion, replacing it with a cosmogony (*Hom.* 6). However, as much as [191] the Jewish religion has a decisive advantage over pagan religion in all these respects, it is nevertheless not ordinary Judaism that the author champions. Rather, he maintains his own view that the writings of the Old Testament are not to be regarded as documents of divine revelation. In his view, the law that Moses handed down to the seventy elders as oral tradition was distorted through erroneous additions that were foreign to the original spirit of Moses, when it was written down by these elders against his will. This is why there are so many contradictory passages even in the Mosaic writings, so many false teachings, unworthy conceptions that are incompatible with a purely monotheistic concept of God that is free of anthropomorphisms (*Hom.* 2.38, 40, 46–52; 8.6–7; 16.13; 18.20). Paganism and Judaism constitute the most general and broadest opposition in the area of religion. Accordingly, within a more narrowly drawn sphere, it is also time and again the same opposition, which is just repeated in another form. Just as the followers of the magician Simon, such as the Alexandrian grammarian Apion, represent paganism in the usual sense, so the magician himself is the representative of the Gnosticism that is configured in a pagan manner. After all, idolatry made him an ally (*Hom.* 2.33), and all of his efforts are aimed at replacing the fallen κατωθεομανία[67] ["madness caused by a lower god"] with an even worse opposition to the teaching of the monarchy of God (*Hom.* 3.3), namely, Gnosticism, which the author of the Clementines does indeed view as a kind of refined and spiritualized polytheism.[68] [192] This is the reason for the serious polemics against the gnostic separation of the creator of the world from the highest God and against all the oppositions that the Marcionite system put forth, especially in this connection. The similarity of Gnosticism to pagan

---

67. [This is how Baur prints the Greek, but in apparent error for Cotelerius's κάτωπολυθεομανίας (i.e., Jean-Baptiste Cotelier, et al., eds., *SS. Patrum, qui temporibus Apostolicis floruerunt, Barnabae, Clementis, Hermae, Ignatii, Policarpy Opera, vera, et supposititia*, 2 vols. [Amsterdam: Wetstein, 1724]), which he cites correctly above; the edition of Bernhard Rehm and Georg Strecker, eds., *Homilien*, vol. 1 of *Die Pseudoklementinen*, 3rd ed., GCS 42 (Berlin: de Gruyter, 1992), here reads κάτω πολυθέου μανίας.]

68. According to the presentation of the author, the teaching of the magician Simon comes, on the one hand, as close to Jewish monotheism as possible and yet, on the other hand, still appears as polytheism. For precisely this purpose, the magician Simon was, as a Samaritan, a very well-chosen person, since Samaritans were regarded just as much Jews as gentiles. This is the reason for the characterization of his false teaching with the words τὴν Ἰερουσαλὴμ ἀρνεῖται, τὸ Γαριζεὶν ὄρος ἀντεισφέρει ["he rejects Jerusalem, and substitutes Mount Gerizim for it" (trans. Smith, Peterson, and Donaldson, modified)]. He also did not completely reject the law. According to *Hom.* 3.2; 18.12.2, he taught that a great unknown power, the highest female ruler, let two angels or gods proceed from her, from which the one created the world and the other gave the law, with each of them presenting himself as the highest god. In so doing he presumed that τὰ τοῦ νόμου ἰδίᾳ προλήψει ἀλληγορεῖ (*Hom.* 2.22 ["the things of the law he explains by his own presumption" (trans. Smith, Peterson, and Donaldson)]). He even observed a certain ceremonial law; at least he celebrated a Sabbath every eleven days (*Hom.* 2.35). He relates to Christianity in the same way. He did not outright contradict the teaching of Christ but ἀντὶ τοῦ ὄντως Χριστοῦ ἡμῶν ἑαυτὸν ἀναγορεύει.... Χριστὸν ἑαυτὸν αἰνισσόμενος, ἑστῶτα προσαγορεύει [*Hom.* 2.22: "instead of our Christ, he proclaims himself.... Intimating that he is Christ, he styles himself the Standing One" (trans. Smith, Peterson, and Donaldson)]. The more error and truth overlap in this way, the more dangerous the deception of such a false teacher is meant to appear.

polytheism in the teaching about the demiurge is, however, only one side of the opposition between Gnosticism and Judaism. The author's polemics are therefore also directed especially against gnostic docetism, which only allows for the divine to be revealed in visions and imaginary appearances, and which thus cannot acknowledge a constant historical connection that only occurs with a revelation that is given externally. It is precisely here, however, that both aspects, the thetic and the antithetic, which must be distinguished in the entire presentation, are very closely intertwined. For in the same way that the author, despite all his polemic, nevertheless has at the same time a mediating and balancing tendency, so he also does not pronounce an absolutely condemning judgment on Gnosticism. Rather, he fully acknowledges in particular the truly speculative element inherent in Gnosticism by [193] constructing his own system in an analogous way and by integrating into it several ideas that are characteristic of Gnosticism, such as the idea of a primitive religion and primitive revelation, and the idea of a development that is mediated through constant oppositions and determined by the law of syzygies.[69] Thus, his polemic is actually always only directed against the one-sidedly anti-Jewish Gnosticism that opposes true monotheism and Mosaism, and in this connection he replaces the deceptive demiurge, who is separated from the highest God and who falsely presents himself as the highest God, with the prophet of truth, who, as the true organ of divine revelation in various figures, in the seven pillars

---

69. [I.e., pairs of opposites. As Peter expresses it in *Hom.* 2.15, "Hence therefore God, teaching men with respect to the truth of existing things, being Himself one, has distinguished all principles into pairs and opposites, Himself being one and sole God from the beginning, having made heaven and earth, day and night, light and fire, sun and moon, life and death. But man alone amongst these He made self-controlling, having a fitness to be either righteous or unrighteous. To him also he has varied the figures of combinations, placing before him small things first, and great ones afterwards, such as the world and eternity. But the world that now is, is temporary; that which shall be, is eternal. First is ignorance, then knowledge. So also has He arranged the leaders of prophecy. For, since the present world is female, as a mother bringing forth the souls of her children, but the world to come is male, as a father receiving his children from their mother, therefore in this world there come a succession of prophets, as being sons of the world to come, and having knowledge of men. And if pious men had understood this mystery, they would never have gone astray, but even now they should have known that Simon, who now enthralls all men, is a fellow-worker of error and deceit. Now, the doctrine of the prophetic rule is as follows..." (trans. Smith, Peterson, and Donaldson).]

of the world, passes through all periods of world history until he, at a determined time, anointed with God's mercy for the sake of his hardships, finds everlasting rest (*Hom.* 3.19-20). Likewise, the author replaces the visionary and ecstatic revelation with the instruction that goes forth from the mouth of the prophet of truth in the form of reliable tradition, being mediated through speech and word. He also replaces the ἄνομος and φλυαρώδης διδασκαλία ["lawless and gossipy teaching"] (see 68-69/125-26 above)—which were the natural fruits of the gnostic anti-Jewish antithesis, with its lack of acknowledgement of any real connection between the later Christian revelation and the earlier Old Testament revelation—with scrupulous respect for everything that was recognized as an authentic part of the Mosaic νόμος. Accordingly, in the author's view, the teaching of Moses and of Christ is essentially one and the same. Just as the author, in this way, has no reservation about acknowledging a certain inner speculative and religious truth in Gnosticism, so he also wants—in great contrast to the flatly rejecting attitude of Judaism, which regarded the gentile world only as the kingdom of darkness and condemnation—to grant all justice and fairness to paganism as well. I include here above all the especially attractive idea—presented so nicely in the story of Clement of Rome [194] being born from pagan parents—that there is an inner drive for truth in human nature, which, according to the Clementines (*Hom.* 1.1-4), can first be seen in the philosophical questions of whether the world is from eternity and exists forever, or whether it had a beginning and will come to an end, and of whether or not humans in particular are annihilated at death, which is followed by the moral question of whether, if souls continue to exist after death, punishment awaits evil people in the next life. Insofar as people, driven by a thirst for truth, search for a solution to these questions in the schools of the philosophers, and out of this same yearning are even prepared to throw themselves into the arms of necromancy, all these strivings and aberrations are, in fact, based on a moral and religious need that cannot deny its truth and that finally—even if it is by way of many detours, as is shown with reference to the example of Clement and his family—leads to the goal. This acknowledgment of a longing for truth in human nature, including in those born as pagans, says, from the standpoint of the author, even more; for in his view revelation is, after all, only an unveiling of what was already present in human nature, given that, as already noted above (74-75/131-33), the seed of all truth is in humans, and what is true springs up from the pure, innate mind. That which is basically only the other side of the same universalism is closely connected with this. Although in the author's view, Christianity is not a new revelation in terms of its content, the era it inaugurates is nevertheless of great importance by virtue of the fact that it seeks to communicate to all the truth that had been hidden and inaccessible for so many up to that point, and to free the entire pagan world from polytheism, idolatry, and lawlessness. Since the truth is deposited only in Judaism and in Christianity, which is identical with the former, it is precisely here that the Judaism of the author comes strongly to the fore, and yet it appears at the same time with a [195] liberality that is supposed to make it as easy as possible for the gentiles to convert to Judaism and that gives clear proof of how much the author is concerned to balance out all the differences that sharply repel each other. The author's Judaism is not at all the ordinary Judaism, but only the Judaism that has been purified of all inauthentic later additions. However, the author's leniency with regard to the commandment of circumcision—which was otherwise observed as a very holy ordinance also by the sects that deviated from ordinary Judaism, and in particular by the Ebionites—demonstrates, in my view, how little the author wanted to tenaciously insist upon something that would necessarily repulse the gentiles and solidify the gap between them and the Jews, even in the case of commandments of Judaism that he undoubtedly regarded as authentic components of Judaism in and for themselves. There is only a single passage in the Clementines in which circumcision is mentioned, namely, only in the *Contestatio pro iis, qui librum accipiunt* [Testimony regarding the Recipients of the Epistle]—which is placed before the homilies—where James reminds the presbyters not to share with anyone else the books in which the sermons of Peter had been sent to him, ἢ ἀγαθῷ τινι καὶ εὐλαβεῖ τῷ καὶ διδάσκειν αἱρεμένῳ, ἐμπεριτόμῳ δὲ ὄντι πιστῷ ["but to one who is good and religious, and who wishes to teach, and who is circumcised, and faithful" (trans. Smith, Peterson, and Donaldson)]. In the homilies themselves, circumcision is never mentioned as one of the conditions for being accepted into the Christian community. On the contrary, it is clear that baptism had replaced this religious custom, while even among Judaizing communities at that time, it was probably no longer customary to insist on the observance of this religious practice. However, as much as the author, out of a certain appeasing leniency, seems satisfied with this surrogate, he insists all the more strongly on the necessity of baptism. It is essential for everyone who believes in the one God to publicly proclaim this by being baptized, because it is an unchangeable law that nobody, not even the most pious person, can be saved without having received baptism (*Hom.* 11.25; 13.21). For it is baptism alone [196] that gives new birth through water to humans conceived from lust, extinguishing the evil fire within them through its water, by the power of an original mercy hovering over the water. Therefore, whoever despises baptism still has an inner spirit of wrath with a fear of the water (*Hom.* 9.26). Besides baptism, the worshiper of the one God is required to refrain from sacrificial meals and from consuming dead flesh and blood, and to wash away all impurities (παντὸς ἀπολούεσθαι λύματος ["to be washed from all pollution" (trans. Smith, Peterson, and Donaldson)])— the very same commandments that God-fearing Jews observed (*Hom.* 7.4–5). Keeping these commandments is seen as so necessary that it is assured that Jesus did not heal the daughter of the Canaanite woman until mother and daughter had adopted the Jewish way of life (νόμιμος πολιτεία) (*Hom.* 2.19). But whoever keeps these basic regulations of true Judaism, for such a one it does not matter whether they are of Jewish or non-Jewish descent; rather, the gentile who keeps not only the moral law but also the ceremonial commandments is a Jew (*Hom.* 11.16).

Returning to the writing's polemics against the apostle Paul, it clearly cannot be denied—in view of the overall character of this writing as we have presented it here—that the author must have taken great offense at the teachings that the apostle Paul put forward concerning the relationship of Christianity to Judaism, and especially at his claim that the ἔργα νόμου were to be completely disdained. The apostle's anti-Judaizing attitude, combined with elements that seemed to have a certain similarity to the character of Gnosticism, provoked the author to let his own polemics against the apostle Paul shine through in his portrayal of the apostle Peter's polemics against Simon the sorcerer. While Paul ventured to come forth as the apostle to the gentiles, and converted gentiles to Christianity, he did not require [197] the converted gentile to recognize and keep the Mosaic law. In this way, he—just like Simon the sorcerer—actually replaced the old form of polytheism with a new, modified form of polytheism that was not in any way compatible with pure Judaism. However, the author does not wish to abandon the idea of an apostle to the gentiles, which Paul embodied, though in the wrong way. Rather, he intends to portray the true apostle to the gentiles as opposed to the false one. The apostle attributes this position to the apostle Peter, who opposes the sorcerer everywhere, as well as to Clement, who, as Peter's pupil, was trained for the same vocation. And just as the sole reason for Paul becoming a false apostle to the gentiles was that he came forth as an apostle of his own authority and believed himself to be called to the apostolic office through appearances that he saw, which cannot count as reliable criteria of the divine, so it is in constant companionship with Peter, the direct disciple of Jesus, and in following in this teacher's footsteps, of which Clement represents the true model, that Paul could have embodied if he had truly wanted to be what he presented himself as. This relationship of Clement to Paul seems to me to be not unclearly suggested in precisely that passage that includes the most visible antithesis to the apostle. It is the passage cited on 63/120 (*Hom.* 17.19), in which Peter closes his lengthy argument against Simon the sorcerer with the following words: "If you have been trained to be an apostle for even an hour by association and teaching, then do not argue with me. If you really and truly wish to be a co-laborer for the cause of truth, then learn first from us as we learned from him, and once you have become a student of truth, then become our co-laborer." Accordingly, even in the case of the magician Simon, Peter (or the author) did not completely reject the thought of him being an apostle or coworker, but it was only that he did not find the required conditions to be fulfilled. By contrast, that which [198] must have been missed in the magician presented itself perfectly in Clement. And Paul could also have become their worthy coworker in the cause of the truth only if he had become, like Clement, a faithful student of the apostles. It seems to me that one can infer that in the person of Clement, the author simultaneously has the apostle Paul in view from a feature, which the author has taken up, probably not without a special reason, into the historical clothing of his writing. When Clement, full of desire to speak to one of those who had seen the Son of God who appeared in Judea, was on the way there, he met with Barnabas in Alexandria, who was proclaiming the teaching of Jesus in that city, not with dialectical art, but faithfully and simply recounting what he had seen and heard. Moreover, it is Barnabas afterwards who introduced the knowledge-desiring Clement to the apostle Peter in Caesarea and brought him into the connection with this μέγιστος ἐν τῇ τοῦ σοφίᾳ θεοῦ (*Hom.* 1.15 ["one who is greatest in the wisdom of God"]), in which he then remained without interruption until the death of the apostle. It is clear that the author wanted to make Barnabas a mediator between Clement and Peter in the same way as he is the mediator between Paul and the other apostles according to Acts 9:27. But just as little as the apostle, through his journey to Jerusalem, could have fulfilled for the author the conditions that he regarded as necessary for an authentic apostle, so little could he also consider the mediation of Barnabas in the same regard as adequate. The subsequent dispute with Peter was regarded by him in any case as the most certain proof that Paul infiltrated the apostolic office only in an illegitimate way. Therefore, while, through the feature taken from Acts and applied to Clement, he wanted to call to mind Paul and a certain relation of identity between Clement and Paul, this did not prevent him from designating Paul as the one whose true antithesis was meant to be established in Peter and Clement.[70]

---

70. The author intentionally chose precisely Clement, who was born from gentile parents [199] and, beyond this, regarded as a student of the apostle Paul according to Phil 4:3, for the role that he assigned to him. As a gentile by birth, he becomes, through his readiness to attach himself to Peter and Judaizing Christianity, the natural mediator between the Jewish-Christian and gentile-Christian parties, in order to gain entrance for the Judaizing Christianity through his authority. Clement appears in the same mediating capacity also already in the Shepherd of Hermas, 50.1, vision 2, end [Herm. Vis. 2.4.3], where the church, appearing in the form of an old woman, commands Hermas to record the new revelation: *scribes duos libellos et mittes unum Clementi, et unum Graptae, mittet autem Clemens in exteras civitates, illi enim permissum est. Grapte autem commonebit viduas et orphanos. Tu autem leges in hac civitate cum senioribus, qui praesunt ecclesiae.* ["Write two little books, sending one to Clement and the other to Grapte. Clement will send his to the foreign cities, for that is his commission. But Grapte will admonish the widows and orphans. And you will read yours in this city, with the presbyters who lead the church" (trans. Ehrman).] With this is connected also the portrayal that the *Epitome de gestis Petri*, ch. 149 (cf. the *Martyrdom of Clement* in Cotelier, ed., *SS. Patrum, qui temporibus Apostolicis floruerunt*, 1:808), gives of the character of Clement, that he, as "the third to sit in the high throne of the Roman church after Peter, taking up that very contest of virtue, followed in the course of the masters, and was himself also proclaiming the apostolic doctrine, and was shining forth with the same manners, and was agreeable not only to Christians, but also to the Jews and to the very gentiles themselves, and he became all things to all people, so that he might thus benefit everyone and bring them to Christ and link them to the true religion" (*tertius post magnum Petrum in excelso romanae ecclesiae throno sedens, ipsumque virtutis cetamen suscipiens, magistri vestigiis insistebat, Apostolicamque doctrinam ipse quoque praeferebat, et similibus moribus effulgebat, non Christianis dumtaxat placens, verum etiam Judaeis ac ipsis Gentilibus, et omnibus omnia factus, ut et sic omnes lucrifaceret Christoque praesentaret ac verae religioni connecteret*). That Clement was thought of in this way as a mediator between Jewish Christians and gentile Christians explains how he would be the bearer of all the traditions regarded as apostolic (the *Apostolic Constitutions* and the *Apostolic Canons*), which were meant to possess an equally binding validity for Jews and gentiles. In this connection, his name appeared to be the best recommendation.

On a side note, I believe that the factual basis that underlies the Clement of the Clementines is derived at least in part from that Flavius Clemens who is spoken of in Suetonius, *Dom*. 15; Dio Cassius (in the edition [200] of Xiphilinus) *Hist. rom.* 67.14; and in Eusebius, *Hist. eccl.* 3.18; and who Cotelier (on Clement, *Rec.* 7.8; in Cotelier, ed.,

132   The Christ Party in the Corinthian Community

[199] A writing such as the Clementines are, according to their whole content and character, probably could have emerged only in the context

---

SS. Patrum, qui temporibus Apostolicis floruerunt, 1:560) called to mind as the "foundation of the fable" (*fundus fabulae*). The agreement cannot indeed be missed, for (1) of both it is said that they were related to the imperial family. Flavius Clemens is called a "paternal cousin" (*patruelis*) of Domitian in Suetonius, *Dom.* 15, the Clement of the Clementine *Hom.* 4.7, ἀνὴρ πρὸς γένους Τιβερίου Καίσαρος ὤν ["being related to the family of Tiberius Caesar" (trans. Smith, Peterson, and Donaldson)], since the whole action falls in the earliest time of Christianity. (2) Just as Clement was led through an inner movement to Christianity according to the Clementines, so Flavius Clemens was also undoubtedly a friend and adherent of Christianity. The ἀθεότης ["atheism"], because of which he was condemned to death by Domitian, with which the ἤθη τῶν Ἰουδαίων ["customs of the Jews"] mentioned in the same context in Dio Cassius (*Hist. rom.* 67.14) are synonymous, is the ordinary pagan designation of Christianity. The "most despicable idleness" (*contemtissima inertia*) of which Suetonius accuses him fits well with this, since he, as a Christian, could have no great interest in the political life of the Romans, which must have been most conspicuous during the time of his consulate, for which reason Domitian had him killed. In the words of Suetonius, "Suddenly, on the slightest suspicion, he killed him, just barely out of his consulship" (*repente ex tenuissima suspicione tantum non in ipso ejus consulate interemit*). (3) As the family of Clement in the Clementines was compelled, as a consequence of a dark fate that hung over it, to leave Rome, and only returned there again after various experiences and fates, then at least the wife of Flavius Clemens, Flavia Domitilla, experienced a similar change of fate. According to Dio Cassius, she was banished to the island of Pandateria for the same reason that brought death to Clement. According to Eusebius, *Hist. eccl.* 3.18, pagan authors who mentioned the persecution of Christians under Domitian reported: ἐν ἔτει πεντεκαιδεκάτῳ Δομετιανοῦ μετὰ πλείστων ἑτέρων καὶ Φλαβίαν Δομετίλλαν— ἐξ ἀδελφῆς γεγονυῖαν φλαβίου Κλήμεντος, ἑνὸς τῶν τηνικάδε ἐπὶ Ῥώμης ὑπάτων, τῆς εἰς Χριστὸν [201] μαρτυρίας ἕνεκα εἰς νῆσον Ποντίαν κατὰ τιμωρίαν δεδόσθαι ["In the fifteenth year of Domitian, Flavia Domitilla, who was the niece of Flavius Clemens, one of the consuls of Rome at that time, was banished with many others to the island of Pontia as testimony to Christ" (trans. Lake and Oulton)]. Afterwards she returned again to Rome, since Domitian, as Tertullian (*Apol.* 4) says about the same measures of persecution, *facile coeptum repressit, restitutes etiam, quos relegaverat* ["He easily stopped that which he had begun and even restored those he had banished"]. On this historical foundation there arose, through transferring to the apostolic Clement, the novel-like narrative, which serves as a nice frame for the content of the writing, which is full of ideas. The death of Flavius Clemens attracted a great deal of interest also among the Romans through the frightening appearances that followed it (*continuis octo mensibus* ["for eight continous months"], Seutonius says, *fulgura facta nuntiataque sunt* ["lightning bolts occurred and were reported"]); all the more can one envisage how this Clement, as one of the first upper-class Romans to convert to Christianity and become a martyr, became interwoven into the Christian saga history.

[200] of the Roman church. There can be no doubt about this because of the role played by the Roman Clement, and by [201] the tradition's presupposition that Peter founded and oversaw the Roman church and named Clement as his successor. Yet another proof seems to be that the hierarchical terms employed so strongly in the Clementines in connection with the fundamental teaching of the monarchy of God are found in reality in no other church to the same extent as in the Roman one. In the writing, the highest respect is found for the necessity of a tradition going back to the apostles themselves (as already demonstrated), and especially for the dignity of the office of bishop. The bishop is the defender of Christ's bride, the church, against the devil, who wages war against her and who afflicts the bishop for the sake of each one of those entrusted to him (Ep. Clem. Jas. 4–17). The bishop is the representative of Christ and God (ὁ προκαθεζόμενος Χριστοῦ τόπον πεπίστευται ["the one entrusted with the place of Christ" (trans. Smith, Peterson, and Donaldson)]). The honor or dishonor given to the bishop reflects back on Christ, and then from Christ back on God; and whoever disobeys the bishop disobeys Christ, and whoever disobeys Christ disobeys God (*Hom.* 3.66). For these reasons, no one in the community [202] should be friends with someone with whom the bishop is at enmity; and any believer who does not want to be considered a destroyer of the church should refrain from associating with anyone whom the bishop does not associate with, if he does not want to be regarded as a destroyer of the church (Ep. Clem. Jas. 18). While the bishop should only command what is good, the seat of Christ and Moses is still to be honored by obedience even if a bad man is sitting on it (*Hom.* 3.66–70). The bishop should not be domineering like the pagan authorities, but should rule the church in a mild and serving manner, as a physician, shepherd, or father. However, he should not disdain external distinction out of humility, for only through it can the masses be deterred (*Hom.* 3.64). Without a doubt, these features and others that so precisely represented the character of the Roman church from early on did not first merge into it from the Clementines, but the author expressed in a more specific and developed manner what he already encountered among the Judaizing party of the Roman church. In particular, the terms κάθεδρα Χριστοῦ and κάθεδρα Μωυσέως, which are repeatedly used to designate the office of the overseer of the church in the Clementines, go together perfectly with the *cathedra Petri*, the common designation for the Roman church, which was at least already employed for it by Cyprian in this sense. To be sure, the Roman provenance of the letter can be opposed, as it seems, by pointing both to the form of the letter written

in the Greek language and to the conspicuous Ebionite ideas and principles that it advocates. These objections, however, do not hold any real weight. The Greek language and the form of the writing cannot be considered oddities in a community that, being largely composed of Jewish Christians and Hellenists, could already for that reason have included members who had become acquainted with Greek education to some extent. With regard to the writing's Ebionism, it is sufficient to note that according to Epiphanius (*Pan.* 30.181 [*Pan.* 2.18.1]), the Ebionites had also spread to Rome (ὁ Ἐβίων καὶ αὐτὸς ἐν τῇ Ἀσίᾳ ἔσχε τὸ κήρυγμα καὶ Ῥώμῃ ["Ebion, too, preached in Asia and Rome"] [trans. Williams]).

[203] On the whole, there cannot be a very large divergence of opinions concerning the time frame in which a writing like our Clementines—with the specific goal of balancing out different prevailing tendencies of that time on the basis of Judaism—might have appeared. Since we find the first traces of the existence of our Clementines (or at least a document that was very closely related to them) in the first half of the third century,[71] they must be dated to the end of the second or the beginning of the third century. Such a date is in complete agreement with the fact that in this very period, the Roman church was vigorously moved by some phenomena that were rather similar to the disposition of our document. It was the time in which Marcion had sparked new interest in Gnosticism for many people through his own unique system, which set up the sharpest contrast to Judaism and provoked a very zealous opponent of that system in Tertullian. This was the time in which Montanism, by inspiring new friends for Judaism but also by being blunt and offensive, drew a sharper division between Jewish Christianity and authentic Christianity, and in which Unitarians like Praxeas, Artemon, and Theodotus [204] shifted the teaching about the Son of God into a condition vacillating between these two opposites. Finally, it was the time in which church leaders such as the

---

71. See Coelln, "Clementina," 18:40: "Origen, in his τόμος on Genesis, which he wrote when he was still in Alexandria (before 231 CE), quotes a long section from discussions of Clement of Rome with his father in Laodicea, which were supposed to have been discovered ἐν ταῖς περιόδοις λόγῳ τεσσερεσκαιδεκάτῳ ["in the fourteenth discourse in the *periodoi*"], and according to a free reworking in the Rufinian translation of the *Recognitions*, but is not read in the Greek Clementines, which otherwise give very similar discussions in *Hom.* 14." Irrespective of how one specifies the relationship of our Clementines to the πράξεις or κηρύγματα Πέτρου (Eusebius, *Hist. eccl.* 3.3) and to the περίοδοι, or the *Itinerarium Petri*, upon which Origen, Epiphanius, and Jerome drew, they undeniably have the character of an original work.

bishop Victor and the presbyter Caius[72] worked with all their might to limit the previous dominance of Judaism as much as possible, and to bring about a direction of thought in the Roman church that was freer from its influence. In a time moved by such phenomena, a man such as the author of the Clementines could have very easily gotten the idea of developing a system that, on the one hand, would argue for everything that could justify the tenets of Judaism, but, on the other hand, would be diverse enough to balance out the oppositions that were at the forefront of the discussion, and that still seemed to create an [205] insecure vacillation between Judaism and paganism in church life in a manner that would satisfy, as much as possible, all interests and justified demands, and yet would also ensure that Judaism maintained its own particular character.[73]

---

72. Caius is known as an opponent of Montanism and Chiliasm, and probably also of the Artemonites. Photius (*Bibl.* 48) says regarding precisely this Roman presbyter Caius, who lived under the bishops Victor and Zephrinus, χειροτονηθῆναι αὐτὸν καὶ ἐθνῶν ἐπίσκοπον ["he was appointed also bishop of the gentiles"]. Whatever else one may understand by this, it certainly points also to a closer relation to the gentile-Christian party. (Did they perhaps have the same office that Clement, according to the passage from the Shepherd of Hermas quoted above, already had in relation to the *exteras civitates* ["foreign cities"], the predominantly gentile communities that had a connection with Rome?) How much interest the question of the extent to which Christianity may retain a Jewish character had in the Roman community, also even later, around the middle of the third century, is shown by the writings of the presbyter Novatian, the still-extant writing about the Jewish food laws, in which he attempted to demonstrate that they are no longer binding for Christians; and two other writings mentioned by Jerome, about the Sabbath and circumcision, in which he had wanted to show "what the true circumcision and the true Sabbath are" (*quae sit vera circumcisio, et quod verum Sabbathum*); Neander, *Allgemeine Geschichte der christlichen Religion und Kirche* 1.3:1166.

73. If the contrast between Jewish Christian and gentile Christian parties had such a significant impact on the conditions of the ancient church, as I believe to have shown, then it is very natural that similar attempts to balance out and communicate between the two sides, as made by the author of the Clementines, had also already been undertaken before. As already noted above (77/136), the Letter of James undeniably has such a tendency. But should not the same point be applied also to the two letters of Peter? The observation that 1 Peter shows conspicuous agreements in language and concepts with the Pauline letters has already been made on multiple occasions (Wilhelm Martin Lebrecht de Wette, *Lehrbuch der historisch kritischen Einleitung in die Bibel Alten und Neuen Testaments*, 2nd ed. [Berlin: Reimer, 1830], 328–29). While this phenomenon does not justify any doubt concerning the authenticity of the letter, it can nevertheless be explained only with regard to the assumption that

the apostle Peter himself felt compelled to indicate, through the whole configuration of his letter, his agreement with the apostle Paul to the communities in Pontus, Galatia, Cappadocia, Asia, and Bithynia, among whom, as could be expected, the opposition of those two parties and directions must have emerged with special prominence. This mediating tendency is even more striking in 2 Peter. This further underlines the suspicion of inauthenticity—which was overwhelmingly strong anyway—since this special intention of the author makes it even more comprehensible why he wanted his letter to be regarded as a letter that was composed by the apostle Peter himself. The ψευδοδιδάσκαλοι (2 Pet 2:1) whom the author combats are opponents who are inclined partly to an immoral libertinism (2 Pet 2:19), which could appear as a natural consequence of the release from the νόμος (cf. οἱ ἄθεσμοι: 2 Pet 2.7; ἄνομα ἔργα: [2 Pet 2:8]; 2 Pet 3:17: ἡ τῶν ἀθέσμων πλάνη) and partly to an oversubtle speculation (2 Pet 1:16: σεσοφισμένοις μύθοις; 2 Pet 2:3: πλαστοὶ λόγοι) that was built upon empty fiction and resulted in docetism (2 Pet 2:1). Both could, as we find it [206] presented in the Clementines, be regarded as an extreme of the Pauline direction. By combating this distorted direction with all seriousness under the name of Peter, the Pauline-minded author grounds even more securely the recognition of the true Pauline Christianity. However, it is especially noteworthy that while the author designates himself as a life companion of Jesus (2 Pet 1:14) and as an ἐπόπτης τῆς ἐκείνου μεγαλειότητος (2 Pet 1:16), he nevertheless appeals for his apostolic authority primarily to the voice from heaven at the baptism and at the transfiguration of Jesus (2 Pet 1:17, 18). Are these not manifestations that fall, so to speak, in the middle between the ἀποκαλύψεις and ὀπτασίαι of Paul, and the criterion that the Judaizing party wanted to be regarded as the only valid one according to the Clementines? On the one hand, they fall in the sphere of the earthly life of Jesus. On the other hand, they were something just as momentary and distinctive as the visions of Paul. By putting that which revealed Jesus's dignity in his life in such moments, the author makes the authentic conviction of the dignity of Jesus just as dependent on individual momentary appearances as was the case in the ἀποκαλύψεις and ὀπτασίαι of Paul. Just as he balances things out here as a Paulinist, so he lets the Petrinist speak more again in the following 2 Pet 1:19–21, where there is talk of the great significance of the προφητικὸς λόγος. Finally, the author most unambiguously expresses the conciliatory aim of his letter—which he places not without reason in the mouth of Peter, who is already near death (2 Pet 1:13–15), in order to make it all the more worthy of acceptance as the last legacy of the apostle—at the end of the letter in 2 Pet 3:15, where he calls the apostle Paul his beloved brother, praises the wisdom granted to him, appeals to his letters, and warns against the misunderstandings that they could cause as well as the misinterpretations that are given to them. Is it not quite obvious that in the whole letter, the author was concerned with the main goal of confronting every doubt about the complete harmony of the two apostles in order to remove everything that could appear to justify the existing opposition?

Bibliography

Ambrose. *Sancti Ambrosii Mediolanensis Episcopi opera*.... 4 vols. Edited by Jacques Du Friche and Denis-Nicolas Le Nourry. Paris: Coignard, 1686–1690.

Athanasius. *Sancti Patris nostri Athanasii Archiepiscopi Alexandriae, Opera quae reperiuntur omnia*. 2 vols. Edited by Lucas Hostenius. Cologne: Weidmann, 1686.

———. *St. Athanasius: Select Works and Letters*. NPNF2 4. Translated by M. Atkinson, John Henry Newman, and Archibald Robertson. Grand Rapids: Eerdmans, 1978.

Basnage, Samuel. *De rebus sacris et ecclesiasticis exercitationes historico-criticae*. Utrecht: Water, 1692.

Baur, Ferdinand Christian. "Abgenötigte Erklärung gegen einen Artikel der Ev. Kirchenzeitung, herausgegeben von D. E. W. Hengstenberg, Prof. d. Theologie an der Universität zu Berlin, May 1836." *TZTh* 3 (1836): 179–232.

———. "Beiträge zur Erklärung der Korintherbriefe." Pts. 1 and 2. *ThJb* 9 (1850): 139–85; 11 (1852): 1–40, 535–74.

———. "Die Christuspartei in der korinthischen Gemeinde, der Gegensatz des paulinischen und petrinischen Christenthums in der ältesten Kirche, der Apostel Petrus in Rom." *TZTh* 4 (1831): 61–206.

———. *Church and Theology in the Nineteenth Century*. Translated by Robert F. Brown and Peter C. Hodgson. Edited by Peter C. Hodgson. Eugene, OR: Cascade, 2018.

———. "Einige weitere Bemerkungen über die Christuspartei in Korinth." *TZTh* 4 (1836): 3–32.

———. *Historisch-kritische Untersuchungen zum Neuen Testament*. Vol. 1 of *Ausgewählte Werke in Einzelausgaben*. Edited by Klaus Scholder. Stuttgart: Frommann, 1963.

———. *Lectures on New Testament Theology*. Edited by Peter C. Hodgson. Translated by Robert F. Brown. Oxford: Oxford University Press, 2016. Orig. ed., Leipzig: Fues, 1864.

———. *Paul the Apostle of Jesus Christ: His Life and Works, His Epistles and Teachings*. 2 vols. London: Williams & Norgate, 1873.

———. *Die sogenannten Pastoralbriefe des Apostels Paulus aufs neue kritisch untersucht*. Stuttgart: Cotta, 1835.

———. "Über den Ursprung des Episkopats in der christlichen Kirche." *TZTh* 3 (1838): 1–185.

———. "Über Zweck und Veranlassung des Römerbriefs und die damit zusammenhängenden Verhältnisse der römischen Gemeinde." *TZTh* 3 (1836): 59–178.

Bauspiess, Martin, Christof Landmesser, and David Lincicum, eds. *Ferdinand Christian Baur and the History of Early Christianity*. Translated by Robert F. Brown and Peter C. Hodgson. Oxford: Oxford University Press, 2017.

Bertholdt, Leonhard. *Historisch-kritische Einleitung in sämmtliche kanonische und apokryphische Schriften des alten und neuen Testaments*. 6 vols. Erlangen: Palm, 1812–1819.

Bèze, Théodore de. *Testamentum Novum, sive Novum Foedus Iesu Christi, D.N. Cuius graeco contextui respondent interpretationes duae....* Geneva: Stephanus, 1589.

Bultmann, Rudolf. "Is Exegesis without Presuppositions Possible?" Pages 289–96, 314–15 in *Existence and Faith: Shorter Writings of Rudolf Bultmann*. Edited by Schubert M. Ogden. London: Hodder & Stoughton, 1961.

Clement of Alexandria. *Klēmentos Alexandreōs ta heuriskomena / Clementis Alexandrini opera, quae extant*. Edited by John Potter. Venice: Zatta, 1757.

Coelln, Daniel Georg Konrad von. "Clementina." *AEWK* 18:36–44.

Cotelier, Jean-Baptiste, James Ussher, John Pearson, William Beveridge, Jean Le Clerc, Gerard Wetstein, and Rudolf Wetstein, eds. *SS. Patrum, qui temporibus Apostolicis floruerunt, Barnabae, Clementis, Hermae, Ignatii, Policarpy Opera, vera, et suppositicia*. 2 vols. Amsterdam: Wetstein, 1724.

Ehrman, Bart D., ed. and trans. *I Clement; II Clement; Ignatius; Polycarp; Didache*. Vol. 1 of *The Apostolic Fathers*. LCL. Cambridge: Harvard University Press, 2003.

Eichhorn, Johann Gottfried. *Einleitung in das Neue Testament*. 3 vols. Leipzig: Weidmann, 1804–1814.

Elwert, Eduard. "Ueber die Lehre von der Inspiration, in Beziehung auf das Neue Testament, ein Versuch." Pages 3–104 in vol. 3.2 of *Studien der evangelischen Geistlichkeit Wirtembergs*. Edited by Christoph Benjamin Klaiber. Stuttgart: Löflund und Sohn, 1831.

Emmerling, Christian August Gottfried. *Epistola Pauli ad Corinthios posterior graece perpetuo commentario*. Leipzig: Barth, 1823.

Epiphanius. *The Panarion of Epiphanius of Salamis*. 2 vols. Translated by Frank Williams. Leiden: Brill, 1987–1994.

Eusebius of Caesarea. *The Ecclesiastical History*. 2 vols. Translated by Kirsopp Lake and John E. Oulton. LCL. London: Heinemann, 1980.

Flacius, Matthias. *Historia certaminum inter romanos episcopos et sextam Carthaginensem synodum Africanasque ecclesias de primatu seu potestae papae, bona fide ex authenticis monumentis collecta*. Basel: Oporinus, 1554.

Flatt, Johann Friedrich. *Vorlesungen über die beyden Briefe Pauli an die Corinthier...*. 2 vols. Tübingen: Fues, 1827.

Gieseler, Johann Karl Ludwig. Vol. 1 of *Lehrbuch der Kirchengeschichte*. 2nd ed. Bonn: Marcus, 1828.

Greenslade, S. L. *Early Latin Theology: Selections from Tertullian, Cyprian, Ambrose and Jerome*. LCC 5. London: SCM, 1956.

Grotius, Hugo. *Opera omnia theologica...*. 4 vols. Paris: n.p., 1641–1650.

Harris, Horton. *The Tübingen School: A Historical and Theological Investigation of the School of F. C. Baur*. Oxford: Oxford University Press, 1975. Repr., Leicester: Apollos, 1990.

Harrisville, Roy A., and Walter Sundberg. *The Bible in Modern Culture: Baruch Spinoza to Brevard Childs*. 2nd ed. Grand Rapids: Eerdmans, 2002.

Heinichen, Friedrich Adolf. *Eusebii Pamphili historiae ecclesiasticae libri X*. 2 vols. Leipzig: Kayser, 1828.

Herbst, Johann Georg. "Ueber den Aufenthalt des Apostels Petrus zu Rom, zugleich als Beytrag zur ältesten christlichen Chronologie." *TQ* 2 (1820): 567–626.

Heydenreich, August Ludwig Christian. *Commentarius in priorem divi Pauli ad Corinthios epistolam*. 2 vols. Marburg: Krieger, 1825–1828.

———. *The Formation of Historical Theology: A Study of Ferdinand Christian Baur*. New York: Oxford University Press, 1966.

Hug, Johannes Leonhard. *Einleitung in die Schriften des Neuen Testaments.* 2 vols. 3rd ed. Stuttgart: Cotta, 1826.

Irenaeus. *St. Irenaeus of Lyons: Against the Heresies.* 2 vols. Translated by Dominic J. Unger and John J. Dillon. ACW 55, 65. New York: Paulist, 1992–2012.

Jones, F. Stanley, ed. *Rediscovery of Jewish Christianity: From Toland to Baur.* HBS. Atlanta: Society of Biblical Literature, 2012.

Käsemann, Ernst. "Einführung." Pages viii–xxv in *Historisch-kritische Untersuchungen zum Neuen Testament.* By Ferdinand Christian Baur. Vol. 1 of *Ausgewählte Werke in Einzelausgaben.* Edited by Klaus Scholder. Stuttgart: Frommann, 1963.

Lactantius. *De mortibus persecutorum.* Translated by J. L. Creed. OECT. New York: Clarendon, 1984.

Martini, Christoph David Anton. *Versuch einer pragmatischen Geschichte des Dogma von der Gottheit Christi in den vier ersten Jahrhunderten nach Christi Geburt.* Rostock: Stiller, 1800.

Mynster, Jacob Peter. "Ueber den ersten Aufenthalt des Apostels Petrus in Rom." Pages 143–66 in *Kleine theologische Schriften.* Copenhagen: Gyldendal, 1825.

Nardini, Famiano. *Roma antica di Famiano Nardini.* 4th ed. Edited by Antonio Nibby. 4 vols. Rome: Lomanis, 1818–1820.

Neander, August. *Allgemeine Geschichte der christlichen Religion und Kirche.* 9 vols. Hamburg: Perthes, 1825–1852.

———. "Der Apostel Paulus und die Gemeinde zu Korinth." Pages 68–102 in *Kleine Gelegenheitsschriften praktisch-christlichen, vornehmlich exegetischen und historischen Inhalts.* 3rd ed. Berlin: Eisner, 1829.

———. *Genetische Entwicklung der vornehmsten gnostischen Systeme.* Berlin: Dümmler, 1818.

Nösselt, Johann August. "Commentatio de Christi cognitione secundum carnem ad locum 2 Corinth. V, 14–17." Page 183–206 in vol. 2 of *Opusculorum ad interpretationem sacrarum scripturarum.* Halle: Hendel, 1787.

Pearce, Zachary. *Epistolae duae ad celeberrimum doctissimumque virum F[ranciscus] V[alckenaer] professorem Amstelodamensem scriptae....* London: Clay, 1721.

Périon, Joachim, ed. *Clementis Romani episcopi, de rebus gestis, peregrinationibus, atque concionibus sancti Petri epitome....* Paris: n.p., 1555.

Photius. *Photii Bibliotheca.* 2 vols. Edited by Immanuel Bekker. Berlin: Reimer, 1824–1825.

Posselt, Ernst Ludwig. Vol. 4 of *Europäische Annalen*. Tübingen: Cotta, 1800.

Pott, David Julius. *Epistola pauli ad corinthios prima*. Vol. 5.1 of *Novum Testamentum Graece: Perpetua annotatione illustratum*. Edited by Johann Benjamin Koppe and Christoph Friedrich von Ammon. Göttingen: Dieterich, 1826.

Rehm, Bernhard, and Georg Strecker, eds. *Homilien*. Vol. 1 of *Die Pseudoklementinen*. 3rd ed. GCS 42. Berlin: de Gruyter, 1992.

Routh, Martin Joseph. *Reliquiae Sacrae: Sive, auctorum fere jam perditorum secundi tertiique saeculi fragmenta, quae supersunt*. 4 vols. Oxford: Oxford University Press, 1814–1818.

Saumaise, Claude. *Librorum de primatu papae, pars prima, cum apparatu*. Leiden: Elzevir, 1645.

Schmid, Christian Friedrich. *De Paulinae ad Romanos epistolae consilio atque argumento quaestiones*. Tübingen: Fues, 1830.

Schmidt, Johann Ernst Christian. *Bibliothek für Kritik und Exegese des neuen Testaments und älteste Christengeschichte*. 2 vols. Hadamar: Neue Gelehrtenbuchhandlung, 1797–1798.

Schrader, Carl. *Der Apostel Paulus*. Leipzig: Kollmann, 1830.

———. *Chronologische Bermerkungen über das Leben des Apostels Paulus*. Leipzig: Kollmann, 1830.

Schröckh, Johann Matthias. Vol. 2 of *Christliche Kirchengeschichte*. 2nd ed. Leipzig: Schwickert, 1775.

Smith, Thomas, Peter Peterson, and James Donaldson, trans. "The Clementine Homilies." *ANF* 8:223–346.

Spanheim, Friedrich. *Dissertatio de ficta profectione Petri Apostoli in urbem Romam, deque non una traditionis origine*. Pages 331–80 in *Tomus Secundus: Qui complectitur miscellaneorum ad sacram antiquitatem et ecclesiae historiam pertinentium*. Vol. 2 of *Opera*. Leiden: Boutestein, 1703.

Storr, Gottlob Christian. *Notitiae historicae Epistolarum Paulli ad Corinthios interpretationi servientes*. Tübingen: Fues, 1788.

———. *Ueber den Zwek der evangelischen Geschichte und der Briefe Johannis*. Tübingen: Heerbrandt, 1786.

Süskind, Friedrich Gottlieb. "Neuer Versuch über chronologische Standpunkte für die Apostelgeschichte und für das Leben Jesu." Page 156–225 in vol. 1 of *Archiv für die Theologie und ihre neuste Literatur*. Edited by Ernst Gottlieb Bengel. Tübingen: Osiander, 1816.

Tafel, Gottlieb Lukas Friedrich. *Olympia*. Vol. 1.1 of *Dilucidationum Pindaricarum*. Berlin: Reimer, 1824.
Tertullian. *Adversus Marcionem*. Edited and translated by Ernest Evans. OECT. Oxford: Clarendon, 1972.
Thilo, Johann Karl, ed. *Acta S. Thomae apostoli ex codd. pariss*. Leipzig: Vogel, 1823.
Usteri, Leonhard. *Entwickelung des Paulinischen Lehrbegriffes in seinem Verhältnisse zur biblischen Dogmatik des Neuen Testamentes: Ein exegetisch-dogmatischer Versuch Verhältnis*. 2nd ed. Zürich: Orell, Füssli & Co., 1829.
Valois, Henri de. *Eusebii Pamphili Ecclesiasticae historiae libri decem....* Paris: Vitré, 1659.
Wette, Wilhelm Martin Lebrecht de. *Lehrbuch der historisch kritischen Einleitung in die Bibel Alten und Neuen Testaments*. 2nd ed. Berlin: Reimer, 1830.
Wettstein, Johann Jakob. *Novum Testamentum Graecum*. 2 vols. Amsterdam: Officina Dommeriana, 1751–1752.
Winer, Johann Georg Benedict. *Pauli ad Galatas epistola, latine vertit et perpetua annotatione*. 3rd ed. Leipzig: Reclam, 1829. First published 1821.
Wocher, Maximilian Josef. "Die letzten Reisen [und Schicksale] der Apostel Petrus und Paulus, nach Clemens von Rom und Dionys von Korinth." *TQ* 12 (1830): 621–48.
Wrede, William. "The Task and Methods of 'New Testament Theology.'" Pages 68–116 in *The Nature of New Testament Theology*. Edited by Robert Morgan. SBT, 2nd ser., 25. London: SCM, 1973.
Zachhuber, Johannes. *Theology as Science in Nineteenth-Century Germany: From F. C. Baur to Ernst Troeltsch*. Oxford: Oxford University Press, 2013.
Ziegler, Werner Karl Ludwig. "Besondere Einleitung in unsern ersten Brief an die Corinthier." Pages 26–96 in vol. 2 of *Theologische Abhandlungen*. Göttingen: Dieterich, 1804.

Ancient Sources Index

Hebrew Bible/Old Testament

Genesis
20 62
41 62

Numbers
12:6–7 63

Proverbs
9:1 56

Daniel
3 62
5 62

Deuterocanonical Books

Wisdom of Solomon
7:27 56

New Testament

Matthew
7:25 70
9:15 116
13:16 110
13:52 75
16:14 63
23:2 64
24:5 70
25:1 116

Mark
13:6 70

Luke
11:52 64
21:8 70

John
3:6 44
3:29 116
20:18 20
20:25 20
21:18–19 122

Acts
1:21 53
9 53
9:27 130
11:20 85
11:30 57
15 65, 85, 119
17:32 32
18 17
18:2 119
18:5 118
18:18 118
19:21 106
21:18 65
21:28 71
22 59
23:11 106
26 59
28:14–15 107
28:31 107

1 Corinthians
1–4 36
1:11 17

1 Corinthians (cont.)		2:17	31, 73
1:12	2, 22–23, 28–30, 32, 36, 42	3	31
1:12–3:23	23	3:1	31, 73
1:13	27, 96	3:6–7	31
1:14	23	3:14–15	31
1:21	27	4:3–4	31
1:26	24, 26	4:7	40
2:1–2	24	5:1–4	40
2:9	109, 110	5:5–14	40
2:10	110	5:12	41, 42, 48
2:11	24	5:14	46
2:12	24	5:15	43, 44
2:14	25	5:16	19, 21, 40, 41, 42, 45, 46
2:15	54	5:17	42
2:16	37, 54	10	48
3:1–2	25	10–13	3
3:3–4	25	10:7	34, 48, 50
3:8–15	53	10:11	50
3:16–18	26	10:12	73
3:21–23	26, 27	10:13	49
3:22	22, 23	10:15	86
4:1	37	10:16	86
4:9	39	10:26	119
4:10	37	11	52
4:15	37	11:1	50, 51
9:1	37, 46, 53	11:2	116
9:5	19, 20, 38	11:3–4	31
9:7–8	38	11:5	48
9:9–12	38	11:5–33	53
9:13	38	11:7–20	51
9:15–16	53	11:12–15	31
9:15–27	38	11:13	35, 50, 51, 52
11:2	117	11:18	41, 52
12:10	2	11:19–20	51
15	32, 34	11:20–33	51
15:7	19, 20	11:22	41, 47, 51
15:8	39	11:26	35
15:10	53	12	52
15:11	39	12:2–4	53
15:12	34	12:4	55
15:32	34	12:22	54
15:56	31		
		Romans	
2 Corinthians		1:8	118
1:19	118	1:9–15	86

1:10	105	Colossians	
1:13	105	4:10	95
5:12–13	75		
7:5	44	1 Peter	
9–11	5	5:12	118
9:5	76	5:13	81, 82, 95, 118
11:1–36	103		
11:14	44	2 Peter	
12:1	103	1:13–15	136
14:1–2	103	1:14	136
15:5–13	103	1:16	136
15:18–19	104	1:17	136
15:20	86, 119	1:18	136
15:22	86	1:19–21	136
15:23	86	2:1	136
15:24	89, 91	2:3	136
16:17–20	104	2:7	136
		2:8	136
Galatians		2:19	136
1	56, 57	3:15	136
1:7	55	3:17	136
1:15–16	59		
1:18	58, 65	1 John	
1:19	19	4:1–2	2
2	55, 56, 57, 73, 79, 85		
2:1	57, 85	Revelation	
2:2	55	19:7	116
2:6	55	21:9	116
2:9	51, 55, 58, 65, 73, 81, 116–17		
2:11	59, 67, 119	Early Christian Writings	
2:11–12	66		
2:12	59, 68	1 Clement	
3:3	44	3	88
6:12	44, 52	4	88
6:15	42	5.1	92
6:16	42	5.1–7	88–89
		5.7	96
Ephesians		47.3	36
5:23	116		
		Ambrose, *Sancti Ambrosii Mediolanensis*	
Philippians		*Episcopi opera*	104, 105
3:1–2	54		
3:3	44	Athanasius, *Apologia de fuga sua*	
4:3	131	18	121

Athanasius, *Sancti Patris nostri Athanasii Archiepiscopi Alexandriae, Opera quae reperiuntur omnia*   121

Clement of Alexandria, *Miscellanies*   111

Clement of Alexandria, *Stromateis*   111

Epiphanius, *Panarion*
30.16	60
30.25	60
30.181	134

Eusebius, *Historia ecclesiastica*
2.13	85
2.14	115
2.15	83, 101
2.22	93
2.25	92, 96, 113, 116
3.1	112
3.1.23	65
3.3	134
3.18	131, 132
3.19	21
3.27	60
3.39	84, 86, 87
4.22	109
5.8	117
5.24	107
5.28	108
6.14	84

Ignatius, *To the Romans*
4.3	80

Irenaeus, *Adversus haereses*
1.26	60
3.1	117
3.3	99
5.33	86

Justin, *Apologia i*
26	85
56	85

Lactantius, *De mortibus persecutorum*
2	100

Letter of Clement to James
4–17	133
18	133

Letter of Peter to James
1	75
2	67

Photius, *Bibliotheca*   135

Pseudo-Clement, *Homiliae*
1.1–4	127
1.15	130
2.10	76
2.15	126
2.17	68, 71, 72
2.19	129
2.22	125
2.33	125
2.35	125
2.38	124
2.40	124
2.42	124
2.43	124
2.46–52	124
3.2	125
3.3	72, 76, 125
3.12	76
3.17–18	75
3.18	73, 75
3.18–19	64
3.19	73, 75
3.19–20	127
3.20	76
3.26	116
3.27	116
3.58	114
3.59	65, 66, 72
3.60	64
3.64	133
3.65	64
3.66–70	133

4.7	132	Tertullian, *Apologeticus*	
4.12–13	124	4	132
5.22	124		
6	124	Tertullian, *De jejunio adversus psychicos*	
7.4–5	129	14	107
8.4–7	73		
8.6–7	124	Tertullian, *De praescriptione haereticorum*	
9.2	124	36	99
9.26	129		
11.16	129	Greco-Roman Literature	
11.25	128		
11.35	70, 72, 73	Dio Cassius, *Historiae romanae*	
12.1	114	67.14	131, 132
13.21	128		
14	134	Suetonius, *Life of Claudius*	
14.2–5	124	25	102
15.4	124		
16–17	114	Suetonius, *Domitianus*	
16.12	76	15	131, 132
16.13	124		
16:14	75	Tacitus, *Annales*	
16.15	75	14.14	98
16.21	69	15.44	94, 98
17.4	56		
17.13	61		
17.16–19	62–64		
17.19	66, 130		
18.11	75		
18.12.2	125		
18.14	56		
18.20	124		
19	114		

Pseudo-Clement, *Recognitiones*
7.8   131

Shepherd of Hermas, Similitudes
9.12   108

Shepherd of Hermas, Visions
2.4.3   131

Tertullian, *Adversus Marcionem*
4.5   112

Modern Authors Index

Basnage, Samuel 81, 92, 121, 122
Bauspiess, Martin vii
Bertholdt, Leonhard 19–20, 117
Bèze, Théodore de 80
Bultmann, Rudolf ix, 13, 15
Coelln, Daniel Georg Konrad von 75, 83, 108, 111, 123, 134
Eichhorn, Johann Gottfried 18, 21–22, 28, 82
Elwert, Eduard 24–25
Emmerling, Christian August Gottfried 46
Flacius, Matthias 79–80
Flatt, Johann Friedrich 19, 33, 41, 44, 48
Gieseler, Johann Karl Ludwig 83
Grotius, Hugo 32, 44
Harris, Horton vii
Harrisville, Roy A. ix
Heinichen, Friedrich Adolf 95–96, 108, 116
Herbst, Johann Georg 82, 85, 120
Heydenreich, August Ludwig Christian 20, 31–32
Hug, Johannes Leonhard 20, 94
Jones, F. Stanley viii
Käsemann, Ernst ix, 1–16
Landmesser, Christof vii
Lincicum, David vii
Martini, Christoph David Anton 108
Mynster, Jacob Peter 83, 117–20
Nardini, Famiano 98
Neander, August viii, 28–29, 33, 69, 71–73, 76, 83, 107, 110, 113, 122–23, 135
Nösselt, Johann August 42–43, 46

Pearce, Zachary 36
Périon, Joachim 114
Posselt, Ernst Ludwig 13
Pott, David Julius 22–23, 26
Routh, Martin Joseph 97, 110
Saumaise, Claude 80, 92
Schmid, Christian Friedrich 104
Schmidt, Johann Ernst Christian 29, 34–35
Schrader, Carl 58, 85, 89, 91, 94
Schröckh, Johann Matthias 82
Spanheim, Friedrich 80–83, 92
Storr, Gottlob Christian 18–21, 31–33, 42, 48, 84
Sundberg, Walter ix
Süskind, Friedrich Gottlieb 57–58
Tafel, Gottlieb Lukas Friedrich 90–91
Thilo, Johann Karl 117
Usteri, Leonhard 44
Valois, Henri de 113
Wette, Wilhelm Martin Lebrecht de 135
Wettstein, Johann Jakob 41–42, 44–45
Winer, Johann Georg Benedict 44
Wocher, Maximilian Josef 90, 93, 95–96, 100
Wrede, William 4
Zachhuber, Johannes vii
Ziegler, Werner Karl Ludwig 18

Subject Index

Apollos, 20, 22–23, 26, 28–30, 118
  party, 2–3, 18, 21, 30, 36
baptism, 3, 23, 115, 128–29, 136
Cephas party, 2, 18–19, 21, 30–33, 36–38, 48, 51–52, 102
  as same as Christ party, 35–36
Christ. *See* Jesus, Messiah
Christian community, 6, 17, 24, 34, 50, 57, 59, 64, 102, 114, 116, 118–19, 128
Christian unity, 26–28, 54, 88
Christ party, 2–3, 28–29, 48, 52
  as based on a written instruction, 21–22
  as identified with James, the brother of the Lord, 18–20
  as neutral, 21–22, 28–29
  as same as Cephas party, 35–36
Ebionites, 72, 110, 128, 134
  view of Paul, 59–60, 70
false apostles. *See* pseudoapostles
gentile Christians, 6, 17–18, 30, 32, 34–35, 81, 103, 111, 131, 135
  relationship with Jewish Christians, 16–17, 34–35
gentiles, 24, 55, 59, 64, 66–68, 73–74, 79, 102, 114, 125, 127–29, 131, 135
Gnosticism, 7, 66, 69–70, 72, 76, 110–11, 123–29, 134
James (the brother of the Lord), 18–20, 33, 35, 51, 56, 59, 64–67, 72, 77, 87, 110, 114
Jesus, 27
  death of, 24, 41, 45, 47, 54, 73, 77, 103
  relation to the head of the Christ party, 18–19

Jesus (*cont.*)
  resurrection of, 19, 48
Jewish Christianity, 3–5, 123, 134
Jewish Christians, 6, 17, 34–35, 46, 54, 56, 65, 68, 77, 87, 102–11, 116, 123, 131, 134–35
  relationship with gentile Christians, 17–18, 34–35
Messiah, 3, 20–21, 34, 36, 45–47
paganism, 37, 66, 71–72, 98, 122–25, 127–28, 132–33, 135
Papias, 83–88, 92, 111, 122
Paul, 22–23, 28–31, 51, 57–59, 65–67, 79–81, 87–90, 93–95, 99–100, 102–3, 106–7, 112, 120, 122, 129–31
  apostolic status, 35–39, 47, 49–50, 52, 55–57
  as viewed by the Ebionites, 59–60, 70
  opponents in Corinth, 25, 30–41, 47–54, 73
  party, 2, 18, 21
Peter, 18–19, 22–23, 28–29, 35–36, 38, 48, 51, 53, 57–59, 77. *See also* Cephas party
  in Galatians, 55, 58–59
  in the Clementine *Homilies*, 56, 60–75
  martyrdom in Rome, 80–82, 92–99, 117
  presence in Rome, origin of the saga, 101–22
  presence in Rome as historically suspect, 81–82, 85–86, 99–100
  presence in Rome on the basis of Caius, 97–99

Jesus (cont.)
    presence in Rome on the basis of Clement, 88–92
    presence in Rome on the basis of Dionysius, 92–96
    presence in Rome on the basis of Papias. *See* Papias
    presence in Rome in connection with Simon Magus, 81, 83–85
    presence in Rome with Mark, 82, 84
    presence in Rome with Paul, 92–95
Petrine party. *See* Cephas party
pseudoapostles, 31, 35, 42, 45, 59, 116
resurrection, 3, 7, 32–34, 39, 62
    of Jesus, 19, 48
Sadducees, 31–33
σάρξ, 41–44, 47, 52, 54
Simon Magus, 60–61, 64, 66–71, 83–86, 113, 116–17, 122, 125
Spirit (of God), 11, 13–14, 16, 24–26, 37–38, 54, 76–77, 84, 105, 110
two parties in Corinth, 29–36
wisdom, 56, 76, 108
    of God, 24, 30, 108, 130
    of this age/the world, 24, 26–27, 30

www.ingramcontent.com/pod-product-compliance
Lightning Source LLC
Chambersburg PA
CBHW031402230426
43670CB00006B/623